SECRET VENICE

KU-330-951

Jonglez

It has taken five years to compile this out of the ordinary guidebook. Five years of research, meeting people, reading, walking or boating have gone into a work which, we hope, will help readers to discover unusual, hidden or as yet little-known aspects of Venice. The research was not always straightforward: we had to be patient until successive doors were opened to us. We also had to leave Venice itself to gain a better sense of the rich history of a city that was an indispensable stopover for travellers from all over Europe, particularly during the Renaissance. So to better understand the city, we made a number of journeys into the Venetian hinterlands, to Tuscany, Rome and even Lisbon. Thematic sections accompany the descriptions of certain sites, highlighting historical events or relating anecdotes that reveal the city in all its complexity.

SECRET VENICE also draws attention to the multitude of details found in places that we may pass every day without noticing. These are an invitation to look more closely at the urban landscape and, more generally, a way of seeing the city with the curiosity and attention it deserves.

Comments on this guide and its contents, as well as information on places not mentioned, are very welcome and will allow us to enrich future editions.

Don't hesitate to contact us:
• Éditions Jonglez, 17, boulevard du Roi,
  78000 Versailles, France
• E-mail: info@jonglezpublishing.com

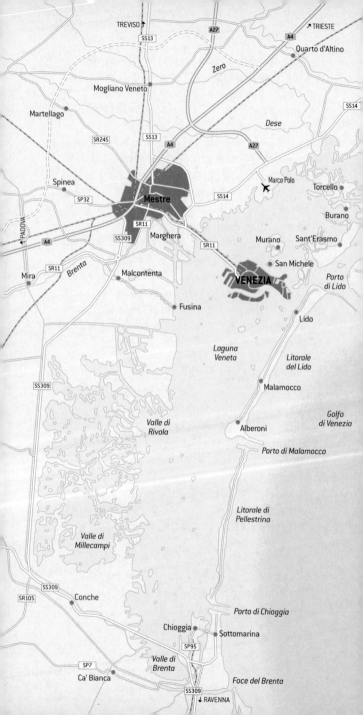

↗ SAN DONA DI PIAVE

SS14

Caposile

Lanzoni

SP43

Porto Grande

SP52

SP42

Eraclea

Piave

SP42

SR43

Jesolo

SP42

Palude
Maggiore

Lido di Jesolo

SP42

Cavallino

Litorale
del Cavallino

MAR ADRIÁTICO

N

0   5   10 km

CONTENTS

SAN MARCO

SANTA CROCE

CONTENTS

CONTENTS

CASTELLO

CONTENTS

DORSODURO

GIUDECCA & SAN GIORGIO

AROUND THE LAGOON

INDEX

SAN MARCO

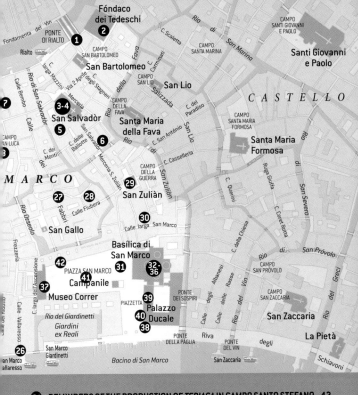

THE *TESTA D'ORO* AT RIALTO ❶

Salizada Pio X
Rialto

> *Custodian of the secrets of a universal panacea*

Almost opposite the entrance to the church of San Bartolomeo at the foot of Rialto Bridge is a small sculpture of a head that can often pass unnoticed. In bronze, it is the old shop sign for the apothecary "Alla Testa d'Oro" (At the Golden Head) and dates from an era when a substantial part of the population was illiterate and had no other way of identifying the shop. We do not know exactly whom the artist took as his inspiration for this depiction of a rather haughty, determined face crowned with laurel leaves. Perhaps it was Virgilio Zorzi, one of the former owners of the apothecary shop, or perhaps it was an imaginary portrait of Andromache or Mithridates. On the wall, you can also see a fragment of an inscription which refers to *Theriaca d'Andromaco*. A sort of universal panacea believed to be efficacious against any number of ills (see p. 44), *Teriaca* was a speciality of this *spezieria* as early as 1603. In fact, its *Teriaca* was considered the best in the city, thus "Alla Testa d'Oro" was authorised to manufacture the potion three times a year, whilst all the other licensed apothecaries in Venice could only do so once a year.

After the Fall of the Venetian Republic in 1797, this apothecary was the only one to go on producing *Teriaca*. It would continue to do so right into the 20th century, even if the recipe was simplified. For example, when regulations regarding pharmaceutical products were introduced in the 1940s, *Teriaca* could no longer include opium, an ingredient that had originally been included for its analgesic properties.

SIGHTS NEARBY

THE GRAFFITI IN THE FONDACO DEI TEDESCHI ❷

The Fondaco dei Tedeschi formerly housed the warehouses, exchange and residence facilities (more than 200 rooms) for merchants from Germany, Austria, Hungary and the north of Europe in general. The interior courtyard was laid out on three floors, the corridors visible through arcades (so the Venetians could keep the activities within under easy surveillance). On the first floor, alongside the monumental clock, there are various bits of graffiti carved into the parapets. These include the schema for a game of Nine Men's Morris, which here seems more likely to be an esoteric symbol than the simple outline of a game (see p. 163).

REMINDERS OF THE COMMUNITY OF *LUCCHESI* NEAR RIALTO

Having been driven out of Lucca (Tuscany) for political reasons, a community of *Lucchesi* settled in Venice in 1317, primarily as merchants and craftsmen working in the manufacture and finishing of silk. The Rialto area that extends from San Giovanni Cristostomo to Calle della Bissa still has traces of their presence, which is sure proof that they did not settle solely within the strict boundaries of the parish of the Cappella del Santo Volto in Cannaregio (see p. 247).

Calle della Bissa is a continuation of Calletta Pistor, which starts directly opposite the main entrance to the Fondaco dei Tedeschi. And at number 5512 in that alley is a pilaster with the carved crest of the *Arte della Seta* (Silk Guild). It depicts a mulberry bush, whose leaves were the staple diet of silkworms.

To the left of the pilaster is the entrance to **Corte dell Tentor**, where dyers exercised their trade, and to the right is **Corte de L'Orso**, which takes its name from the Orso family that had originated in Lucca but then settled here. The buildings around this small courtyard reach up to six floors. It is interesting to note that this is fairly unusual in Venice, but is not restricted to the area of the Ghetto as is commonly believed. In zones occupied by those who were from the same geographical region or engaged in the same trade, there was also the tendency to build upwards and thus exploit limited ground area.

Calle della Bissa owes its name to its serpentine layout (*bissa*, or *biscia* in Italian, means grass snake). It was once also known as *Calle dei Thoscani* because of the Lucchesi who lived there. Their parish church was **San Giovanni Crisostomo**, a short distance from which is **Corte Amadi** (or **dei Amai**), which was home to the wealthy Amadi family that had originated in Lucca.

Behind the church of San Giovanni Crisostomo, the street towards the Malibran Theatre passes numerous warehouses that were used to store silk. At number 5864, there is still evidence of important premises of the **Silk Inspectors Offices** (*Provveditori alla Seta*). The merchants and silkweavers from Lucca had, in fact, obtained authorisation from the Venetian State to set up their own magistracy, responsible for resolving disputes amongst them. Above the entrance to what is now a restaurant, the Latin inscription reads *Provisores Sirici*, with the date *1515* and the crests of the *provveditori*: the Lucca families of the Paruta (escutcheon with three roses); the Sandei (lion rampant); the Ridolfi (escutcheon with sea waves); Amadi (esutcheon with three hills and a bird); and the Perducci (escutcheon with three batons). On the architrave, which dates from later, is the date *1578* and other (now indistinct) crests.

In **Campo Nuovo** at Rialto (close to which is also **Calle Toscana**), there were other premises of the *Ufficio della Sera* (Silk Office). At number 553, the doorframe is again carved with a mulberry tree, the symbol of the guild of silk producers.

THE "PALA D'ARGENTO" IN THE CHURCH OF SAN SALVADOR ❸

Church of San Salvador
• On public display three times a year:
From 25 December to 1 January (inclusive)
From Easter Sunday to the following Sunday (inclusive)
From 6 August (The Feast of the Transfiguration) to 13 August (inclusive)
• sansalvador@inwind.it

A Titian that disappears to make way for another masterpiece...

Whilst the basilica of St. Mark's has its *Pala d'Oro*, the church of San Salvador has its *Pala d'Argento*, a masterpiece of Venetian silverwork that probably dates from the end of the 16th century.

The work, however, is little known to tourists because it is put on public display only three times a year: at Christmas, Easter and the Feast of the Transfiguration (for precise dates, see above).

Most of the time the masterpiece is located directly behind Titian's *The Transfiguration of Christ,* which – thanks to a system of weighted pulleys – at these key moments of the year literally disappears into the altar itself, leaving the *Pala d'Argento* visible.

Just like the *Pala d'Oro* in St. Mark's – and most of the other such altarpieces that once adorned Venetian churches (almost all of which have since disappeared) – this *pala* was an object of particular veneration, and was only put on display during the major events linked with the church itself. Given that the church of San Salvador (The Holy Saviour) is dedicated to Christ, those essential moments were, therefore, Christ's birth (Christmas), Transfiguration (see opposite) and death and Resurrection (Easter).

As Renato Polacco shows in a study published in 2000, the *pala* probably dates from the very end of the 16th century. Depicting the central theme of the Transfiguration (just like the Titian painting itself), the altarpiece was originally a small triptych, but today comprises five horizontal parts (see photo). In fact, initially, the *pala* was intended to close shut, the central panel (depicting the Transfiguration) being covered over by panels immediately above and below it. When in this closed position, what was visible was the back of these two panels, which now form the top and bottom sections of the *pala* as we see it, the parts decorated with cherubim and the Lamb of God. The message is clear. The Lamb is the symbol of the sacrifice that opens the gates of Paradise (and the *pala*), a Paradise symbolised here by the transfigured Christ surrounded by the Virgin, saints and prophets.

WHY DOES THE FEAST OF THE TRANSFIGURATION ALWAYS FALL ON 6 AUGUST?

This date had figured in the rite of the Byzantine Church since the 7th century. Tradition had it that this was the date of the consecration of the very first basilica built on Mount Tabor, where Christ's Transfiguration was said to have taken place. Later, in 1456, Pope Callixtus III would confirm this as the official date of the feast day for the Roman Church. However, whilst he was thus adapting a date that was already widely recognised, he was also celebrating a happy coincidence. The victory of the Christian army over the Turks at Belgrade had occurred on 22-23 July that same year, but news of it only reached Rome on 6 August.

WHAT IS THE TRANSFIGURATION?

Mentioned in three of the Gospels (Matthew 17:1-9, Mark 9:2-9 and Luke 9:28-36), the Transfiguration took place shortly after the miracle of the loaves and fishes. Accompanied by Peter, John and James, Christ retired to a hill upon which he appeared transfigured, bathed in a dazzling white light. Alongside him appeared the prophets Elijah and Moses, who then disappeared as a heavenly voice spoke to Peter, saying, "This is my beloved son in whom I am well-pleased. Listen to him." Indeed, the Transfiguration heralds the Resurrection, which had already been announced by various prophets, represented here by the figures of Moses and Elijah.

Traditionally, the site of the Transfiguration is held to be Mount Tabor, near the Sea of Galilee. However, the Maronites argue it occurred on Mount Lebanon and others say it was Mount Hermon (on the border between modern-day Syria and Lebanon).

SACRISTY OF THE CHURCH OF SAN SALVADOR

Church of San Salvador
- Open daily from 9am to 12pm and 3pm to 6pm
- Visits upon request or upon e-mail reservation
- sansalvador@inwind.it

A hidden gem

Built in 1546, in the relatively tight and dark space between the church and the monastery of the same name, the sacristy at San Salvador is a hidden gem.

It can be visited upon request or by making a reservation via e-mail. You thus gain access to a room with frescoes (artists unknown) that are a small masterpiece of taste and refinement. The magnificent proportions of the space are reminiscent of one of the finest rooms in Palazzo Grimani (near Santa Maria Formosa; visits by appointment every day except Sunday). In the centre of the ceiling is the figure of Christ blessing the faithful, but all around are delightful *trompe-l'oeil* depictions of trees and shrubs with both local and exotic birds. Contrary to certain other monasteries in the city (for example, those at Il Redentore or San Francesco della Vigna), the one at San Salvador had no space for a garden, as it was right in the centre of Venice. The space of its two cloisters was already taken up by the wells from which the monks drew water. Hence, the painters of the frescoes created a sort of virtual garden, glimpsed through *trompe-l'oeil* windows. Note in particular how the branches and foliage continue from one "window" to the next.

SIGHTS NEARBY

THE FORMER REFECTORY OF THE MONASTERY OF SAN SALVADOR
Telekom Future Center
- Open upon request, daily from 10am to 8pm

At present occupied by Telecom Italia, the former monastery of San Salvador, alongside the church of the same name, has maintained two pretty cloisters (probably designed by Jacopo Sansovino and generally accessible during biennales) and the former refectory, sometimes used for meetings and conferences.

Whilst the space has been modernised to meet modern needs, it still has its frescoes. Mostly in a rather poor state, they are attributed by some to Polidoro da Lanciano (active in Venice between 1530 and 1565), whilst others argue they were painted in 1545 by Fermo Ghisoni. Born in Caravaggio in 1505, Ghisoni was one of the best pupils of Giulio Romano, and helped his master in the work on the frescoes of the Palazzo Te and the ducal palace in Mantua in 1538. Note the absence of the figures of the prophets. They were stolen at some point.

At the entrance to the refectory is a small collection of antique phones, and a fine door in carved wood.

CASINO VENIER

Venice premises of the Alliance Française
San Marco 4939
• Open Monday to Friday from 9am to 1pm and from 3pm to 6pm, or with prior reservation for groups.
• Tel: 041 522 70 79
• alliancefrancaise@libero.it

> *One of the last and most charming of the Venetian casini*

The Venice premises of the Alliance Française since 1987, the Casino Venier is one of the last and most charming of the Venetian *casini* (see following double page). Its interior decoration, dating from 1750-1780, is still intact, with floors of cemented marble (not the typical Venetian *terrazzo*), stuccowork, frescoes and mirrors. The whole forms a little bijou of a place, particularly since the restoration of 1981-1993, financed by the Comité de Sauvegarde Français de Venise. The *casino* or *ridotto* – a place where the aristocracy met for gaming and conversation – belonged to Venier, the Procurator of St. Mark's, but is primarily associated with his wife, Elena Priuli. The layout of the rooms reflects that of a typical Venetian palazzo, with a number of different chambers off a long central hall/salon. Above the entrance staircase, the two grilles in gilded and carved wood enclosed the space for the musicians, who could thus play without being seen by – or seeing – those who were arriving. On the left at the end of the central hall is the dining room, decorated with attractive stuccowork depicting birds and plants and a fresco of the *Triumph of Bacchus*. Note the serving hatches concealed within cabinets.

In the end room on the right is a very pretty fireplace in Delftware, as well as a fresco attributed to Guarana. The room also contains the so-called *liago*, a sort of enclosed balcony giving onto Ponte dei Baretteri. It allowed those inside to watch the comings and goings below without being seen.

A SPY HOLE FOR A QUICK GETAWAY

During your visit, do not miss one particular floor panel in the entrance. This panel could be moved to enable those upstairs to look down and see who was outside at the door waiting for admission. Should the new arrival be unwelcome for some reason, this spy hole made it possible to make a quick getaway, via the "emergency exit" in the first room on the right. Probably concealed within a cupboard at the time, this exit no longer exists.

THE CASINOS IN VENICE

The casinos – or, to use the proper Italian plural, *i casini* – were small private places where a select company met to gamble, talk and enjoy themselves. The first written mention of a *casino* (literally "little house" in Italian) or *ridotto* (club or "withdrawing room") dates from 1282.

While certain casinos were places of romantic assignation, this was far from true for most of them, which were dedicated primarily to the great Venetian passion for gambling.

Indulgence in betting, however, became so dominant a passion – some lost their entire fortune in a single night – that the Venetian authorities felt bound to impose legal restrictions. In 1506, cards and dice were banned from casinos – a ban that was never obeyed even if the penalties for infraction were severe. A nobleman caught gambling in a casino risked a fine of 300 ducats and exclusion from all public office for ten years, whilst a member of the lower classes could be banished from the city for ten years. In 1609, the legal sanctions were extended: anyone who worked in a *casino* risked six years' imprisonment, after his nose and ears had been cut off. And a second-time offender would serve a double prison term.

Nevertheless, the Venetians continued to gamble and to frequent the most attractive of the *casini*. So, in the end, it was the government that gave in, authorising these premises (in 1638) so that they could exercise control over them.

New bans were introduced, however, in 1774. Still, the 118 *casini* that existed in 1744 had grown in number to 136 by the fall of the Republic. Many of these premises were subsequently destroyed and today only a dozen or so remain (see below).

THE OLD *CASINI* OPEN TO THE PUBLIC

Casino Venier (see p. 25).

Casino Sagredo (see p. 203) at Santa Sofia.

Casino Zane, near the Frari. Now within the Centre de Musique Romantique Française (Fondation Bru Zane, established in 2008), it can be visited during the regular concerts held here, so once again it serves the purpose for which it was created three centuries ago.

Casino Contarini dal Zaffo (former Casino degli Spiriti – see p. 209).

Casino del Comercio in St. Mark's Square (above Café Lavena, entrance behind the café). The space can be rented for events; two rooms overlook St. Mark's Square.

Casino Dandolo (the Ridotto – see p. 53).

Casino Contarini at San Beneto (see p. 37).

HEAD OF AN OLD WOMAN 7

Corte del Teatro
San Luca

> **The good,
> the poor
> and the miserly**

Halfway up a house in Corte del Teatro, there is a curious marble sculpture of an old woman's head, which originally seems to have been the shop sign of the Farmacia "La Vecchia" in Campo San Polo. There is an amusing story about it.

A miserly old woman (*vecchia*) of the parish of San Paternian (see p. 33) used to hide her money in the lining of an old cloak that she kept in the attic. One winter's day, her son, Vincenzo Quardio, knowing nothing about the hiding-place, took pity on a local pauper and gave him the cloak.

A week later, the woman went to add to her savings but could not find the garment. To convince her son to go and get it back, she told him that it contained all the money that she had intended to leave to him. The son then set out in search of the pauper, even disguising himself as a beggar on the steps of Rialto Bridge. Finally, he found him and, voicing charitable concern about the bitter cold, suggested a swop – his own thick cloak for the threadbare one he had given him before. With the money he got back, the son was then able to open a flourishing apothecary's business, the rear of which was decorated by a sculpture showing his mother seated and himself standing.

Today, all you can see of the high-relief is the woman's head, flanked by an image of a cedar tree (the shop sign of another nearby apothecary that has since disappeared), the arms of the Bembo and Moro families, and the crest of the Confraternity of San Rocco. In the 16th century, this house had passed from the Bembo to the Moro and then to the confraternity.

SIGHTS NEARBY

THE EMBLEMS ON THE FLAG POLE IN CAMPO SAN LUCA 8

On the base of the flag pole in Campo San Luca are the emblems of the two confraternities that played a part in defeating the conspiracy led by Bajamonte Tiepolo (see p. 61): the Scuola della Carità (Confraternity of Charity) and the Scuola dei Pittori (Guild of Painters).

GRAFFITI OF A MAN WITH A PIPE ❾

Second column in Palazzo Loredan
Riva del Carbon

> *Biagio's miraculous sacrifice*

L ooking at Palazzo Loredan, the second column in from the left has a graffiti depiction of a man with a long pipe. It is inspired by the remarkable legend of a local fisherman called Biagio. A firm favourite with one and all, this old man used to spend a lot of time outside Palazzo Loredan, touting for small jobs amongst the residents of the district. During the moments of rest that he allowed himself, he liked to stand and look out along the canal while smoking his pipe. One day, however, when the city was very quiet, the wake left by a passing gondola suddenly turned red. The waters of the canal parted, leaving the gondola suspended in midair, whilst the panic-stricken gondolier dived to one side and swam to the bank.

At this point two enormous black arms ending in terrible claws came out of the water and snatched away the *felze* (the small cabin that used to be located at the centre of a gondola). Biagio caught a glimpse of two young girls seized by the claws, whilst a monstrous twin-horned head emerged from the water. Biagio had no doubt that it was Satan himself.

Later, it emerged that the two young girls were members of the Gradenigo family, and it was said that Satan was probably taking revenge upon their father, whose dabbling in the secrets of magic had unwittingly offered the devil the chance to seize hold of these innocent souls.

Faced with this terrifying spectacle, Biagio did not think twice. He hurled his pipe into the water and yelled at Satan to take him rather than the two girls, extending his arms to show that he offered himself in sacrifice. Now it was Satan's turn to mock Biagio for believing he was some sort of Christ figure. However, he did promise to release the two girls if Biagio's extended arms could embrace the entire world. No sooner had he said this than Biagio's arms were painlessly detached from his body and, followed by a host of cherubim, flew off in either direction around the globe. The Devil was left speechless and released the two girls, leaving untouched the old Biagio whom God had protected.

SIGHTS NEARBY

THE PLAQUE OF THE FIRST FEMALE GRADUATE ❿

On the wall of Palazzo Cavalli, at the corner of Riva del Carbon and calle Cavalli, a plaque placed about 4 metres high recalls the fact that the first woman in the world to graduate from a university was born here in Venice, in 1646. Elena Lucrezia Cornaro Piscopia graduated from the University of Padua (then under Venetian rule) with a degree in philosophy in 1678. The first university to welcome female students opened in Zurich in 1867.

PLAQUE COMMEMORATING THE CHURCH OF SAN PATERNIAN

11

Campo Manin

> **The destruction of a rare polygonal bell-tower**

On the ground at the northwest corner of the Manin monument in the centre of the campo is a plaque indicating where the old church of San Panternian stood prior to its demolition in 1871. Built in the 10th century, it had a superb bell-tower dating back to 999, thus making it the second oldest in Venice after St. Mark's bell-tower (which itself collapsed a few years after the demolition of this church). The San Paternian bell-tower was distinctive because it was polygonal on the outside but circular inside, rather like the mysterious medieval towers you find in the Irish countryside.

The entire church was demolished to make way for the monument to Daniel Manin, which now stands directly in front of one of the city's few real eyesores, the premises of the Cassa di Risparmio bank. Hailed by a *tiny* minority as a fine work of Modernist architecture, it was built in 1964-1971 to designs by Angelo Scattolin and Pier Luigi Nervi. It is significant that, since its completion, no further authorisation has been given for a modern building to be raised in the old city centre.

The church is also commemorated in the name of Ponte San Paternian, which leads towards Campo Sant'Angelo.

In the northwest corner of the campo, a discreet plaque commemorates the former existence here of the house of Aldo Manuzio, the inventor of italic print and probably the greatest printer in Renaissance Venice (see p. 150).

THE LAST TRACES OF THE ANCIENT CHURCH OF SANT'ANGELO
Campo Sant'Angelo

In the middle of Campo Sant'Angelo, a discreetly-placed paving stone bears the Latin inscription *V TEMPLUM ARCHANGELI M AMOLITUM A MDCCCXXXVII FORUM SILICE STRATUM AERE CIVICO A MDCCCXLI.* It refers to the fire that destroyed the old church of Sant'Angelo in 1837. The very first church on this site, built in the second half of the 10th century, it had been dedicated to St. Maurus, and was renamed San Michele Archangelo in the second half of the following century. Thereafter, it was always known to the Venetians simply as Sant'Angelo. After the fall of the Republic, the church became a warehouse, with the parish being transferred to Santo Stefano, then only a monastery church.

CHURCH OF SANT'ANGELO DEGLI ZOPPI OR DELL'ANNUNZIATA
Campo Sant'Angelo 30124 Venice
Open Saturday morning

Often overlooked, the tiny church of Sant'Angelo degli Zoppi (or dell'Annunziata) is open on Saturday morning. Founded in the 10th century by the Morosini family, it was rebuilt in the 12th and then again in the 18th century and was occupied by the Confraternita dei Soti (in Italian *zoppi* means "lame"), which had been charged by the Venetian government to provide care for old and invalid sailors. Inside is a *Nativity of the Virgin* by Giuseppe Cesari, known as Il Cavaliere d'Arpino.

THE RUBELLI COLLECTION

Archives at Palazzo Corner Spinelli
- Palazzo Corner Spinelli 3877
- Visits by appointment only
- Tel. 041 2417329
- museo@rubelli.com
- The venue is sometimes used for public exhibitions
- For information, consult the site: www.rubelli.com

A treasure chest of fabrics

Housed within Palazzo Corner Spinelli, the historic archives of the Rubelli Company can be visited by appointment, which also gives you a chance to see the inside of this very fine Renaissance *palazzo*.

The archives cover the output of the family company over five generations, since the business was founded by Lorenzo Rubelli in the 19th century. Since then, textiles for the company have been designed by the likes of Vittorio Zecchin, Guido Cadorin and Giò Ponti, and their work goes together here with some 5000 fabrics dating from the end of the 15th century to the middle of the 20th. These include late-15th-century velvets of cut silk with loops of gold thread (that is, with a raised weave of gold through the fabric), Baroque damasks and brocades with floral motifs, exotic fabrics inspired by the taste for *chinoiserie*, and other opulent textiles dating from the 18th century.

Amongst the numerous designs and patterns, the collection has numerous pieces of great historical interest. These include a sample of 16th-century *altobasso* velvet (such as that used for the robes of Venetian *Procuratori*), elegant 18th-century tailcoats, and velvets produced for the Royal House of Italy in the early 20th century. Having existed for over a century now, the archive also has fabrics from America, Africa and the East.

The palazzo is also the Rubelli showroom.

SIGHTS NEARBY

THE DUTCH CERAMICS IN THE FORMER CONTARINI *CASINO*

Palazzo Corner Contarini dai Cavalli
San Marco 3780

Now housing the offices of the public administration, Palazzo Corner Contarini dai Cavalli still contains the remains of the old *casino*. If the offices that now occupy that space are not being used, it is theoretically possible – upon request – to gain admission to this room, which is covered in Dutch tiles depicting animals, houses and windmills, all in the purest Dutch style.

SIGHTS NEARBY 🔟

THE FORMER PREMISES OF THE CONFRATERNITY OF GERMAN SHOEMAKERS
La Crosera 3127a

At the corner of Calle Crosera and Calle dei Orbi, the bas-relief of a shoe is carved at about 2 metres from ground level on the façade of the house at number 3127a. This marks the fact that the building was the premises of the Confraternity of German Shoemakers, founded in 1383; the building itself dates from 1482. The first premises of the Scuola dei Calegheri Tedeschi were not far from the church of Santa Maria della Carità (the present-day museum of the Accademia).

> The old *scuola* of the (non-German) shoemakers is to be found in Campo San Tomà (see page 159).

> Opposite Caffè Lavena in St. Mark's Square there is another inscription – this time in the pavement – honouring the city's shoemakers.

CHURCH OF SANTI ROCCO E MARGHERITA 🔢
Istituto Ciliota- Calle delle Munaghe (Santo Stefano)- San Marco 2976
• Tel: 041 5204888 • www.ciliota.it info@ciliota.it

Built in the 18th century and now officially closed to the public, the church of Santi Rocco e Margherita can however be visited by going to the Istituto Ciliota (which has 51 rather functional rooms available for students and tourists; prices range from €50 to €140 per room). A polite request at the reception will almost always get you permission to look around the church. The Istituto and the church itself are part of the old convent of Augustinian nuns founded in 1448 (some sources say 1488), by the patriarch Maffeo Girardi, to replace an old oratory that had been dedicated to Santa Suzanna. Suppressed during the period of Napoleonic rule, the convent was not however demolished. The main surviving traces are parts of the ancient cloister (substantially "restored", they provide a nice location for tables and chairs in the summer months) and the church, which is sometimes still used by the Istituto Ciliota for private services. There is nothing extraordinary to see inside the church, which owes its name to two facts: that the Confraternity of San Rocco was established in the old oratory in the 15th century, and that the nun (Sister Chiara) who founded the Augustinian convent herself came from the Convent of Santa Margherita on Torcello.

SIGHTS NEARBY

THE FORMER PREMISES OF THE CONFRATERNITY OF STONEMASONS
San Marco 3216

On the second floor of the house at number 3216 you can – by stretching a little – make out a discreet emblem carved here in 1482. Combining a set-square, trowel, plumbline and hammer, this identifies the place as the former premises of the Scuola dei Mureri (Confraternity of Stonemasons), founded in 1220. The patron saints of these craftsmen, also called *cazziole* in Venetian, were St. Thomas and St. Magnus.

THE VENETIAN "PANTHEON" AT PALAZZO LOREDAN

Venetian Institute of Science, Arts and Letters
Campo Santo Stefano, 2945
30124 Venice
• Tel: 041 124 77 11
• www.istitutoveneto.it
• Open weekdays during office hours

Palazzo Loredan in Campo Santo Stefano has been home to the Venetian Institute of Science, Arts and Letters since 1810. This makes it possible for the public to enter this superb palazzo, whose entrance hall forms a sort of Venetian "Pantheon" with busts

Doges, architects, painters...

of some sixty figures who played an important part in the city's political or cultural life (doges, painters, architects, etc.). The earliest of these busts dates back to 1847, with the collection originally being housed in the Doge's Palace. Their setting here was entirely revamped in 2009 by Fabrizio Plessi, using a colour scheme that recalls some of the main attributes of the former Venetian Republic: red (the colour of Verona marble), yellow (Vicenza stone) and white (Istrian stone).

SIGHTS NEARBY

A FORGOTTEN TRACE OF THE AUSTRIAN OCCUPATION

Just above the entrance to Palazzo Loredan is an inscription that is easy to overlook. The curious thing is that it is in German. Reading K.K STADSUNDFESTUNGS COMMANDO, it is one of the rare existing traces of the Austrian occupation and identifies this building as the premises of the Austrian military forces in Venice.

REMINDERS OF THE PRODUCTION OF *TERIACA* IN CAMPO SANTO STEFANO

21

Campo Santo Stefano, outside number 2800

> **A trace of the divine potion**

Just opposite the pharmacy on the corner between Campo Santo Stefano and the aptly-named Calle Spezier (a *spezier da medicina* was an "apothecary" in Venetian), an often overlooked detail survives. About 5 metres from the façade of the pharmacy are three circular depressions in the ground, marking the space that once contained the cauldron in which the apothecary prepared the famous *Teriaca*, a magical potion that was said to cure any number of ailments (see opposite and following double page).

THE PRODUCTION OF *TERIACA*: A CAREFULLY-PLANNED CEREMONIAL

Not all apothecaries were licensed to produce *Teriaca*. Of the 90 in Venice, only about 40 had a licence to do so. These were known as *teriacanti*, who made the potion in the street itself using bronze cauldrons. The place where these cauldrons were set in the ground can still be seen around the city: in Campo Santo Stefano (see opposite) or in front of the Farmacia Alle Due Colonne (see p. 189).

Its most common ingredient being vipers (said to have restorative properties for ageing skin), *Teriaca* was produced once a year, in the period when vipers were captured (that is, towards the end of spring or during summer).

The success of the beverage led to an increase in demand, and some apothecaries - for example, Alla Testa d'Oro at Rialto — were allowed to produce it three times a year. In order to guarantee the quality of the product, Venice imposed strict rules. When making *Teriaca*, each apothecary was required to put all the ingredients he intended to use on public display outside his shop for three days. For the public, the best part in all this was the sight of live vipers, writhing inside lattice-work cages. When the mixing of ingredients began, the apothecary was watched by both the public and by State officials.

OTHER TRACES OF *TERIACA* IN VENICE
An inscription above the old sign at the apothecary "Alla Testa d'Oro" (see p. 17).
A depression in the pavement at San Canciano, in front of the modern-day pharmacy "Alle Due Colonne"; this was where the cauldron was placed for the preparation of the beverage (see p. 189).
Note that numerous pharmacies still have a jar marked *Theriaque*, even if such jars are unlikely to be originals. The old pharmacy at number 412 behind the Basilica of St. Mark's — now an art gallery — has an inscription regarding *Teriaca* on its wooden shop-fittings.

TERIACA: A MIRACULOUS POTION?

The legend goes that, in the second century BC, a physician-poet named Nicandre living in Colophon (Ionia) wrote a poem entitled *Ta Theriaca*. This treatise on the treatment of bites from wild animals, in particular serpents and other poisonous creatures, took its name from the Greek word *therion* (literally "viper" or "serpent", and by extension, "poison" in general). In 65 BC, Mithridates, King of Pontus (the Black Sea coastal region in the north-east of present-day Turkey) brewed the famous potion for the first time. Totalling 46 ingredients, the recipe was then completed by Andromachus, personal physician to Nero, who added a further 25 substances. Criton, physician to Trajan, then coined the name *Teriaca*, and the philosopher/physician Claudius Galenus (131-201) was responsible for establishing its reputation. As it developed in the years to follow, a whole host of recipes were concocted, generally changing according to the city where the potion was produced: Paris, Venice, Strasbourg, Poitiers or elsewhere. Amongst the recurrent – or most extravagant – ingredients that might be cited: powdered viper (made from live vipers), opium, dried wine lees, powdered stag's testicle, the horn of a unicorn (in fact, a narwhal, such as you can see nowadays in the Museo Correr) and so on. The claims made for the potion were infinite. Some of the things it was said to heal were: the plague and all infectious diseases; scorpion stings; viper and rabid dog bites; tuberculosis; putrid fever; stomach ailments; sight defects... By the 17th century, Venice had established a Europe-wide reputation for its own *Teriaca*, produced under the supervision of the State health authority and then exported not only throughout Europe but even to Turkey and Armenia. Such success inevitably stimulated greed, with some Venetian monasteries – for example, that of Santi Giovanni e Paolo – taking advantage of the fact that they were not under State control to produce vast quantities of the stuff. Even more seriously, there were "fakes", either of the product itself or of the label and packaging under which it was sold. This could lead to the apparently legal exportation of potions that were either inefficacious or even dangerous. A victim of the abuses arising from its own success, *Teriaca* ceased production in the 19th century.

WHY DID VENICE'S PHARMACEUTICAL PRODUCTS ENJOY SUCH A REPUTATION?

Up to the 19th century, Venice's pharmaceutical products enjoyed an international reputation. Often made using spices imported from the East, these products obviously benefited from the near monopoly that Venice had over trade with that area, which meant that the city could obtain good-quality ingredients at reasonable prices. From 1468 onwards, all these imports (together with the crews of the ships that carried them) were, upon arrival, held for forty days at the island of Lazzaretto Nuovo in order to avoid any risk of contagion within the city.

Thanks to the importance and prestige of its publishing and printing industry, Venice also became the place that produced the most significant books and anthologies of texts dealing with medicine and pharmacology. The present-day collection in the Biblioteca Marciana, for example, contains all the fundamental texts of Arabic medicine by such writers as Avicenna, Averroes, and others. And it was these works that would provide the intellectual and scientific background for the organisation of production of various types of medicines.

Similarly, as this area of manufacture took on increasing importance, the city introduced severe laws to impose quality control, thus opening up a wider export market for products that came with a certain guarantee.

Venice had up to 90 apothecaries who not only sold, but also produced

medicines. The craft was a prestigious one, recognised as a "noble art" (which meant that apothecaries could marry into patrician families). In the 16th century, the trade in medicines grew at such a rate that Venice had to impose limits. After 1616, no apothecary could set up within 100 paces (around 35 metres) of an existing *spezier da medicina*.

THE WINGED HORSE OF PALAZZO MOROSINI ㉒

Palazzo Morosini
Campo Santo Stefano
San Marco 2802

> **An alchemical symbol of the search for Philosopher's Gold**

The main entrance of Palazzo Morosini gives onto Campo Santo Stefano, whilst the other side of the building is bound by the Rio Del Santissimo. Although there is a bridge over the small *rio*, it is nevertheless difficult to see the amazing sculptures that decorate this side of the building. You either have to have your own boat or else ask the gondolier to halt here as you go past. One of the sculptures is a surprising depiction of a winged horse flanked by two winged gryphons.

The horse is Pegasus ("winged horse" in Greek), an animal which in Greek mythology was said to have been born from the blood of Medusa after Perseus beheaded the monster. Where Pegasus's hoof struck the ground of Mount Helicon, it caused water to flow forth. This "Horse Spring" (Hippocrene) would become identified as the source of poetic inspiration and associated with the immortality of poetry. Pegasus was subsequently immortalised by Zeus, who turned him into the constellation Pegasus within the northern hemisphere. Ultimately, the winged horse would also become a symbol of the Primordial Tradition of Alchemy, its flanks said to be made of gold (a reference to the Philosopher's Gold which was the ultimate aim of the Great Work of Alchemy).

It is no accident that this sculpture is placed here, over a very quiet canal. It symbolises Divine Wisdom, referring to Pegasus' ability to create, with a mere blow of its hoof, a miraculous spring that can give humans immortality.

This divine wisdom is also represented by the two winged gryphons alongside. They symbolise the phase of sublimation in alchemy (see following double page). Traditionally, these creatures were said to mate with a mare, the fruit of the union being a hippogryph. There is a medieval expression, *Jungentur jam grypes equis*, which means "to cross a gryphon with a mare" and was used to refer to something that was considered impossible. Hence, the hippogryph symbolises both love and impossibility. In medieval legends, this imaginary animal was often associated with knights in love with a lady who was impossible to conquer. Similarly, it would become the symbol of those engaged in the magical arts, who achieved the apparently impossible by submitting the material to the laws of the spiritual.

SIGHTS NEARBY

THE ONLY UNDERGROUND CANAL IN VENICE ㉓

If you have your own boat – or want to add to the wealth of one of the gondoliers – you can enjoy the thrill of travelling along the one underground canal in Venice, a stretch of the Rio del Santissimo that passes right under the choir of the Church of Santo Stefano. The place is also well-known to young Venetians, who come here to smoke without being disturbed. At high tide, be careful not to hit your head!

THE SYMBOLISM OF THE GRYPHON

In the alchemical bestiary, the gryphon is a mythological animal with the head and wings of an eagle and the body of a lion. It was said to make its nest near treasure and itself to lay golden eggs in a golden nest.

The first mention of this fantastic creature is found amongst the Babylonians, Assyrians and Persians, who depicted it in both sculpture and painting. In Ancient Greece it was believed that gryphons lived near the mythical place known as Hyperborea* and that they were the birds of Zeus (Jupiter). From around the 12th century, the gryphon began to appear on the escutcheons of numerous aristocratic European families, given its associations with a range of virtues (courage, purity, etc.) and its exemption from all defects. The gryphon also became a symbol of the Libra zodiac sign, given its keen sense of justice, the value it put on arts and intelligence, and the fact that it dominated the skies and the heavens.

In alchemy, the gryphon symbolised the relation between fixed and volatile principles. Thus, it was associated with both salt and mercury – not the material elements as such, but rather their "subtle essence". The *fixed* and the *volatile* could also be a reference to "water and air", to "the male and the female". Hence, the gryphon became a symbol of the Hermetic Cup (also known as the Philosopher's Cup or the Philosopher's Egg). This was a specially-shaped ceramic bottle used as a condenser in the process that alchemists called *sublimation*, the final phase in the transmutation of coarse elements into subtle ones.

According to legend, gryphons mated with horses, producing a creature called a hippogryph (see previous double page). A fine sculpture of such a creature by Antoine-Louis Barye is in the Louvre (Paris).

* In Greek, this literally means "beyond the Boreus" (the North Wind). In Greek mythology, *Hyperborea* was the paradise of the gods.

THE REMAINS OF THE OLD BELL-TOWER OF SANTA MARIA DEL GIGLIO

An unfinished bell-tower

It is easy to miss the fact that the small souvenir shop standing opposite the side entrance to the Church of Santa Maria del Giglio is housed within what remains of the church's old bell-tower.

As can be seen from Jacopo de'Barbari's famous *View of Venice*, published in 1500 (see below), the bell-tower was still unfinished at the end of the 15th century, even if the church itself dates back to the 10th century. It is amazing to note that the bell-tower, as depicted in that wood-cut of 1500, appears exactly the same as the one standing today, even if quite a few things have happened since. We know, for example, that the bell-tower was finally completed in the 16th century, but it leant at such an angle that it was considered a threat to nearby housing and was demolished in 1775. At that point, the Senate ordered it to be rebuilt, but the work clearly was never finished.

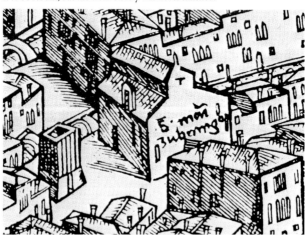

THE ORIGIN OF THE WORD *ZOBENIGO*
This alternative name for the Church of Santa Maria del Giglio comes from that of the Jubenico family, who contributed to the foundation of the church at the beginning of the 10th century.

SIGHTS NEARBY

THE CHAMBER OF RELIQUARIES IN THE CHURCH OF SANTA MARIA DEL GIGLIO

• Open Monday to Saturday from 10am to 5pm • Mass on Saturday at 6pm and on Sunday at 11:30am and 6pm. Weekday mass at 9:30am

Immediately to your right when you enter the church is a door that leads into an amazing hall of reliquaries. Its contents include a fragment of the Veil of the Virgin and reliquaries of St. Stephen, St. Theodore and St. Catherine of Siena, plus a fragment of the skull of St. James the Apostle and an ivory sculpture that probably depicts Mary Magdalene at the foot of the Cross. Curiously enough, this depiction shows the saint's left breast emerging from her dress.

For more information on reliquaries, see pages 76-77.

Contrary to what you might think, here you are encouraged to go behind the high altar to admire the paintings of the Evangelists. *St. Mark* and *St. Matthew* were painted by Tintoretto in 1552.

The Church of Santa Maria del Giglio is also the Venice seat of the Order of the Holy Sepulchre, whose mission is primarily to protect Catholic interests in Jerusalem (for more information, see our guide *Secret Rome*). The Order is also the guardian of the little-known reliquary of Christ's Crown of Thorns in Notre-Dame-de-Paris (see our guide *Secret Paris*). The Cross of the Order of the Holy Sepulchre can be seen on the main doorway to the church.

THE ORIGIN OF THE NAME OF CAMPIELLO FELTRINA

Between San Maurizio and Santa Maria del Giglio is the Campiello della Feltrina. The name is due to the fact that, up to the 18th century, the Palazzo Malipiero housed the "hostel" of the city of Feltre. Various cities of the Venetian Republic, including Bergamo, Brescia, Chioggia, Feltre and Vicenza, had the right to maintain such hostels to accommodate dignitaries visiting Venice.

THE ROOMS OF THE *RIDOTTO* AT THE HOTEL MONACO E GRAND CANAL ㉖

Calle Vallaresso 1332
- For information: 041 5200211
- Open admission or upon request
- maiolbox@hotelmonaco.it
- www.hotelmonaco.it

> *Venice's first state-run gambling house*

T he Hotel Monaco e Grand Canal near St. Mark's Square contains the recently restored rooms of an old *ridotto*, now open to the public. Immediately to your right upon entering the hotel lobby, a fine staircase leads up to the *piano nobile*, which opens onto a richly decorated central hall off which are located a total of eight rooms; the layout was designed by the 18th-century architect Maccaruzzi. The walls and ceiling of the largest room (which rises to the height of two floors) are luxuriously decorated in faux marble, complete with mirrors and stuccowork of flowers, fruit and foliage. The other rooms also have decoration in marble and stucco of floral and shell motifs combined with ribbons and volutes.

The palazzo originally belonged to the Dandolo family. In the 16th century, it housed the French embassy and then, in 1638, was rented to the State, which transformed it into a public gaming-house, or *ridotto*. Open during Carnival, which at the time lasted a full two months, the *ridotto* was run by *barnabotti*, aristocrats who had fallen on hard times (so called because they lived in the San Barnaba area, in accommodation provided for them by the State). With the exception of the croupiers, all those in the *ridotto* had to wear masks.

Even though it was well-known throughout Europe and made a substantial contribution to the State's coffers, the *ridotto* was closed in 1774 (see page 267). After a period of neglect, in recent times the rooms were used first as a cinema and then as a theatre. Nowadays, they are used for events organised by the Hotel Monaco (conferences, parties, banquets and concerts).

The *ridotti* – literally meaning "withdrawing rooms" – were small assembly rooms where Venetians could enjoy gambling, maintain social and political contacts, and also indulge in the pleasures of the flesh (see page 267). The term itself dates back to the 13th century. Tradition has it that initially games of chance were played in the open air, between the two columns in the Piazzetta leading from St. Mark's to the waterfront (the same place where executions were carried out, see page 99). However, it did not take long before gambling spread, so the State decided to restrict such pleasures to the interior of specially designated locations.

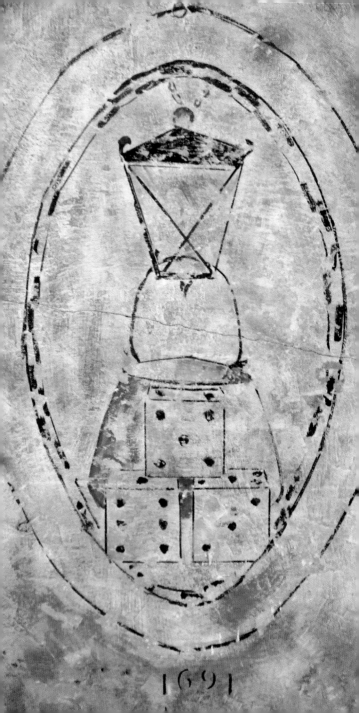

1691

FRESCO OF A DICE GAME

Rio Terà de le Colonne (to the southeast corner of Calle dei Fabbri)

> *A game once played between the columns in the Piazzetta*

As its name indicates, the Rio Terà de le Colonne occupies the site of a filled-in canal. The location of the old *fondamenta* (quayside) is now indicated by the small *sotoportego* (covered walkway). At the junction with Calle dei Fabbri (on the southeast corner), you can see a fresco showing a game of dice and a lantern on the ceiling of this *sotoportego*. Whilst the accompanying date reads 1691, it would seem that the work is actually modern.

The first place where the playing of dice was legal in Venice was between the two columns in Piazzetta San Marco, and the reason for this is very curious. For a long time, these monumental columns – which had been brought to the city from the East – were left lying on the ground as no-one had found a way of raising them into position. Then, in 1172, the Bergamo engineer Nicola Starantonio Barattiero, who had built the first Rialto Bridge, had the ingenious idea of holding one end of the column fixed and tying ropes that were solidly fixed to the ground around the other end. When the ropes were wet, they would expand then shrink in length and slide a few centimetres down the shaft of the column, raising the head of the column off the ground. Wooden blocks then kept it in place, while dry ropes replaced the wet ones, and the process was repeated, until finally the columns stood upright.

As a reward for this idea, Barattiero was granted authorisation to hold a dice game between the two columns, and even to organise an open-air gambling den. Dice games had, up to that point, been strictly forbidden within the city.

SIGHTS NEARBY

THE ARMENIAN CHURCH OF SANTA CROCE DEGLI ARMENI

• Open once a month for mass, on the last Sunday of the month at 10:30am

The little-known church of Santa Croce degli Armeni is – along with the monastery on the island of San Lazzaro degli Armeni and Palazzo Zenobio (see p. 347-349) – the only other mark of the Armenian presence in the city. Once a month, the Armenian community gathers here for mass. However, the church itself is of no particular artistic or historic interest.

THE FAÇADE OF THE CHURCH OF SAN GIULIANO

㉙

Church of San Giuliano (*San Zulian* in Venetian)
Campo San Giuliano

> *A specific
> application
> of hermetic
> theories*

The curious façade of the church of San Giuliano in the eponymous square contains Alessandro Vittoria's statue of Tommaso Rangone, an extraordinary Renaissance figure who made his fortune from a natural "remedy" for syphilis brought from South America (see double page overleaf).

Part of his wealth went to finance the 1553 restoration of this church, which was by then in a parlous state.

Rangone, shown seated on a sarcophagus and wearing a professorial gown, seems to be in the act of proffering part of his vast knowledge – an attitude befitting a far from modest man who was convinced of his own special destiny. The hemispherical space within which he is depicted is a symbol of the Heavens above the Earth. Hence, there is a conscious reference to the hermetic theories that enjoyed such a vogue in the Renaissance. Arguing that "all that which is above is just as that which is below", these ideas aimed to describe the action of cosmic and sidereal energies upon the sublunary world (see p. 174). The globe to the right of Rangone is shown inclined at 44° 30' (the latitude of Venice) and is engraved with the constellations as they were on the date of his birth (18 August 1493; his zodiac sign – Leo – is shown at the centre of the heavenly sphere). In combination with the cube on which it rests, this celestial globe symbolises motion and stability, Heaven and Earth, and the finite and the infinite. To the left, a terrestrial globe is shown on a table, together with some books. Inclined in the opposite direction to the celestial globe, it shows at its centre the Atlantic Ocean between Europe and South America (where Rangone's "remedy" had been discovered). Between these two globes, Tommaso is shown seated and holding a book in his left hand within which the word DEUS and the abbreviation HIQ (*Hinc Illincque*) can be read, which might be translated as meaning "on one side and the other" or "on each side". The message is that God can be contemplated in both the microcosm and microcosm, on Earth as in Heaven.

In his right hand, Rangone holds the plant discovered in South America, to which he would give the name of "Indian wood" or "holy wood". The divine presence thus manifests itself on both sides of the Atlantic, just as it does in both the celestial and terrestrial spheres.

There are three inscriptions on the façade. The one in Latin gives biographical and juridical information, that in Greek praises Rangone's cultural achievements, and that in Hebrew recalls the possibility of achieving on Earth the divine project of living to the age of 120 (see p. 59).

TOMMASO RANGONE, A VERY CURIOUS FIGURE

Born in Ravenna on 18 August 1493, Tommaso Rangone died in 1577 at the age of 84 (not 94 as Tassini claims). A scholar and scientist, his reputation suffered somewhat from his marked taste for self-celebration. The effigy on the façade of the Venetian church of San Giuliano (see previous double page) came only after he had failed in his attempts to get a statue of himself erected on the façades of the church of San Geminiano (where he was a procurator) and of the Scuola Grande di San Marco (where he was the *Guardian Grande*). Rangone had already had himself included in the paintings Tintoretto was commissioned to produce for the Scuola Grande. However, the works had been rejected by the monks, who were sick of Rangone always having himself depicted in the place of honour. To get the pictures accepted, Tintoretto had even proposed painting over the figure of the pushy scholar. The high opinion that Rangone had of himself comes across continually, both in his repeated references to his vast learning in astrology, medicine and languages, and in the boast that his own personal library formed one of the Seven Wonders of the World.

Even in death, he managed to push himself forward. The plans for his funeral stipulated that his body was to be carried through the city on its way to San Giuliano, preceded by a long file of people bearing open books. Each one of these was to illustrate a specific subject: Ravenna (Rangone's birthplace), the bird of paradise, a pair of ravens (symbols of long life), the peony (the most ancient and celebrated of medicinal plants), the movement of the heavenly orbs and constellations, and so on...

Rangone had made his fortune through the discovery of a "cure" for syphilis, though he denied the disease was transmitted solely via sex. According to his theory, it was the result of natural causes and his remedy came from the recently-discovered New World, where the natives had long been expert in finding natural remedies for different diseases. Rangone also founded a university college in Padua, which provided free accommodation for 32 students who studied astronomy, Hebrew, Chaldee, Syriac, Persian and the interpretation of Holy Scripture. Taking his lead from the Bible — where (in Genesis 6:3) it is said of mankind "his days shall be an hundred and twenty years" — Rangone also wrote a treatise entitled *Sul Come condurre la vita fino a 120 anni**, mentioning all the various ancient philosophers and biblical patriarchs who had lived up to (or beyond) that age. The book was then presented to doges and popes, and Rangone even had a compilation of extracts made for the benefit of the populace of Venice. His recipe involved a healthy lifestyle, minimal consumption of medicines, rigorous self-discipline and frequent prayer to one's guardian angel and to the stars.

* How to Live to 120 Years

ADDI XV GIVGNO MCCCX

THE SCULPTED PLAQUE OF AN OLD WOMAN ㉚ WITH A MORTAR

Mercerie, at the corner of the Sotoportego del Cappello
Mercerie, 149

> **A reminder of a conspiracy in 1310**

Often overlooked, this sculpted plaque just a few steps from St. Mark's Square is a reminder of a remarkable incident in the history of the Venetian Republic that took place on 15 June 1310.

In order to overthrow Doge Pietro Gradenigo, the Tiepolo and Querini families banded together with various other aristocratic families (see p. 120) in a plot led by one Bajamonte Tiepolo. However, things did not go as planned. Forewarned by informers, the doge's guards cut off access to the Palace and fighting started in St. Mark's Square. Soon, the rebels had to beat a hasty retreat, making for the Rialto via the Mercerie.

Looking out on these events from her balcony at the beginning of that street, an old woman – whom some records identify simply as "Giustina", others as "Lucia Rossi" – dropped a heavy mortar onto the fleeing rebels, hitting Bajamonte Tiepolo's standard-bearer and killing him on the spot.

The old woman subsequently asked for a reward for her daring-do, requesting that thereafter on 15 June and all public holidays she be allowed to hang the banner of St. Mark from her balcony, and that the rent for her house never be raised (neither for her nor her daughters after her). A munificent ruler, the doge accepted her requests, and ruled that the fixed rent should be enjoyed by the old woman's heirs in perpetuity.

More than 500 years later, in 1861, the sole occupant of the house, Elia Vivante Mussati, had this plaque carved. Bearing the date of the rebellion, it depicts the old woman throwing the mortar.

There are other reminders of the Bajamonte Tiepolo conspiracy in Venice. An engraved stone in Campo San Agostino (near Campo San Polo) identifies the location of Bajamonte's house, which was demolished. In its place, a "column of infamy" recording his crime was initially set up. It was then replaced with the paving stone that recalls the episode (see p. 151).

Other traces are the marks that were set on the homes of each of the conspirators as well as the emblems of the confraternities that helped bring about the defeat of the conspiration, on campo San Luca (see p. 29).

Directly below the sculpted plaque in St. Mark's is a small white stone indicating where the mortar fell. It also shows the date in Roman numerals.

WHY IS THE CLOCK FACE ON THE CLOCK TOWER DIVIDED INTO 24 HOURS?

After centuries of sundials, the first mechanical clocks made their appearance in Europe at the end of the 13th century. They marked a real revolution, as an hour finally became a fixed unit of length. By the end of the 14th century, most cities had abandoned time as measured by the gnomon of a sundial for time as measured by their church clocks.

Each day actually began at sunset and was divided into 24 hours (see below), so the first clock faces were calibrated from I to XXIV. However, it was quickly seen that counting up to 24 strokes of a bell to tell the time could be annoying and lead to error. In the 15th century, the system was thus simplified, with the bells striking only 6 times instead of 24. Such a simplification was also rapidly applied to the clock faces themselves, which were now divided from I to VI. Known as "Roman clock faces", some of these still exist. There is one in the Sala dell'Avogaria in the Doge's Palace and various others, mainly in Italy (see our guides *Secret Rome* and *Secret Tuscany*).

During the Napoleonic wars in Italy, the "Italian" system was replaced by the "French" one, with clock faces being divided I to XII and days beginning at midnight.

VENETIAN CLOCKS WITH 24-HOUR FACES
Fondaco dei Tedeschi, at Rialto
Church of Santi Apostoli, near Rialto
Church of San Giacomo, at Rialto
Clock Tower in St. Mark's Square
Doge's Palace

GO TO THE TOP OF THE CLOCK TOWER
Curiously, people often forget that it is possible to go up the clock tower. Although quite expensive (€12 per person), the hour-long guided visit is very interesting and you will probably have the guide all to yourself while admiring the superb panorama from the top. Commentaries are given in Italian, English and French.
Tickets from the Museo Correr or by telephoning 041 520 90 70.

THE SYMBOLIC SIGNIFICANCE OF THE MOORS ON THE CLOCK TOWER

Far from depicting Moorish slaves or the victory of Christian Venice over Islam, the two Moors on the top of the clock tower represent the chaos and primordial darkness that preceded the Creation. Armed with hammers to strike a large bell, they are a reminder that it was through the ringing sound of the Word (*Fiat Lux*) that the world was created.

THE SYMBOLIC FLAGPOLES IN FRONT OF ST. MARK'S BASILICA

St. Mark's Square

③

> ### The symbols of Candia, Morea and Cyprus

The three flagpoles located directly in front of St. Mark's Basilica can sometimes be overlooked. They symbolise the three kingdoms conquered by Venice during the course of its history: Cyprus, *Candia* (modern-day Crete) and *Morea* (the Peloponnese), whose flags used to fly here.

The term *Morea* for the Peloponnese was adopted in the 12th century by the Crusaders. It was inspired by the fact that the peninsula's overall shape is similar to that of the leaf of the mulberry (or *morus*) bushes which are common here. As for the name "Peloponnese", it comes from the name of Pelops, the son of Tantalus, king of Lydia (in the west of modern-day Turkey). The Ottoman Turks conquered *Morea* and the last Venetian possessions on Crete in 1715, even if the war dragged on to 1718.

The term *Candia* comes from the Latin *Candicus* (moat), which was the original name for the island's main city, Heraklion. In the Middle Ages, the term was used to refer to either the island or the city. Candia was under Venetian rule from 1204 to 1648, by which time Venice had control of only three cities on the island: Gramvoussa (which fell to the Ottomans in 1691) and Spinalonga and Souda (both of which fell in 1715).

Cyprus was Venetian from 1489 to 1571, thanks to the marriage of the Venetian Caterina Cornaro to James II de Lusignan, king of Cyprus. The marriage contract stipulated that the throne should pass to Caterina Cornaro if the king died without an heir. It is said that the Venetians promptly poisoned the son born to the couple.

Nowadays, the flags of Venice, Italy and Europe fly from the flagpoles.

A SIMPLE CHANGE OF SYMBOLS TO SAVE THE FLAGPOLES

In the period of Napoleonic rule, a certain Giuliani protested that the flagpoles should be torn down as they were symbols of tyranny. After long debate, it was decided to keep them – with the official declaration that they actually symbolised Freedom, Virtue and Equality.

THE PORPHYRY LOZENGE IN THE ATRIUM OF ST. MARK'S BASILICA

32

St. Mark's Basilica
In front of the main doorway
• Open daily from 9:45am to 5pm
• Sundays and holidays from 2pm to 5pm (4pm from November to Easter)

> **The exact spot where Frederick Barbarossa knelt before the pope in 1177**

In front of the main doorway in the atrium is a very discreet lozenge in porphyry which marks the spot where the Holy Roman Emperor, Frederick I – known as Barbarossa – knelt before Pope Alexander III on 24 July 1177 before being received in the Doge's Palace. Humiliating for a man who had seen himself as the heir of the Roman emperors and wished to control the same vast regions of territory, this gesture signified Barbarossa's acceptance of Alexander III as the sole pope of Christendom, and his abandonment of his own claim to be able to appoint bishops.

Shortly after Alexander III's election in 1159, Frederick Barbarossa had, in fact, had a college of cardinals under his own control elect an anti-pope*, Victor IV, who was then followed by two other anti-popes (Pascal III and Calixtus III). The great Catholic States of Europe (France, England, Sicily and the Iberian kingdoms) were at the time involved in a power struggle with the German Empire and so recognised Alexander III as their pope, who excommunicated Barbarossa in 1160. War broke out and, after Frederick's

defeat at Legnano in 1176, Venice offered itself as "neutral" ground for the reconciliation of pope and emperor. This was a very important event because, by serving as an intermediary between them, Venice placed itself at the same level as the two figures, thus acquiring considerable prestige. Approaching the city via Ravenna and then Chioggia – while the pope himself was already in Venice – Barbarossa had to abjure his nomination of anti-popes before making his entrance into the basilica.

* Anti-pope: a figure elected pope when there was already a pope on the Throne of St. Peter. Not officially recognised by the Catholic Church, most of these anti-popes were nominated by individual sovereigns to serve their own political ends.

THE MYSTERIOUS LETTER OF GREETINGS FROM PRESTER JOHN

Legend has it that after signing their peace treaty, the pope and emperor received a letter from the mysterious Prester John. Considered by some to be the emperor of the East, this figure's legendary reputation was in part due to the Templars, who claimed that he lived in a mysterious realm somewhere in Asia, that he was both simultaneously pope and emperor, and that he had actually been crowned by the Mother of God.

It would seem that this letter – which congratulated Alexander III and Barbarossa on having reached a peace agreement and then continued with reflections upon the Virgin Mary and upon peace and concord between the different peoples of the world – was actually fabricated by the Templars themselves. The maritime expeditions of the Portuguese were in part inspired by the legendary figure of Prester John, in the hope of forging an alliance between Western Europe and Christian Asia against the Muslims of the Middle East. See our guide *Secret Lisbon*.

THE ORIGIN OF THE NAME *BUCINTORO*

Tradition has it that, after the conclusion of peace between pope and emperor, Alexander III gave the doge a ring in thanks for his work of diplomacy. This was the ring which was at the origin of the custom of the "Wedding of the Sea" on Ascension Day, when the doge would throw a ring into the waters of the Adriatic. The vessel which carried the doge on these occasions only became known as *Il Bucintoro* around 1311, which also happens to be the year in which the Templars were exterminated in France. One of the explanations for the origin of the name says it is a composite of *bucio* or *bucin* (a medieval vessel powered by a number of oars) and *oro* (in reference to its rich gilding). However, others say the name comes from *Beaucéant*, the name of the standard of the Knights Templars, who had provided hospitality for the pope in 1177 (see page 144). The Templars were also Alexander III's bodyguard; furthermore, their fleet and their possessions in the Holy Land played a major role in maintaining Venetian trade with the East (see p. 243). The name *beaucéant* itself is a composite in *langue d'oil* of the terms *beau* (beautiful) and *céant* (within) – that is, a reference to interior or spiritual beauty.

THE MOSAIC OF THE DODECAHEDRON

Exit from St. Mark's Basilica
• Open daily from 9:45am to 5pm
• Sundays and holidays from 2pm to 5pm (4pm from November to Easter)

> *The dodecahedron and cosmic harmony*

On the floor of St. Mark's, just in front of the main doorway on the left, is a curious mosaic of a starred dodecahedron. It is attributed to Paolo Uccello, the famous Florentine Renaissance artist (1397-1475), who here was perhaps influenced by Luca Bartolommeo de Pacioli (1445-1517), even though the latter was only thirty at the time of the artist's death. De Pacioli was a Franciscan monk and a famous mathematician and is considered to be the father of modern bookkeeping. He was also the author of a treatise entitled *De Divina Proportione*, published in Venice in 1509, which was primarily concerned with the "golden ratio" and its application in architecture and painting.

By extending the faces of the dodecahedron so that they meet to form "pyramids", a star is obtained, hence the "starred dodecahedron" made up of twelve pentagons. The basis of the pentagram (the five-pointed star made up of five straight lines), this figure was, for the wise men of Antiquity, a symbol of Venus, the planet governing Venice (see page 86), which explains its presence here.

In traditional symbolism, the dodecahedron was the form that best represented the manifestation of God in Nature. For Plato, it was the symbol *par excellence* of cosmic harmony. It is also a three-dimensional representation of the symmetry of the pentagon and of the "golden ratio" that occurs throughout the natural world. This "golden ratio" or "golden mean" (1.618), described by Kepler in his *Mysterium Cosmographicum* as "a gem of geometry", is the essential property of the dodecahedron and also the other geometrical forms that Plato described as "celestial". Totalling five in number, they were the model for all the forms to be found in the natural world (see following double page). These universal forms are systematically organised in a geometrical form in which each figure has its own mathematical and philosophical interpretation, hence their use in religious art and religious architecture.

There is another dodecahedron below the iconostasis (visible from rather far away by standing at the Pala d'Oro entrance).

THE FIVE BASIC SOLIDS AND SACRED GEOMETRY

Sacred geometry is a world vision according to which the basic criteria for existence are perceived as being *sacred*. Through them can be contemplated the *Magnum Misterium*, the Universal *Grand Project*, by learning its laws, principles and the inter-relationships of shapes. These universal shapes are systematised in a geometric complex in which each figure has its own mathematical and philosophical interpretation. They are applied in projects of *sacred architecture* and *sacred art*, which always use the "divine" proportions in which Man reflects the Universe, and vice versa. It is a common belief that *sacred geometry* and its mathematical relationships, which are harmonic and proportional, are also found in Music, Light and Cosmology. Man first discovered this system of values in prehistoric times, in the megalithic and Neolithic cultures, for example, and some consider it to be a universal facet of the human condition.

Sacred geometry is fundamental to the construction of sacred structures, such as synagogues, churches and mosques, and also plays a role in creating the interior sacred space of temples, through the altars and tabernacles. Passed down from Graeco-Egyptian culture and exported to ancient Rome, *sacred geometry* in the European Middle Ages inspired the creation of the Roman and Gothic architecture of Europe's medieval cathedrals, which incorporate this geometry of sacred symbolism.

It is said that Pythagoras (Samos, *c.* 570 BC -- Metapontum, *c.* 497 BC) was the one who founded the system of *sacred geometry* in his school in

Croton, Greece. This Greek philosopher and mathematician is believed to have brought the knowledge he acquired in Egypt and India back to Greece. Using the golden ratio (1.618) and applying it to the geometric forms of the five basic solids, Pythagoras created the mathematical method universally known as *Pythagorean geometry*.

To create the five solids (the tetrahedron or pyramid, the hexahedron or cube, the octahedron, the dodecahedron and the icosahedron), about which Plato would later philosophise (to such a point that they would become known as the *five Platonic solids*), Pythagoras was inspired by the Greek myth about the child-god Dionysus' toys: a basket, dice, top, ball and mirror. On a cosmic level, the *basket* represents the Universe; the dice, the *five Platonic solids* symbolising the natural elements (ether, air, fire, water, earth); the *top* is the atom of matter; the *ball*, the Earth's globe; and, finally, the *mirror* reflects the work of the Supreme Geometrist (*Dionysus*), which itself is the universal manifestation of Life and Consciousness, of God towards Man and vice versa. Each of the five Platonic solids also represents a planetary energy that is connected by its form to a natural element. Thus, the *dodecahedron* is traditionally linked to Venus and ether, the natural quintessence, expressed by a temple's dome. The *octahedron*, linked to Saturn and the air, represents the transept's cross. The *tetrahedron*, linked to Mars and fire, is symbolised by the openings in the temple through which light gushes forth. The *icosahedron*, linked to the Moon and water, establishes the harmony of forms in the temple *design*, constructing the connecting lines between the altars and columns. Finally, the *hexahedron* (cube), fixes the Sun to its element, the earth, by determining the shape of the temple's foundation or floor.

The main purpose of *sacred geometry* is thus to create Universal Perfection through perfect mathematical forms and calculations, and, by using *sacred architecture*, to connect the Multiple to the Single in a space that is geometrically dedicated to this end.

THE MOSAIC OF THE RHINOCEROS

St. Mark's Basilica
Open daily from 9:45am to 5pm
Sundays and holidays from 2pm to 5pm (4pm from November to Easter)

A rhinoceros in the basilica...

The long and rich history of the basilica means that its walls now enclose some quite extraordinary features.

One of them is just to the left of the side doorway, opposite the chapel of St. Isidor: an astonishing mosaic of a rhinoceros. Its origin is still the subject of scholarly debate. Some claim it dates from the 13th century (like most of the other mosaics in the basilica), whilst others argue for the 15th, 16th, 18th or even 20th centuries.

Though the animal's existence is mentioned by Pliny the Elder, Strabo, Solinus and Isidor of Seville, the first recorded presence of a rhinoceros in Early Modern Europe dates from 1515, when one was presented as a gift to King Manuel I of Portugal by the Sultan of Cambay (modern-day Gujarat in India). In Lisbon, a combat was organised between the newcomer and an elephant, which rapidly fled, confirming the claims made by the Ancients that the rhinoceros was the only animal that could defeat an elephant. Sent on to Pope Leo X, the rhinoceros would prove such a curiosity that the French king, François I, would come to admire it while it was being transported by ship off the coast of Marseilles. The animal later died in a storm at sea during that voyage, and certain sources claim that it was stuffed so that it could be presented to the pope anyway. Albrecht Dürer produced a famous engraving of the animal that same year (1515).

It would seem that the first time a rhinoceros came to Venice was in 1751, during a European tour organised by its owner, the Dutchman Douwe Mout

van der Meer. Nicknamed "Clara", it was one of the attractions at that year's Carnival and was painted by Pietro Longhi.

Some claim that the tree shown behind the rhinoceros in this mosaic is a symbol of strength and fortitude. Others argue that the presence of the rhinoceros itself is intended to ward off illness.

OTHER CURIOSITIES IN THE BASILICA

The **icon of the Virgin Nikopeais** is said to have been painted by St. Luke himself. The **black and white columns** of the atrium around the main entrance are said to come from the Temple of Solomon in Jerusalem (even though some say the marble comes from the Pyrenees).

The columns that flank the two mosaic angels to each side of the high altar are said to come from **the house of Pontius Pilate**.

The stone that serves as an altar in the baptistery is said to be that on **which Christ stood when preaching at Tyre**.

The stone upon which St. John the Baptist was beheaded, complete with what were said to be traces of his blood, was once also to be seen in the baptistery. Now it is in the basilica's storerooms.

RELICS AND OTHER EXTRAORDINARY POSSESSIONS OF THE TREASURY OF ST. MARK'S

Venice certainly did not lag behind in the rush to gain possession of relics which, from its very beginnings, had always been part of Christianity (see following double page). Along with the famous relics of St. Mark and such "classic" relics as a part of the True Cross, a finger of St. Mary Magdalene and the thumb of St. Mark, the basilica possesses various other surprising relics, some of which are on public display in the Treasury.

A **phial of Christ's blood.** Threads of cotton soaked in the blood and water that flowed from the crucified Christ's wound when his side was pierced.

A small portion of the **Column to which Christ was bound at the Flagellation** (the largest part is in Rome; see our guide *Secret Rome*).

A part of the rod on which the crucified Christ was offered **a sponge soaked in vinegar** ("Sacra Arundine").

A **piece of the fabric (linen)** Christ used when washing the Apostles' feet ("Santo linteo").

A reliquary containing the **Virgin's milk** was long on display, but is now in the storeroom.

A **lock of the Virgin's hair.**

The **sword with which St. Peter cut off Malchus' ear** in the Garden of Gethsemane.

A **fragment of John the Baptist's skull.**

St. Mark's thumb: the saint is said to have cut off his thumb in a gesture of humility, so that he would not be considered a suitable candidate for the priesthood.

The **arm with which St. George** is said to have held the lance that killed the dragon.

The **tooth of a hippopotamus**, which was once thought to be a rhinoceros horn; there are also three "unicorn" horns (actually narwhal teeth) now in the storeroom. The Museo Correr has a large narwhal tooth that is magnificently carved with the Tree of Jesse.

THE CULT OF CHRISTIAN RELICS

Although rather neglected these days, with their devoted following greatly diminished in numbers, saints' relics had extraordinary success from the Middle Ages onwards. Their presence today in numerous churches across Europe is a reminder of those exceptional times.

The cult of Christian relics goes back to the beginning of Christianity, to the deaths of the early martyrs and the creation of the first saints. The function of these relics was threefold: they bore witness to the example of a righteous and virtuous life to be copied or followed; they possessed a spiritual energy and power that could even work miracles (it was believed that the miraculous powers of the saints themselves was retained by their relics); and over time, with the rise of the contested practice of granting indulgences, relics bestowed indulgences on those who possessed them (see opposite).

As demand dictated supply, it was not long before unscrupulous parties were competing to invent their own relics, aided in their task by the Church which, for political reasons, canonised a great number of undeserving individuals (see opposite). Over-production went to absurd extremes: if the authenticity of all their relics was to be accepted,

Mary Magdalene would have had six bodies, and St. Biagio a hundred arms. These excesses, of course, raised suspicions and the popularity of relics gradually waned, although many people still believe that the true relic of a saint possesses spiritual power. How else can the numerous pilgrimages in the footsteps of Father Pio throughout Italy be explained?

There are around 50,000 relics scattered around Europe, from some 5,000 saints.

Note that most of the world's other religions also worship relics, or used to do so.

21,441 RELICS FOR 39,924,120 YEARS OF INDULGENCES! The greatest collector of relics was Frederick III of Saxony (1463-1525), who procured 21,441 of them in all, 42 of which were fully preserved bodies of saints. Based on this unique collection, he calculated that he had amassed a grand total of 39,924,120 years and 220 days of indulgences! However, under the influence of Luther, who opposed indulgences, he abandoned the cult of relics in 1523.

WHEN SAINTS ARE NOT SO HOLY: ST. GEORGE, ST. CHRISTOPHER, AND ST. PHILOMENA, STRUCK FROM THE LIST...

From the Middle Ages onwards, the pursuit of relics continued, as did their falsification. Not only relics were fabricated, however. Sometimes, even the saints themselves were a fabrication.

Recently – an event that passed almost without comment – the Church purged St. George, St. Christopher and St. Philomena from its calendar, the very existence of all three now being in doubt.

The totally abusive canonisation of certain real personalities also took place, allowing the objects connected with them to feed the market for saintly relics.

For diplomatic reasons linked to the Counter-Reformation of the 16th century, canonisation was often based on political rather than religious or moral criteria. As a result of this *Realpolitik*, many rulers of the time were thus sanctified in a bid to ensure their subjects' allegiance to the Roman Catholic Church, then under pressure from the Protestant movement. St. Stanislas of Poland, St. Casimir of Lithuania, St. Brigitte of Sweden, St. Stephen of Hungary, St. Margaret of Scotland, St. Elizabeth of Portugal, St. Wenceslas of Bohemia ... The list is long, indeed.

RELICS OF THE FEATHERS OF THE ARCHANGEL MICHAEL, THE BREATH OF JESUS, AND EVEN THE STARLIGHT THAT GUIDED THE THREE WISE MEN!

Leaving no stone unturned in their efforts to make money at the expense of the most naive believers, relic merchants showed unparalleled imagination in their quest for sacred paraphernalia and invented some fascinating objects, such as the horns of Moses or the feathers of the Archangel Michael, recorded as having been on sale at Mont-Saint-Michel in 1784.

The most highly prized relics were of course those of Christ. Unfortunately for relic hunters, as Christ had ascended to Heaven, his body was by definition no longer on Earth. Imagination again came to the rescue in the form of the quite extraordinary relic of the breath of Jesus (!) which was preserved in Wittenberg cathedral, Germany, in a glass phial.

The remains of Christ's foreskin, recuperated after his circumcision seven days after birth, and of his umbilical cord (!) were preserved at Latran, Rome (in the Sancta Sanctorum) while bread from the Last Supper was kept at Gaming, Austria. Certain medieval texts lost to us today even spoke of the relic of the rays of the star that guided the Wise Men, also preserved at Latran.

Nowadays, a church becomes a basilica by papal decree as a result of its extensive spiritual influence or the exemplary nature of its devotions.

THE STONE MARKING THE BURIAL SITE OF DOGE FRANCESCO ERIZZO'S HEART

- Visible during visiting hours for the Pala d'Oro
- Daily 9:45am to 5pm
- Sunday and holidays: 2pm to 5pm (4pm from November to Easter)

> *A doge's heart buried in the basilica*

Just a few steps away from the Pala d'Oro, visitors on their way to the exit inevitably tread upon one special paving stone without even noticing it. It is marked by a heart and the ducal *corno* (ceremonial hat) and indicates the place where, in compliance with the wishes in his last will and testament, the heart of Francesco Erizzo (1566-1646; doge from 1631 to 1646) was buried. The rest of his body lies in the Church of San Martino in Castello, near his birthplace. The black shape under the *corno dogale* symbolises a hedgehog (*riccio* in Italian), which was the symbol of the Erizzo family because of the assonance between the two words.

HOW TO VISIT ST. MARK'S BASILICA WITHOUT THE TOURISTS

After the official closing at 5pm, St. Mark's opens for the lucky few. On the north side of the church (not far from the clock tower) is a door that gives access to those going to Vespers (5:30pm in winter; 6pm in summer) and to the 6:45pm mass (which is preceded by a saying of the Rosary at 6:30pm). Before going through the door, put away your camera. The sacristan only lets in those who are coming for religious worship. Once inside, you definitely cannot walk about. Sit down quietly on one of the seats, and avoid coming in too late or leaving before the end of service. Another, much more expensive, way of avoiding the tourists costs around €400 for up to 50 people: an official reservation for a nocturnal visit to the basilica and its crypt. Reservations at 041 2702424 or 041 2708334.

WHAT IS A BASILICA?

During the Roman Empire, a "basilica" was the place where the king (*basileus*) meted out justice. After the Edict of Milan (313), which put an end to the persecution of Christians, the Emperor Constantine had four so-called major basilicas built in Rome and donated them to the pope. These were St. Peter in the Vatican (the supposed place of St. Peter's martyrdom), St. Paul without the Walls (the supposed site of St. Paul's martyrdom), Santa Maria Maggiore (the first Christian church dedicated to the Virgin) and San John Lateran (in homage to the apostle "beloved of Jesus"). All other basilicas (in Rome or elsewhere) are classified as "minor"; under the protection of the pope, they are associated with one of the four major basilicas.

A DEPICTION OF PIETRO ARETINO

Entrance to the sacristy
• Door can be seen during the visiting hours of the Pala d'Oro
• Daily 9:45am to 5pm
• Sunday and holidays: 2pm to 5pm (4pm from November to Easter)

> **A libertine anti-clerical poet within the basilica**

When you look closely at the bronze heads that project from the doors leading from the sacristy to the basilica of St. Mark's, you will be surprised to see that one is a bust of Pietro Aretino, a libertine anti-clerical poet; the portrait is by Sansovino.

The door can be seen by those who pay to go through to see the Pala d'Oro. It is to the left if you are standing with your back to the Pala.

Pietro Aretino was an Italian writer born in Arezzo in 1492, hence his surname, meaning "an inhabitant of Arezzo". He was famous for his *Sonetti Lussuriosi* (Licentious Sonnets) and for writings that derided the sacraments. Having quickly become hostile to the papacy, he took refuge in Venice, the Italian city of the day which was the most fiercely independent of the pope. Author of numerous satirical writings that often ridiculed the great and powerful, he died in Venice in 1556.

ARETINO IN THE CHURCH OF SAN LUCA
To the side of the high altar in the church of San Luca, there were once certain paintings by Alvise Dal Friso in which you could see depictions of this scandalous author, who – in the latter part of his life – lived in this area (on Riva del Carbon; see p. 129). However, these paintings were removed in 1845 because tourists were coming more to admire Pietro Aretino than to pray. Aretino's tomb once stood in this church as well, but that too was removed for the same reason.

"THE VENETIANS KNOW NOTHING ABOUT FOOD AND DRINK"
The libertine poet Aretino was not afraid of speaking his mind, even when his opinions were hardly likely to be shared. Thus, for example, he had no problem proclaiming that "the Venetians know nothing about food and drink." Another commentator, for his part, would observe that it was sad that a city's main culinary boast should be dried ship's biscuit, whose prime quality was that it seemed to last forever. Certain dried biscuits that had been left in Crete in 1669 were still judged edible in 1821!

SYMBOLISM OF THE "VENETIAN CROSS"

In Venice, you frequently encounter a cross whose arms end in rounded forms (see, for example, the one above St. Mark's Basilica or at San Martino). In effect, these are stylisations of the *fleurs-de-lis* that figure in one type of Cross: three at the end of each arm (symbolising the Trinity) and four radiating from the angles of the cross-joint (symbolising the world). All in all, that makes sixteen *fleurs-de-lis* – as can be seen in the cross suspended in the apse of St. Mark's Basilica.

This original version – the St. Mark Cross – was created when the Archdiocese of Venice, founded in 775, became a Patriarchate and St. Mark's Basilica became its patriarchal church. (Note in passing that the Patriarch of Venice, upon his investiture, acquires the right to sit in the Consistory of Cardinals, enjoying the title of Cardinal-Patriarch.) Though following the Latin rite of the Roman Catholic Church, the Venetian Church maintains a certain autonomy, preserving the Byzantine principles which date from the arrival of Christianity in this region (and Venice in particular) around 568.

It was upon the creation of the Patriarchate of St. Mark's that the Order of St. Mark was founded, which though short-lived was primarily responsible for the spread of the "Venetian Cross". Created by the government of the Venetian Republic, the Order was under the protection of the Evangelist Mark and its members were all those – Venetian or otherwise – who had performed some service for the State.

The *fleur-de-lis* is a symbol of divine royalty (see following double page); it also symbolises God's Power and Wisdom, and thus joins with the symbolism of the Winged Lion of St. Mark.

SYMBOLISM OF THE ARMORIAL BEARINGS OF THE PATRIARCH OF VENICE

As was traditional within the Catholic Church, a cross with two horizontals was that of archbishops and cardinals (the rank enjoyed by the Patriarch of Venice; see opposite). The upper arm bears the inscription of Pilate's phrase *Iesus Nazarenus Rex Iudaeorum* ("INRI": Jesus of Nazareth, King of the Jews), whilst the lower one was that to which Christ was nailed. This form is also to be seen in the Cross of Lorraine, even if it originally comes from Greece (where it is still common). The cross with three horizontals has, since the 15th century, been solely a papal symbol, the three arms symbolising a pope's crown, a cardinal's biretta and a bishop's mitre. The cross with one horizontal is associated with bishops. The armorial bearings of the Patriarch of Venice also include the phrase *Sufficit Gratia Tua* (Your Grace Suffices). There is also a boat under the star of Venus (see p. 86), whose eight rays represent the symbolic number of Christ's perfection.

THE SACRED SYMBOLISM OF THE *FLEUR-DE-LIS*

The *fleur-de-lis* is symbolically linked to the *Iris* and the *Lily* (*Lilium*). According to Miranda Bruce-Mitford, Louis VII the Younger (1147?) was the first king of France to adopt the iris as his emblem and use it as a seal for his letters patent (decrees). As the name *Louis* was then spelled *Loys*, it supposedly evolved to "*fleur-de-louis*", then "*fleur-de-lis*", its three petals representing Faith, Wisdom and Courage.

In reality, even if there is a strong resemblance between the iris and the *fleur-de-lis*, the French monarch merely adopted an ancient symbol of French heraldry. In AD 496, an angel purportedly appeared before Clotilda (wife of Clovis, king of the Francs) and offered her a lily, an event that influenced her conversion to Christianity. This miracle is also reminiscent of the story of the Virgin Mary, when the Angel Gabriel appeared to her, holding a lily, to tell her she was predestined to be the mother of the Saviour. This flower is also present in the iconography of Joseph, Christ's father, to designate him as the patriarch of the new Holy dynasty of divine royalty.

In 1125, the French flag (and coat of arms) depicted a field of *fleurs-de-lis*. It remained unchanged until the reign of Charles V (1364), who officially adopted the symbol to honour the Holy Trinity, thus deciding to reduce the number of flowers to three. The flower's three petals also referred to the Trinity.

The lily stylised as a *fleur-de-lis* is also a biblical plant associated with the emblem of King David as well as Jesus Christ ("consider the lilies of the field ..." Matthew 6:28-29). It also appears in Egypt in association with the lotus flower, as well as in the Assyrian and Muslim cultures. It became an early symbol of power and sovereignty, and of the divine right of kings, also signifying the purity of body and soul. This is why the ancient kings of Europe were godly, consecrated by the Divinity through sacerdotal authority. Thus, theoretically, they were to be fair, perfect and pure beings as the Virgin Mary had been, she who is the "Lily of the Annunciation and Submission"

(*Ecce Ancila Domine*, "Here is the Servant of the Lord," as Luke the Apostle reveals), and patron saint of all royal power.

The lily thus replaced the iris, which explains why, in Spanish, "*fleur-de-lis*" becomes "*flor del lírio*", and why the two flowers are symbolically associated with the same lily.

Botanically, the *fleur-de-lis* is neither an iris nor a lily. The iris (*Iris germanica*) is a plant of the Iridaceae family that originates in northern Europe. The more commonly known lily species (*Lilium pumilum*, *Lilium speciosum*, *Lilium candidum*) are members of the Liliaceae family that originates in Central Asia and Asia Minor. The true *fleur-de-lis* belongs to neither the Iridaceae nor the Liliaceae family. It is the *Sprekelia formosissima*, a member of the Amaryllidaceae family that originates in Mexico and Guatemala. Known in other languages as the Aztec lily, the São Tiago lily, and the St. James lily, *Sprekelia formosissima* is the only species of the genus. It was named in the 18th century by botanist Carl von Linné when he received a few bulbs from J. H. Van Sprekelsen, a German lawyer. The Spanish introduced the plant to Europe when they brought bulbs back from Mexico at the end of the 16th century.

THE FORGOTTEN SYMBOLISM OF THE WORD "VENICE": WHY DID THE VENETIAN REPUBLIC SEARCH OUT THE BODY OF ST. MARK?

Venice gets its name from the *Veneti*, a people of biblical origin whom the Judaeo-Roman historian Flavius Josephus (AD 30-100) identifies with the Paphlagonians, who originated in the south of Russia. According to him, they were the descendants of Rifath, son of Gomer, grandson of Japheth and great-grandson of Noah. The Greek epic poet Homer also wrote that the *Veneti* lived in Paphlagonia. An enterprising, war-like people, the *Veneti* were deeply religious, worshipping a supreme female deity called Reithia (comparable to the Greek Hera and the Roman Juno). The name (Reithia) is, in fact, the same that the Paphalgonians gave to the planet Venus, the "Upright, Just and Noble" goddess. It was this association with Venus that led the Huns and Romans to name them the *Veneti*. Furthermore, the goddess, who was associated with the planet Venus, was also referred to by the epithets "the Splendid and most Serene". The latter title of *Serenissima* would subsequently be used for the autonomous Venetian State, whose antecedents date from well before the Romans and reflect the influence of the Goddess- Earth Mother. The term *Venetia* (or *Henetia*) comes from the Latin *Uenus* (Venus), which itself incorporates the two Sumerian terms *W* and *Anu*, meaning "daughter" and "heavens", respectively. They thus combine to make "daughter of the heavens", and Venus is the planet that is visible in the sky immediately before sunrise and immediately after sunset. In Graeco-Roman mythology, Venus was the goddess of the evening and the patron of love and sensuality (two things with which Venice would be associated during the course of its history). She was also the goddess of the morning, presiding over warlike actions and conquest (again, a field in which the enterprising warriors of the *Veneti* excelled). According to legend, the city was founded in AD 811, on 25 March, the day on which the *Veneti* celebrated their feast day. Close to the spring equinox, this day marked the entrance of the Sun into the sign of Aries and its conjunction with Mars (Ares and Mars being the Greek and Roman names for the god of war). In another account, Venus is the daughter of the Moon and the sister of the Sun, her mother having been the goddess of the Underworld. This all suggests a link with the terrestrial or "lunar" waters within the lagoon, and with the mythical beast or "crocodile" that was said to live there and was associated with the gods of the underworld, of night and of the mystery of hidden things. The diurnal cycle of Venus, which appears in both the east and west, also makes the planet a symbol of death and rebirth. In the ancient world, this pairing of end/beginning is said to have inspired the tradition of placing a mask upon the dead - and, of course, the Venice Carnival would become famous for the masks that brought together aspects of the festive and the tragic. It is therefore no coincidence that the city should take for itself the remains of the apostle St. Mark (from the Indo-European world *makara*, which literally means "crocodile"). The feast day of Venice's patron saint now falls on 25 April, after *Pascoela* (the Sunday after Easter), when the Sun (represented by the lion) enters into the sign of Taurus, the sign of the zodiac which contains the planet Venus.

THE FORGOTTEN SYMBOLISM OF CARNIVAL: WHEN THE MASK REVEALS THAT WHICH LIES IN THE VERY DEPTHS OF THE INDIVIDUAL...

Throughout his existence, man is torn between his aspirations towards a better life and his lower instincts. The ox and ass that figure to either side of the infant Christ in the crib symbolise respectively these beneficent or maleficent impulses; a similar symbolism is to be found at the moment of the Crucifixion, in the good and bad thief. Note also that in his Palm Sunday entry into Jerusalem, Christ rode upon an ass (symbolising his victory over the forces of evil).

All of this encapsulates the significance of Carnival. The occasion channels the forces of evil, allowing them to find expression within a well-defined framework for a short period of time.

In accordance with the same principle, most masks are ugly distortions; they depict humankind's lower instincts. Following this logic to its conclusion, the mask that each individual chooses for him/herself does not actually conceal. Far from it, the mask reveals to one and all the real nature of the most powerful maleficent forces within the individual.

It is interesting to note that, by the 18th century, Carnival had been extended so much that it lasted for a number of months. It thus lost its very *raison d'être*, becoming further proof of the decline of the Venetians in the period before the fall of the Republic.

THE PLAQUE COMMEMORATING THE DESTRUCTION OF THE FIRST CHURCH OF SAN GEMINIANO

Sansovino's was not the first church of San Geminiano to be demolished. A dozen or so metres away to the right – just in front of Café Florian – a stone commemorates the destruction in the 13th century of the church of Saints Geminian and Menas, which had been built on this spot in the 6th century by Narses, exarch of Ravenna.

THE PLAQUE INDICATING THE SITE OF THE CHURCH OF SAN GEMINIANO

Sotoportego San Geminian

❸❼

I n front of the entrance to the Museo Correr is a plaque that commemorates the existence here of the church of San Geminiano (built by Sansovino in 1557), which was demolished in 1807 to make way for the Ala Napoleonica that closes off this end of St. Mark's Square. On that occasion, the bodily remains of the banker John Law and Sansovino (now in St. Mark's Basilica) got mislaid – carelessness that

A church destroyed by Napoleon but perhaps never beloved of the Venetians themselves

caused an eruption of imperial anger from Napoleon himself. It is interesting to note that contrary to what might be supposed from nostalgic regrets, a number of Venetians actually found Sansovino's church rather unappealing. Cicognara* considered that the faults in the design of the interior could not possibly outnumber those in the design of the exterior! Visentini, in his *Osservazioni sugli Errori degli Architetti* (1771-1775), was no less severe with regard to the design of the façade. To be fair to Sansovino, when he undertook work on this church he was already involved in such demanding projects as the monumental staircases of the Biblioteca Marciana and the Doge's Palace.

In order to leave some trace of the church within the place-names of the modern-day city, on 18 January 1973, Venice Council voted that the previously-unnamed *sotoportego* that contains the plaque should be called Sotoportego San Geminian.

The high altar from the church can now be seen in the Church of San Giovanni di Malta [see p. 289], to which it was transferred.

*Together with A. Diedo and G. Selva, the author of the book *Le fabbriche e I monumenti cospicui di Venezia.*

THE NARRATIVE OF THE COLUMN CAPITALS ❸❽ IN THE DOGE'S PALACE

Piazzetta di San Marco

> **The Doge's Palace: a book in stone**

The seat of power, the Doge's Palace was a symbol of Good Government and of the strength of the Venetian Republic. Its columns end in capitals that are adorned with 600 carved images, forming a narrative that weaves together the created world and divine majesty. Mixing allegory and moral precept, history and myth, the sacred and the secular, the "text" draws upon sources from the Bible to Claudius Ptolemy's *Tetrabiblio* (Astrological Predictions) and comprises scenes that celebrate justice, wisdom and prayer.

The works on the outside of the building were sculpted in the years 1340-1355 by the craftsmen of the local Stone-Carvers Guild under the direction of two *protomagister* (master craftsmen): Pietro Baseggio and Henricus *tajapiera* (the stone-cutter). Recent studies have suggested that the Renaissance attribution of the work to Filippo Calendario is less worthy of credit than was once thought. However, Calendario is named in 14th-century documents as supplying stone used in the palace – and as having been arrested and executed for his part in the Marin Falier conspiracy.

The corner sculptures.

Given their central role in the overall narrative, the three corner sculptures (depicting *Adam and Eve*, *The Drunkenness of Noah* and *The Judgement of Solomon*) are much bigger than the others and serve to highlight the role of Christian precepts as the bases for the political structure of the Venetian Republic. The palace, in effect, is a sort of open book. You begin reading at the southwest corner (*The Creation of Adam*, the hinge around which the symbolical narrative pivots) and – passing left to right across the "book in stone" – end at the southeast corner (*The Drunkenness of Noah*). Near the two free-standing columns in the Piazzetta (southwest corner), you find the creation of Adam, the eating of the forbidden fruit and the Archangel Michael (who stood guard over the gates of Paradise). This combination serves to mark the opening of human history as such. However, the archangel is also placed in the ideal position to guard the nearby chamber of the Grand Council (*Maggior Consiglio*), where the patricians of the city hopefully exercised the qualities of wisdom and judgement extolled in the column capitals. This is the same chamber that would later be dominated by Tintoretto's massive painting of *Il Paradiso*. At the corner of the palace nearest the Bridge of Sighs (southeast side) is *The Drunkenness of Noah*. While Cham derides his father, two other sons hurry to cover up his nakedness. The latter, together with the archangel Raphael (patron saint of the young, and wise counsellor to Tobias, son of Tobit, who is also depicted), serve to symbolise both filial devotion and hope in the resurrection.

Near the Porta della Carta (northwest corner) is *The Judgement of Solomon*, together with archangel Gabriel; both images are associated with the Good News of the Messiah. This corner sculpture is, however, a later work and is attributed to Bartholomeo Bon (*c.* 1435).

The thirteen capitals in the arcades.

The numbers cited here are those given by scholars and can be used to identify the original capitals in the Museum of the Palace Fabric inside the building. In this scheme, number one is the sculptural group of *The Judgement of Solomon* near the Porta della Carta, with the series then extending to number 36 (the sculptural group of *The Drunkenness of Noah* by the Ponte di Paglia, parallel to the Bridge of Sighs).

Birds with their Prey (35). Here depicted in realistic detail, birds were, according to Claudius Ptolemy, affected by the signs of the solstice and equinox and symbolised the life of the senses. Here a bird can be seen eating a fish, a stork devouring a serpent and an ibis twisting down to preen its chest plumage.

The Latin Peoples (34). This depiction, also known as "The Family of the Crusader", comprises the head of a soldier and that of other male and female figures of various ages. In the Middle Ages, the characteristics of peoples from different latitudes were said to be influenced by the planets and signs of the zodiac that ruled over these different territories, a notion linked with Ptolemy's "universal astrology".

Kings and Emperors (32). Here is a line of monarchs, from the wise Nebuchadnezzar (his *fleur-de-lis* sceptre symbolises Good Government founded upon the purity of the soul) to the Roman Emperor Trajan (whose sword symbolises military power and a sense of justice). Astrologically, each of these is placed under the domination of Jupiter (the doctrine of planetary conjunctions serving to explain the birth, rise and fall of dynasties and kingdoms).

Latin Women (31). Comparable to the depiction of the Latins, this capital of Latin women, under the influence of Mars and Jupiter, comprises a series of fine female heads whose headwear and hairstyles reflect their age and social status.

Seven Deadly Sins (27). The seven deadly sins are depicted together with Vanity. Each allegory conveys a powerful didactic message that is underlined by the Latin inscription. Lust is a young woman wearing a diadem of pearls, who uncovers her breast as she gazes at herself in the mirror; Gluttony is a figure raising his cup of wine as he sinks his teeth into a leg of meat; Pride is a warrior wearing the horned helmet of Satan and bearing a shield depicting a fire-spitting dragon; Wrath is shown hair streaming in the wind as he tears his clothes; Avarice, an old woman, grasps two money bags in her fists; Sloth is an idle young woman whose apathy drains away her life (as symbolised by the leafless branches of the tree that envelops her); Vanity is crowned with flowers (thus linked symbolically with Lust) and is glared at furiously by Envy, an old woman shown with various demonic animals (a dragon, a serpent biting at her girdle and another serpent coiled atop her head).

The Peoples of Various Latitudes (21). The peoples of the Earth, here depicted with great realism, represent a theme linked with astrology. It is possible to make out a Moor in a turban, a pug-nosed Tartar and an old man wearing a cap decorated with two small lions of St. Mark shown *in moeca* (literally, in "crab form", due to the similarity of the enveloping wings to crab claws). This latter figure may represent such peoples as the Cretans, who were under Venetian rule.

Solomon and the Seven Sages symbolising the Liberal Arts (20). Shown in a thoughtful pose with crossed legs, these seven wise men symbolise the liberal arts of the *Trivium* – that is Grammar (Priscian), Dialectics (Aristotle) and Rhetoric (Cicero) – and the *Quadrivium* – Arithmetic (Pythagoras), Geometry (Euclid), Music (Tubal, the first ironsmith and, according to medieval tradition, the inventor of the art) and Astronomy (Claudius Ptolemy, author of the *Tetrabiblios* that was a source of inspiration for this entire decorative scheme). Solomon comes first as the master of these wise men, a symbol of the superiority of divine wisdom.

The capital reminds us that human wisdom and knowledge are derived from divine knowledge. It shows that the exercise of Good Government can open the gates to Paradise, to which we can never gain access except through knowledge of the laws governing the universe.

The Houses of the Planets (19). The Creation of Adam is the pivot around which hinges the narrative on the two external sides of the Doge's Palace. Described by the English Critic John Ruskin as "the finest in Europe", the capital containing this scene draws both on the Book of Genesis and on Greek mythology. The seven planets are sculpted in association with the twelve signs of the zodiac and the different seasons of human life.

Depicted as a young man, Adam is shown immediately after he has been formed by God the Father, seated on a throne (side 1). Saturn, a bearded old man, is shown (side 2) seated on Capricorn and raising the jug of Aquarius; his toes are shown sticking out of his shoes (this planet was associated with poverty, the exhaustion of old age, and with captivity and famine). Jupiter is shown between Pisces and Sagittarius, represented here by the centaur Chiron, who raised Achilles and Jason (side 3), whilst Mars, seated between Libra and Scorpio, is represented as a warrior armed with a sword and a shield adorned with flames burning upon water (an alchemical symbol that refers to the inscription *Sono di Ferro* – "I am Iron" – on his standard) (side 4). The Sun, a young Phoebus crowned with rays of light, is seated in Leo and bears up the solar star (side 5), whilst Venus – the morning and evening star – holds Libra, is seated on Taurus and looks at herself in a mirror (side 6). Dressed in a toga, Mercury is shown between Virgo and Gemini (side 7) and is followed by a young girl in a boat whose hair is streaming in the wind; she is the symbol of the Moon which presides over childhood and over the winds and tides. Identified with Selene, she bears up the lunar star and touches a crab, the symbol of Cancer (side 8).

Saint and Stone-cutters (18). In homage to the guild of *tajapiera* (stone-cutters) responsible for this work, there is a depiction of the Christian martyrs Claudius, Symphorian, Simplicius, Castorius and Nicotratus – all considered as the patron saints of stone-cutters. They alternate with various disciples: the "excellent", the "Tartar" (almond-shaped eyes and pug nose) and the "incredulous" or infidel (wearing a turban and a caftan).

Animals with their Prey (17). Various animals are shown seizing their prey in their jaws: a lion, a wolf, a fox, a gryphon (the only mythological beast; see p. 49), a boar, a dog, a cat and a bear. Under each head is a branch, which suggests a network of associations between the plant and animal world.

Crafts (16). Of the various arts and crafts depicted, some are "manual", for example the "mechanical" crafts of the smith and the shoemaker. But there is also a notary, whose work was the fruit of memory and intellect, and a goldsmith, whose craft was ennobled by the value of the materials with which he worked. There are also various *arti agrichole* of peasant life: the stone-cutter, the carpenter and the "measurer" of cereals and vegetable crops. Professional status is indicated by headwear. Master craftsmen, such as the goldsmith, the notary and the stone-cutter, have large hats; paid craftsmen have a cap (smith and carpenter), whilst those performing more menial tasks are bare-headed (cobbler).

Months of the Year (12). The astrological year started with Mars (March), as did the Venetian calendar. So, reading anticlockwise, we begin with the windy spring season of the Ram, symbolised by a man playing a double-belled horn. Then come April and May, governed by Venus and surrounded by flowers; the first holds a small bull in her lap (the zodiac sign of Taurus) whilst the second holds a rose in her hand. June has cherries, whilst in July the wheat is harvested and in August the tubs for the grape harvest are prepared. Adorned, like Bacchus, with vine branches and bunches of grapes, September treads the grape. October and November (unfortunately both damaged) winnow the grain and store it. December slaughters the pig whilst January, wrapped in hair and warming his numb body at a fire, is shown with three eyes and two noses, indicating the two faces looking backward and forward to the old and new year. February grills fish on an open grate (an allusion to the zodiac sign of Pisces).

Fruits (10). Claudius Ptolemy's *Tetrabiblios* describes how the ascendance of planets at different times and seasons influences the fecundity of animals and plants, and the flow of water and wind. Solstices and equinoxes have a large influence upon the weather and the seasons, which in turn affect the fruits of the Earth. This capital shows baskets filled with the fruit of each season: cherries, pears, cucumbers, peaches, pumpkins, melons, figs and grapes.

Following restoration in the late 19th century, 42 of the capitals were replaced by copies (13 in the external arcades, 29 within the gallery). Visitors can now enjoy a close view of the originals within the six rooms of the Museum of the Palace Fabric in the Doge's Palace itself (1 April to 31 October, open 9am to 7pm, and from 1 November to 31 March, 9am to 6pm. The ticket office closes an hour before closing time, and the museum is closed on 25 December and 1 January).

THE PINK COLUMNS OF THE DOGE'S PALACE ㊴

I n the upper gallery of the Doge's Palace, two pink columns stand amongst all the other white ones. Legend has it that the doge used to stand between these two during official ceremonies. It was also from here that death sentences were announced to the crowd below (the pink thus recalling the colour of blood).

Why are two of the columns in the Doge's Palace pink?

The most common place for the gallows was between the two columns overlooking the waterfront in the Piazzetta. Across the far side of St. Mark's Square was the clock tower, and so the condemned man could see the exact time of his demise.

St. Mark's bell-tower itself was sometimes used for punishments, when a cage (*cheba*) containing convicted criminals was hung from a point half-way up the structure.

SIGHTS NEARBY

THE LAMPS OF THE DOGE'S PALACE ㊵

On the southwest side of the Doge's Palace are two small lamps that are always kept lit. They commemorate one of the rare occasions when the Republic admitted to a miscarriage of justice.

One morning, as he was going to his bakery, baker Piero Tasca tripped over an object lying on the gleaming flagstones. Bending down to pick it up, he saw it was the sheath of a dagger. A few feet away lay the body of a man. Tasca was arrested for his murder, ultimately "confessing" under torture and consequently executed on 22 March 1507, opposite the south side of the basilica. The real murderer was discovered shortly after his execution.

TRACES OF AN OLD WELL IN ST. MARK'S SQUARE ㊶

A dozen or so metres in front of Café Florian (slightly to the right), a discreet inscription marks the site of the last public well to exist in St. Mark's Square.

THE AXIS OF THE BASILICA ㊷

St. Mark's Basilica is not exactly aligned with St. Mark's Square. Under the arcades in the square, opposite Sotoportego de l'Arco Celeste, is a small metal medallion which indicates the exact line of the basilica's axis.

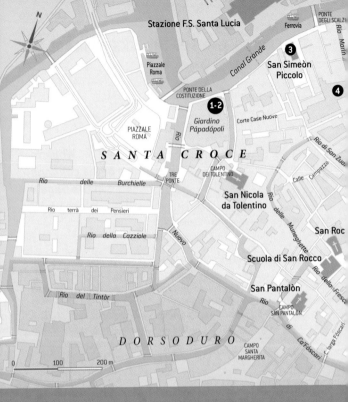

SANTA CROCE

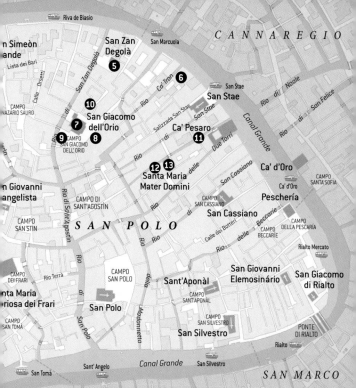

THE COLUMN OF THE FORMER CHURCH OF SANTA CROCE ❶

Fondamenta del Monastero, at the corner of Fondamenta Santa Croce

> **Where they cut off criminals' hands?**

By the foot of the Santa Croce bridge, at the corner between the Papadpoli gardens and the Rio dei Tolentini canal, an old column can be seen embedded in the wall. This is said to be the last remnant of the church of Santa Croce and its monastery, which were demolished in the 19th century during the period of Napoleonic rule. The first trace of a church here seems to date back to the 9th century, which in the 12th century was ceded to the Benedictines, who founded a monastery and rebuilt the church. In 1470, apparently due to behaviour that was out of keeping with the morals of the day, the monastery became a convent of the Poor Clares (Franciscan nuns). Then, at the end of the 16th century, the church was rebuilt again (see lower right), to ultimately be destroyed in the 19th century.

The column itself has been the subject of some debate. The similarity between its capital and the inscriptions found on the single column in front of the baptistery of St. Mark's Basilica (a column apparently brought to Venice in 1256 from Ptolemais) have led some to argue that it might have a similar origin. Others, however, argue that it comes from the tomb of Doge Domenico Morosini or Doge Orio Mastropiero (Malipiero), who were both buried in the church of Santa Croce. There is even source evidence suggesting that the capital in fact comes from the city of Tikhil in the Caucasus (see following double page).

Certain historians argue that it was in front of this column that criminals were tortured and their hands severed before they were led to their place of execution.

SYMBOLS ON THE CAPITAL FROM THE FORMER CHURCH OF SANTA CROCE

The column of the former church of Santa Croce
Fondamenta del Monastero, at the corner of Fondamenta Santa Croce

> **Tikhil, a city on the Caucasus with links to Venice?**

Whilst the column that actually stands at the foot of the Santa Croce bridge (see previous double page) would seem to be fairly recent (probably dating from the 19th century), its capital is probably of medieval origin.

Standing on tip-toe, you can see that the back of the capital is decorated simply with a Byzantine cross. However, the inscription on the front is much more mysterious. With some difficulty, the letters T I K H I L, forming a stylised interwoven pattern, can be made out. This spells out the name of a city in southwest Russia that, over the centuries, was linked with the Armenian Church. In the past, as now, it has had a presence within Venice (see p. 347). Indeed, Tikhil and the surrounding region was home to the original *Veneti*, who came here across the Caucasian mountains (see p. 86).

The rounded parts – particularly that on the right (even if worn down at the top) – are also seen to resemble the ansate Egyptian cross, the *ankh*, which takes its name from the root *ansa* or *asa*, a term that means "to rise up" or "to develop" and thus refers to the Resurrection.

Besides this literal explanation of the inscription, the capital itself also seems to form the letter H, which some take as a symbolic reference to hermeticism. The double ansate crosses linked by the horizontal bar of the H could be a hermetic symbol of the Resurrection.

The same sources also see significance in the location of this capital, the ancient church of Santa Croce (the "Holy Cross", which is obviously linked with Christ's Resurrection). Similarly, there were close links of location and organisation between this church and the monastery of Santa Croce which was said to house one of the three nails used in Christ's crucifixion (see p. 178).

A LATIN MASS: THE RITE OF SAINT PIUS V

Mass at the church of San Simeon Piccolo is said in Latin, following the rite of Saint Pius V (or the "Roman Rite", which was established in 1563 at the Council of Trent, hence its other name of the Tridentine Rite). Though a new Roman Catholic missal was introduced in 1970, the Roman Rite was never actually abolished, as Pope Benedict XVI confirmed in 2007.

Founded by Pope John Paul II in 1988, the Fraternity of St. Peter continues to use the Tridentine Rite, as they believe the Latin mass communicates a more powerful sense of sacred mystery.

THE UNDERGROUND CEMETERY
AT THE CHURCH OF SAN SIMEON PICCOLO

Church of San Simeon Piccolo
698 Santa Croce
• Open for Mass on Sunday at 11am (service lasts about 1 hour
40 minutes)
• First Saturday of each month: Mass at 6:30pm
• padrek@libero.it • http://venezia.fssp.it/pages/benvenuto.php
• Tel.: 041 719438

*A forgotten
cemetery*

Known as the San Simeon Piccolo, the
church is actually dedicated to saints
Simeon and Jude. The present structure
was built in 1718-1738 (based on designs by
Giovanni Scalfarotto) and stands on the site of
a church that dated back to the 9th century. The floor of the existing building
is raised above street level and, beneath it, you can still find the subterranean
spaces that served – and still serve – as a cemetery.

Though there are no officially organised visits, it is sometimes possible to
gain access at the end of Sunday mass by asking one of the members of the
Fraternity of St. Peter (to whom the Patriarch of Venice entrusted the church
as a mass chapel).

The visit itself is fascinating. By the light of a lamp, you enter a relatively
large underground space whose walls are largely covered with 18th-century
frescoes inspired by the themes of Death, the Last Judgement and Christ's
Passion. Of rather mediocre artistic value, these works have suffered from the
humidity that has severely damaged most of them.

The cemetery is laid out around an octagonal room, which is probably
where mass was celebrated. From here, four corridors run out to each of the
various burial chambers. Human bones can still be seen abandoned in one of
these spaces.

At just over 3 metres high, San Simeon Piccolo has the lowest bell-tower
in Venice.

WHY IS SAN SIMEON PICCOLO BIGGER THAN SAN SIMEON GRAND?
In relation to the nearby church of San Simeon Grande, the church of saints
Simeon and Jude acquired the name San Simeon Piccolo (St. Simeon the
Small) for two reasons: firstly because, before its reconstruction in the 18th
century, the old church of San Simeon Piccolo was actually smaller than
that of San Simeon Grande; secondly, because the word "Grande" does
not refer to the church's size but its titular saint, the prophet Simeon, also
known as Simeon the Great.

GARDEN OF PALAZZO SORANZO CAPPELLO ❹

Santa Croce 770
Rio Marin
• Visitors can enter during office hours

A romantic secret garden

The garden of Palazzo Soranzo Cappello is one of the most beautiful in Venice. The building itself houses administrative offices, but during normal working hours the public are allowed to enter through the gate that leads directly into the garden, as long as they remain quiet and discreet, of course.

The garden itself is laid out in two main parts. Opposite the palazzo is a court with statues of Julius Caesar and the eleven Roman emperors who came after him – a clear allusion to the wealth of the Soranzo family, who had the palazzo built in the 17th century. This court opens onto the main garden, at the end of

which is an eight-column pavilion surmounted by statues of allegorical figures. To the right is the second part of the garden, which is occupied by a pergola and a lawn with various fruit trees.

Upon acquisition of the palazzo by the Italian Ministry of Culture, the garden was restored on the basis of a 1709 engraving by Vincenzo Coronelli that showed the layout in some detail. However, the wise decision was made to leave part of the garden wild, as this is how it is described in Gabriele d'Annunzio's *Il Fuoco* and Henry James' *The Aspern Papers*. The romantic result is a great success.

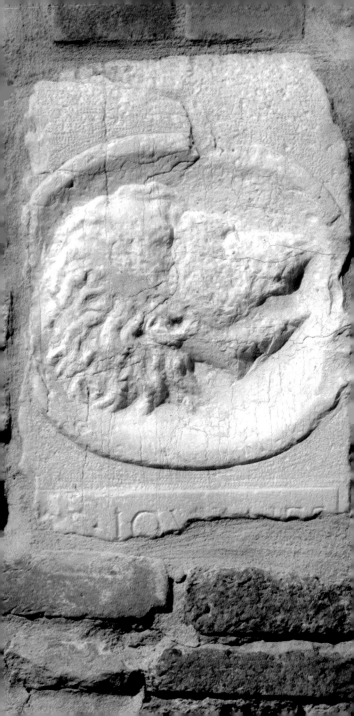

THE HIGH-RELIEF OF ST. JOHN THE BAPTIST ❺

Church of San Zan Degolà (San Giovanni Decollato)
Campo San Zan Degolà
• Open 10am to 12pm daily, except Sundays and holidays
• Mass: Saturday at 7pm
• Ukrainian mass on Sunday morning

A delicious stew of child's flesh

On the southeast side of the church façade is a haut-relief that recalls a very macabre story. The work depicts St. John the Baptist and, until the middle of the 20th century, it was actually located on the facade of Palazzo Gidoni-Bembo, beyond the bridge opposite the church. It was notoriously used by local residents to scare disobedient youngsters, by telling them that the figure portrayed was a certain Biasio, who had killed a number of children.

In the 16th century, this Biasio had a tavern in the area and gradually made a name for himself with a delicious meat stew that attracted people from all over the city. Everything went well, until one day a customer found a finger joint in his meal. He reported the matter, and it was discovered that Biasio's secret was quite simply that he used tender children's flesh in preparing his recipes.

Found guilty, the child murderer was dragged behind a horse to his tavern, where his hands were cut off and hung around his neck (it was traditional in Venice for a criminal's hands to be severed at the very place where they had "offended"). His flesh was then torn with tongs and he was taken to St. Mark's Square, where he was hung by the neck between the two columns in the Piazzetta. What was left of his body was then cut into four pieces, each piece being strung up in a different part of the city. His home and tavern were also razed to the ground.

In spite of this terrible story, the quayside here is still called Riva de Biasio, and there is even a vaporetto stop of the same name. A similar story is told concerning the Palais Royal in Paris. There, it was a barber who used to cut his clients' throats to pass on their carcasses to his neighbour, the butcher (see *Secret Paris*).

WHERE DOES THE NAME SAN GIOVANNI DECOLLATO COME FROM?

San Giovanni Decollato recalls the famous "decollation" (beheading) of St. John the Baptist, which Salome requested of Herod at the behest of her mother, Herodias. The saint had, in fact, reproached Herod for marrying Herodias because she had been the wife of his half-brother, Herod Philip.

THE REMAINS OF CASINO TRON

Calle Tron 1957
• Open during university hours (without booking); Monday to Friday,
9am to 7pm
• Information: 041 2572300

> ## Traces of past magnificence

The Urban Planning Department of the Architecture Faculty is housed in a magnificent palazzo that was restored in 1971. It is reached by the Calle Tron and stands near the San Stae vaporetto stop. Overlooking the Grand Canal, the building has retained a lot of its charm, with the well-preserved interiors maintaining some of the splendour it must have had at the time of the Tron, the wealthy family that used to own it.

On the first-floor *piano nobile* are various family portraits along with frescoes of Old Testament subjects (by the French artist Dorigny) intended to celebrate the glory of the Tron family. In the *salotto da parata* (main drawing room) is a fine late-15th-century fireplace and a typical Venetian floor which reveals a fine blend of different colours.

Little is left of the Palazzo Tron's gaming pavilion (*casino*), which dated from the 18th century. It stood at the end of the garden – beyond the paved courtyard – and was demolished at the beginning of the 19th century after the death of Cecilia Tron, the last member of the family. All that remains now are two grooved columns surmounted by Ionic capitals in Istrian marble, together with a statue of St. George defeating the Dragon. In its heyday, the *casino* had magnificent rooms decorated with mirrors, stuccowork, paintings by Dorigny, and frescoes by Guarana. A setting for passionate intrigue, this *casino* also served as a luxurious ballroom for the parties given by the powerful *procurator* Andrea Tron (so powerful that he was simply known as *El Paron*, "the boss"). In 1775, a reception was held here for the Austrian Emperor Joseph II.

CECILIA TRON, CAGLIOSTRO'S MISTRESS

Cecilia Zen, wife of Francesco Tron, was a fascinating and lively woman. She inspired the poet Angelo Barbaro and the writer-priest Giuseppe Parini. Enchanted by her charms, the latter recalled her in an ode dating from 1787, revealingly entitled *Il Pericolo* (Danger). A lover of *la vie mondaine*, Cecilia gave magnificent receptions for any sovereign passing through the city. Furthermore, her luxurious palazzo was also home to a literary salon that attracted men-of-letters and other talented individuals. She even had a love affair with Count Cagliostro, which came to an abrupt end when the adventurer had to make a rapid departure after being accused of stealing from a rich Venetian merchant.

THE MIRACLE OF THE VIRGIN ❼
AT THE CHURCH OF SAN GIACOMO DELL'ORIO

Church of San Giacomo dell'Orio
• Open Monday to Saturday, 10am to 5pm
• Masses on Sunday at 8am, 11am and 7pm. During the week at 6pm in winter and 7pm in summer (April to September)

Severed arms ...

There are a number of remarkable curiosities at the church of San Giacomo dell'Orio, one being the painting that stands directly to the right of the entrance. The work of artist Gaetano Zompini (1702-1778), it depicts a little-known miracle performed by the Virgin, as told in numerous literary works, such as Jacques de Voragine's *Golden Legend*.

This texts tells how, after her dormition (Christian tradition has it that the Virgin did not die but solely fell asleep prior to her Assumption into Heaven), the Virgin's body was being carried by the faithful when a non-believer by the name of Jephonias tried to touch it, in an attempt to demonstrate that the Virgin was not a saint. However, as soon as he touched the sarcophagus containing the body, his hands were severed and the man fell to the ground. This is the spectacular episode depicted in the painting, which shows the man on the ground, with his arms as raised stumps and the severed hands above.

A painting of the same episode can be seen in the sacristy of the church of San Zaccaria.

TRACES OF THE COMPOSTELA PILGRIMAGE IN VENICE
The church of San Giacomo dell'Orio was the Venice starting-point of the pilgrimage to the church of St. James of Compostela (Spain). A trace of this can still be seen on the bell-tower: the figure of a man identified by a clamshell, the symbol of the pilgrimage.

AN APOCRYPHAL MIRACLE PERFORMED BY ST. JAMES
Above the entrance to the first chapel on your left after you enter the church is a painting by Antonio Palma (early 16th century) depicting an apocryphal miracle attributed to St. James. Whilst on the pilgrimage to Compostela, a couple stopped with their son at an inn. The daughter of the innkeeper fell in love with the young man and decided to put a few gold coins in his bag, so that the youth would be accused of theft and made to stay. The plan worked. The young man was arrested after his parents had continued on their pilgrimage. Upon their return, the couple found their son unjustly accused. However, according to legend, it was decided that he would be declared innocent of the crime if he could bring back to life two cooked chickens that had already been served up on the kitchen table. St. James, shown waiting in the upper left of the painting, did just that in response to the parents' prayers, and the young man was freed immediately.

THE UNALIGNED BALCONIES OF PALAZZO PEMMA ❽

Santa Croce 1624
Campo San Giacomo dell'Orio

> ## *The Jew who wanted to be spared the sight of a Catholic church...*

Built in the 17th century, Palazzo Pemma looks peculiar because the axis of the entrance and the supports for the balcony do not look straight, as they would in any traditional building. When you look closely, you see that these features are slightly shifted to the right, towards the Calle Larga, rather than facing directly forward, towards the bell-tower of the Church of San Giacomo dell'Orio. Legend has it that this feature is due to the fact that the palazzo was once bought by a Jew who wanted to be spared the sight of a Catholic church…

REMAINS OF AN ANATOMY THEATRE

9

Campo San Gioacomo dell'Orio
Santa Croce 1507

• To see the interior doorways, ring at the OCRAD bell (offices of the Regional Government of the Veneto) during normal opening hours: Monday and Thursday from 9am to 12:30pm and from 3pm to 5pm; Tuesday, Wednesday and Friday from 9am to 12:30pm

On the façade of the building alongside the church, which is still known as the *Ex Vida*, is the inscription D:O:M: MEDICORUM PHYSICORUM COLLEGIUM. The building, in fact, was once part of an old *Teatro Anatomico*, hence the name of the nearby courtyard and bridge (Ponte and Corte dell'Anatomia). On the outside, all that is left of the original structure are two 16th-century doorways, one giving onto the campo, the other onto the canal. The upper floors have been heavily restored to make them habitable, but inside you can still see two old doorways surmounted by mascherons (or masks) in Istrian stone, which date from the period when the structure was used for anatomy lessons.

Opened in 1671, the magnificent anatomy theatre was a room with three levels of banked seats from which doctors could watch dissections. The upper floor housed a fine library, plus archives and meeting rooms reserved for physicians and surgeons. The entire structure was gutted by a fire in 1800. It was entirely rebuilt in less than six months, but just a few years later the anatomy room was moved to the city hospital.

There are still perfectly preserved anatomy theatres in Padua, Bologna, Pistoia (see *Secret Tuscany*), London (see *Secret London*) and Barcelona (see *Secret Barcelona*).

AN "ISLAND" SET APART FROM THE WORLD

10

Extending from Campo San Giacomo dell'Orio is a small district of the city that remains hidden from curious eyes. Approached by two parallel alleyways (*rami dell'Isola*), this was in fact once a real island entirely surrounded by a canal. However, the waterway was filled in to make Rio Terà dell'Isola and Calle della Vita (where the paving is seen to be different to that found elsewhere in the former island). An iron foundry from the days of the Venetian Republic once stood at the corner of the small alleyway leading into the island.

SIGHTS NEARBY

BAS-RELIEFS OF THE EVANGELISTS ON PALAZZO AGNUSDIO

11

Palazzo Agnusdio
Fondamenta Pesaro 2060

Standing alongside a quiet canal near Ca' Pesaro, Palazzo Agnusdio has a five-lobe central window that is rather surprisingly decorated with the symbols of the four evangelists: eagle, lion, ox and man (see opposite).

It would seem that the palazzo does not take its name from the aristocratic Venetian family of the Agnusdei (which was extinct by 1242), but rather from its magnificent sculpture of the *Agnus Dei* (Lamb of God), a mystic symbol that, like the other fine decorations, bears witness to the devotion of the owners of the palazzo who commissioned it.

WHY ARE THERE FOUR EVANGELISTS?

In the first century AD there were a number of gospels relating the life of Christ, including the gospels of St. Thomas, St. Judas and St. Peter, all of which are now considered to be apocryphal. It was in the second century AD that Irenaeus of Lyons claimed that, just as there were four distinct regions in the world and four main winds, so the Church, which extended throughout the world, should be based on four gospels. The correspondence between the four gospels of Matthew, Mark, Luke and John and the four "living creatures" (see above) probably played a part in these texts becoming the ones that were officially accepted. Others have argued that the so-called apocryphal gospels did not propound ideas concordant with the message that the early Church, largely inspired by the preachings of St. Paul, wished to propagate in order to nurture the growth of Christianity within the Roman world. In fact, some of these texts were considered Gnostic in content, reserving salvation to a few chosen initiates rather than to all mankind. Others presented Jesus not as a God-made-man, but rather as a Jewish prophet-king striving to help the Hebrews free themselves from the yoke of Roman occupation.

THE ORIGIN OF THE ANIMAL SYMBOLS FOR THE FOUR EVANGELISTS

In numerous churches in Venice and throughout the world, depictions of the four evangelists show them accompanied by an animal.

St. Mark: a lion

St. John: an eagle

St. Luke: an ox

St. Matthew: a man

The explanation for these pairings was given by St. Jerome (348-420) who argued that: St. Matthew was paired with a man because his Gospel begins with the human genealogy of Jesus (Matthew 1:1-17);

The lion was associated with St. Mark because the first lines in his Gospel refer to "the voice which cried in the wilderness", which – St. Jerome claims – cannot be other than the roar of the lion (Mark 1:3);

The ox, a sacrificial animal, was associated with St. Luke because his Gospel begins with a reference to the sacrifice offered in the Temple of Jerusalem by Zachariah (Luke 1:5);

And the eagle was associated with St. John because this evangelist soared to the very peaks of Christian doctrine, just as the eagle soars to the peaks of mountains.

Historically, the attribution of the four symbols to the evangelists is rooted in the prophet Ezekiel's vision of God in his glory (the four "living creatures" mentioned in Ezekiel 1:5) and the vision of the throne of God in the Book of Revelation (4:6), which again mentions "four beasts" around the throne of God: "And the first beast was like a lion, and the second beast was like a calf, and the third beast had a face as a man, and the fourth beast was like a flying eagle." Irenaeus of Lyons, in his anti-Gnostic treatise *Adversus haereses* (written around AD 180), was the first to exploit the link of the four evangelists and the four living creatures. As for St. Jerome's explanation, it was first introduced in the Vulgate (his Latin translation of the Bible in the 5th century), which explains why it then became widespread within Western Christendom. In fact, the pairing of evangelists and animals was not accepted by the Eastern Church, which explains why there are very few representations of evangelists with these symbols within Byzantine art. The few exceptions occur where there was an influence of the West – for example, at St. Mark's Basilica in Venice. Another point that St. Jerome makes is that the four living creatures symbolise four fundamental moments in Christ's life: the incarnation of God (man), Jesus tempted in the desert (lion), his sacrifice (ox) and his ascension into Heaven (eagle).

THE ERASED IMAGE OF A LION ON CA' ZANE ⓬

Campo Santa Maria Mater Domini
Ca' Zane
Santa Croce 2120 and 2121

A lion identifying the homes of the conspirators of a plot in 1310

Following the Bajamonte Tiepolo conspiracy in 1310 (see the stone that marks the place of the column of infamy, p. 151, and the haut-relief of the mortar, p. 61), a Lion of St. Mark was carved on the houses of each of the conspirators. Obviously, the owners of the houses had this mark of infamy removed as quickly as possible. In the charming Campo Santa Maria Mater Domini, on the façade of Ca' Zane (opposite the bridge, at numbers 2120 and 2121), you can see the place of the old sculpture showing clear scrape marks.

The other houses marked with lions were:

Cà Longo opposite I Servi
Cà Querini in Calle delle Rasse
Cà Querini at the bridge of S. Giacomo dell'Orio
Cà Loredan in S. Canciano
Cà Molin at La Bragola
Cà Corner by the bridge of S. Fosca
Cà Corner at S. Beneto, at the entrance to Rio Menuo
Cà Garzoni in Campo S. Bartolomeo
Cà Donà at S. Polo, on the campo and at the Ponte dei Cavalli

SIGHTS NEARBY

THE DISCOVERY OF THE TRUE CROSS BY TINTORETTO

Church of Santa Maria Mater Domini - Campo Santa Maria Mater Domini
Open in the morning from 10am to 12pm, and on Sunday from 5pm to 7pm

As it is tucked away within a dark alley, it is easy to miss the church of Santa Maria Mater Domini. Certainly, it does not attract large numbers of tourists, and the restricted visiting times make matters no easier. However, the interior of the church is charming, and it houses a neglected masterpiece by Tintoretto, *The Discovery of the True Cross*, which depicts a forgotten episode in the history of the Roman Church (see below for more details). The work was originally painted for the Scuola de la Croce, founded in 1561. Tradition had it that, in 4th-century Jerusalem, Helena, mother of Constantine (the first Roman emperor to embrace Christianity) found the Cross on which Christ had been crucified. On the site of the discovery, she had the church of the Holy Sepulchre built. Although its original foundation dates from the 10th century, the church of Santa Maria Mater Domini has been altered several times.

CAN THE TRUE CROSS BE TRACED BACK TO ADAM, SOLOMON AND THE QUEEN OF SHEBA?

According to the *Legenda aurea* (*Golden Legend*) by Jacobus de Voragine (1228-1298), Adam in his great age asked his son Seth to procure oil from the Archangel Michael to anoint him before he died. The archangel refused but instead gave him a small branch from the Tree of [Knowledge of] Good and Evil with the command to place it in Adam's mouth at the moment of his burial. This small branch would then grow from Adam's body into a great tree that would save him from his sins, ensuring his salvation. Much later, when King Solomon was having the Temple of Jerusalem built, this tree was cut down to be used in the construction, but it so happened that the beam kept changing size and was either too short or too long for its intended use. The workmen got rid of it by casting it into the River Siloe to use as a footbridge. The Queen of Sheba, who had journeyed to visit Solomon, had a premonition as soon as she stepped on the bridge: this beam of wood will one day be used for the crucifixion of Christ and the reign of the Jews will come to an end. In order to avoid this tragic fate, King Solomon had the beam taken away and buried. At the time of Jesus' trial, however, the beam sprang miraculously from the soil and was ultimately used for the cross on which he was crucified. In order to avoid crosses becoming cult objects, they were buried and forgotten until the Roman Emperor Constantine, while fighting his rival Maxentius, had a vision of an illuminated cross on which was inscribed: *"in hoc signo vinces"* ["In this sign, conquer"]. His army having won the decisive battle of the Milvian Bridge by following the sign of the cross, Constantine wished to recover the Cross of Christ and sent his mother Helena to Jerusalem to look for it. After torturing a Jew who knew the burial site of the three crosses (Jesus and the two thieves) for seven days, Helena rediscovered them. A miraculous event then revealed which of the three was the True Cross: a young man who had just died was instantly revived when his lifeless body touched the wood of the Cross of Christ. Part of the Cross was retained in Jerusalem while another fragment was taken to Constantinople, the new imperial capital.

SAN POLO

THE *CAPPELLINA* IN THE CHURCH OF SAN CASSIANO

Church of San Cassiano
Open daily from 9am to 12pm and 5:30pm to 7:30pm. Mass at 7pm
You have to ask for the light in the *cappellina* to be switched on

> *A little-known chapel set with precious stones*

To the left of the choir in the church of San Cassiano, a small opening leads on the left to the sacristy, and on the right to a wonderful little chapel largely unknown to the public. Designed in 1746 by Father Carlo dal Medico (who died in 1758), this Cappella di San Carlo Borromeo is a little 18th-century gem, complete with polychrome marble, semi-precious stones and walnut choir stalls. The painting of *Christ in the Garden of Gethsemane* on the wall is attributed to Leandro Bassano. The altarpiece, *The Virgin and Children with Saints Carlo Borromeo and Filippo Neri*, was painted by G. B. Pittoni, as was the ceiling fresco.

AN UNKNOWN MASTERPIECE BY TINTORETTO

Whilst it lies off the usual tourist track, the church of San Cassiano is home to one of Tintoretto's masterpieces, *The Crucifixion*, painted in 1568. To the left behind the main altar, this work is stunning both for its palette and for the power of the composition. The 50 eurocents it costs to turn on the light is money very well spent.

SIGHTS NEARBY

AN INSCRIPTION RECORDING THE CAPTURE OF BUDA FROM THE TURKS ❷

On the façade of the house at number 1686, just at the end of the Ponte della Chiesa in Campo San Cassiano, is the following inscription: *1686 – ADI 18 ZVGNO – BVDA – FV ASSEDIATA ET ADI 2 – SETTEMBRE FV PRESA*. This commemorates the capture of the city of Buda (which later formed half of the Hungarian capital, Budapest) by the Hapsburg forces. The city had been under Turkish rule since 1541 but was retaken after a siege that started on 18 June 1686, and ended on 2 September.

THE CAPITALS IN THE FISH MARKET

Pescheria Nuova
Rialto

A catalogue of marine life

Those buying fish here rarely notice the capitals of the columns around the outside of the *Pescheria Nuova* (New Fish Market). The capital of the central column shows four carved human heads and commemorates the year (1905) in which the first part of the building was constructed by architect Domenici Rupolo to a design by painter Cesare Laurenti (whose name is engraved on the capital).

The capital of one of the side columns depicts boats laden with *vieri* (the large baskets that were used to bring the fresh fish to market). All the other capitals are decorated with sea creatures: crabs and large-clawed lobster, fish of all sizes, squid and octopus, and majestic seahorses. If you look carefully, you can see that the names of Domenico Rupolo and Cesare Laurenti are also engraved here.

The period when the *Pescheria* was built was one when Symbolism was at its height. This is reflected in the capitals of the inner columns, which have floral or maritime symbols in a sort of Art Nouveau style (a wind rose, a clamshell, a winkle, a water-flea, a crustacean, a crab and a fish) as well as other more esoteric symbols (the Sun, the moon, the stars and a blank heraldic escutcheon).

THE PESCHERIA: A NEO-GOTHIC BUILDING DATING FROM 1907
Contrary to what you might think, the Pescheria is a relatively new building. It was officially opened in 1907 and the decoration was the work of the artist-craftsman Umberto Bellotto.

SIGHTS NEARBY

THE INSCRIPTION *PISCIS PRIMUM A CAPITE FOETET* ④

The first floor of the building overlooking the area where the stalls of the Pescheria Nuova are laid out is occupied by the *Procura della Repubblica* (State Courts). Access is via a large staircase with rather remarkable banister "pommels": stone carvings of a pine cone, a squid, a shellfish and a fisherman's head. Beneath the stairs are two (permanently closed) gates in wrought iron. On the larger one, a curious inscription adapts a Greek saying that Erasmus of Rotterdam translated into Latin in the 16th century: *piscis primum a capite foetet* (fish begins to stink from the head).

This is a truth which is well known to anyone who knows anything about fish. And while it might be read as a warning to the inexperienced customers buying fish here, it could also be taken as a metaphorical warning against the dangers of power corrupting those who possess it, with the "head" being the first part of the body politic to go rotten. As such, this adage might be intended for the local authority employees responsible for running the market (their offices are located within the building).

THE PRIVILEGE OF BEING A FISHMONGER

The ancient trade of the *compravendi pesce* (fishmonger) was restricted to old fishermen from Poveglia (an island in the south of the lagoon) and San Nicolo (on the Lido) who had worked at least 20 years at sea and were over the age of 50. As a reward for their hard work, the Venetian Republic set aside this trade exclusively for them, allowing the men to end their working life away from the risks of the sea. The *compravendi pesce* had St. Nicholas as their patron saint and used to gather in the church of the Beata Virgine ai Carmini.

MEASURING FISH

On the Grand Canal side of the building that stands behind Pescheria Nuova is a marble plaque that shows the lengths which the city council established each type of fish must have before it could be sold. These regulations were rigorously enforced and were intended to protect the fish during the breeding season. The rules still apply today.

There are similar marble plaques in Campo Santa Margherita, on the Fondamenta della Tana (near the Arsenal) and within the Palazzo dei Dieci Savi (the building that housed the authorities responsible for the Venetian lagoon and its waterways).

WAR RATIONING

During the Second World War, the first floor of the building in the Pescheria Nuova was occupied by the office which supplied the people of Venice with their ration cards.

A PORTRAIT OF PIETRO ARETINO: A REMINDER OF HIS STAY IN VENICE

On the façade of the Pescheria Nuova are two works by Cesare Laurenti: a Lion of St. Mark and a statue of St. Peter the Fisherman (perhaps a self-portrait).

To the right is a modern work by the artist Guerrino Lovato. It is a terracotta depiction of Pietro Aretino and is copied from a medallion that the sculptor Alessandro Vittoria created for the satirist, who originally came from Arezzo.

The plaque was unveiled in 2001 and commemorates the fact that, from 1527 to 1556, the libertine and art critic lived in Palazzo Bollani, opposite the Pescheria, on the Grand Canal. The bas-relief also features an inkwell and quill – a reference to Aretino's polemical writings – and a cartouche containing a quote from Aretino himself: *Veritas filio temporis* (Truth, the daughter of Time).

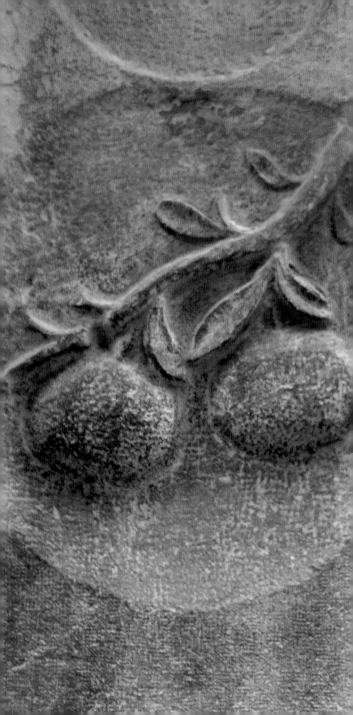

SIGHTS NEARBY

THE COLUMN WHERE FRUIT WAS SOLD

The column that marks the corner between Ruga dei Spezieri and Ramo do Mori (numbers 379 and 395) bears a carving of two peaches with intertwined stalks. It is the symbol of the Confraternity of Merchants of fruit and of *persicata* (the *Confraternita della Persicata e dei Fruttaroli*). *Persicata* was a peach preserve, very similar to quince preserve, which was a great delicacy during the Renaissance.

At number 374, you can see two similar fruits hanging from a branch.

THE LEANING HOUSE AT SAN POLO 965A

In Calle del Sansoni (at the end of Calle Arco), the house at 965a has a ground-floor doorway that must be one of the most heavily sloped of any in the city.

RAMO DELLA DOGANA DA TERRA

The name of this alleyway recalls the existence nearby of a *Dogana da Terra*, a Customs House for products brought into the city from the mainland. Up to 1414, all merchandise entering the city had been offloaded at San Biagio in Castello. However, when the site became unable to handle the amount of traffic, two Customs Houses were created. One, the still famous *Dogana da Mar*, was for merchandise brought from overseas, while the other, the no longer existing *Dogana da Terra*, was for all merchandise from the mainland.

A "BARREL" DOORWAY

San Polo 456 – Calle Arco

I n the labyrinth of small alleyways behind Rialto, there is a striking curiosity at number 456. The ground-floor doorway in stone is heavily splayed to make it easy for the movement of the wine barrels once stored here.

A splayed doorway: easier for wine barrels

SIGHTS NEARBY
THE HIGH-RELIEF OF A BARREL

In Campo Rialto Novo – so called because it dates from long after the Campo di Rialto at San Giacometto – can be seen a number of columns dating from the 16th and 17th centuries that are carved with the symbols of various guilds. At number 551 there is a barrel, the symbol of the Confraternity of Coopers (called *boteri*), whose warehouses were in the area (see, for example, the "barrel" doorway). The name of the guild also figures in the nearby Calle dei Boteri, close to the Fish Market.

THE CONFRATERNITA DEI BOTERI

The makers of barrels, the *boteri*, had their *scuola* opposite the church of the Gesuiti (near Fondamenta Nuove), a fact still recalled in the street name. Normally, they used oak of good quality to produce barrels that were lighter and easier to manage. However, they also sometimes used chestnut and conifer wood. The *boteri* were required to repair the barrels of the doge's household free of charge.

At number 553, you can also see a depiction of a mulberry bush, the symbol of silk-makers, who had warehouses for their merchandise in this area (see p. 19).

PALLADIO'S DESIGNS FOR THE RIALTO BRIDGE

In the Gulbenkian Museum (Lisbon), you can see a fine painting by Guardi which shows the design for the Rialto Bridge which Palladio proposed in the 16th century. The picture depicts the Grand Canal as if the bridge had actually been built; as so often in his paintings, Guardi combines real features of the setting with imaginary elements (here taken from Palazzo Chiericati in Vicenza). The first real Rialto Bridge was built in wood in 1264. After it had been rebuilt several times and in various forms – a Carpaccio painting (now in the Accademia) shows a wooden structure with a drawbridge in the middle – the idea was mooted in 1507 that there should be a stone bridge, with the decision finally being taken in 1525. Four years later, Michelangelo submitted his own proposals, which aroused such conflicting opinions that any decision on the matter was put off again. Then, in 1551, various architects were invited to draw up plans, with Palladio, Scamozzi, Sansovino and Giacomo Barozzi Vignole all submitting proposals. However, it was the fittingly-named Antonio da Ponte whose scheme was adopted in 1588. Audacious for the day, his proposal of a single-arch bridge facilitated the movement of shipping along the very busy Grand Canal. The new bridge was finally competed in 1591. Nevertheless, there are now a number of people (both in and outside Venice) who judge the final result to be rather heavy and inelegant, bitterly regretting that Palladio's fine design for the Rialto was not the one chosen.

THE LEGEND OF THE DEVIL AT THE RIALTO BRIDGE

A local legend has it that the Devil himself put in an appearance during the building of the bridge in the 16th century, threatening that work would never be completed if he was not promised the first living soul to cross the finished structure. The architect, Antonio da Ponte, accepted, thinking to outsmart the Devil by having a cockerel be the first to cross the bridge. But, having got wind of the trick, Satan appeared at the architect's house and told his pregnant wife her husband was waiting for her at the worksite. The wife was thus the first to cross the bridge, and tradition has it that the soul of the infant – who was still-born – haunted the area for ages before finally being helped "to the other side" by a gondolier.

CIVIL WAR UPON THE RIALTO BRIDGE

The last cannon to be fired in Venice was located on the Rialto Bridge. Furious at their leaders for having allowed Napoleon's troops to invade the city, the populace began to sack the homes of those they held responsible for the fall of the Republic. To quell the revolt, the provisional government, on 2 May 1797, gave orders to fire upon the crowd from cannons installed at the top of the Rialto Bridge.

THE STORK: THE HERALDIC SYMBOL OF THE FAMILY OF DOGE PASQUALE CICOGNA

The stork carved in a medallion on the southeast corner of the bridge commemorates the fact that the structure was built when the doge was Pasquale Cicogna, whose surname means "stork".

OTHER NEVER COMPLETED PROJECTS

Two fanciful projects of the late 19th century

Enthusiasm for the city's industrial development and the increasing focus on its role as a tourist destination actually resulted in plans for trains to arrive directly at St. Mark's Square. This very odd idea involved the creation of a railway station on the island of San Giorgio Maggiore, which thus would have facilitated the flow of tourists into the very heart of Venice. In 1852, the entrepreneur Busetto, nicknamed *Fisola*, also defended the project of the architect Cadorin for a magnificent **Grand Hotel Thermal** on Riva degli Schiavoni, very close to the Doge's Palace (see opposite). However, the project never got beyond the drawing-board stage.

The first project for an Accademia Bridge, rejected in the 19th century

Ever since the 16th century, there had been talk of the need to build another bridge over the Grand Canal. By itself, the Rialto Bridge did not make it easy to pass from one side of the waterway to the other. The first project was, however, only presented in 1838, by the engineer Giuseppe Salvadori, head of the Public Works office in Venice. This structure would have linked Santa Maria del Giglio (in the *sestiere* of San Marco) to the *sestiere* of Dorsoduro, where the Zattere was becoming one of the hubs of commercial activity within the city. However, it was ultimately the English engineer Neville, owner of the iron foundry at San Rocco and a specialist in the building of steel structures, who designed the first bridge, built in 1853. This bridge remained in use until 1933, when it was replaced by the wooden structure that was subsequently replaced by the bridge that exists today.

A fourth bridge over the Grand Canal in the 19th century

As work was beginning on the filling-in of a number of canals in order to make it easier to move about the city, Neville suggested a quicker link between the railway station and Campo Santo Stefano, creating a link through the area close to his own foundry in San Rocco. The engineer had already acquired a certain reputation for his two iron bridges over the Grand Canal (Accademia and Scalzi), but this project was never approved. To achieve its purpose, it would have required the creation of a wide new street and another steel bridge (this time crossing the Grand Canal near the San Tomà traghetto stop).

Le Corbusier's new hospital: started but never completed

Le Corbuiser's new hospital was to stand in the area of the new city abattoir of San Giobbe, yet the plan was never put into effect. In 1965, the famous Swiss architect signed the contract defining the specifications and the actual timetable of the work, but he died a few months later. The buildings were left as they stood, empty, and have only recently been refurbished to house the Economics Faculty of Ca' Foscari University. The project plans can be seen in the library of the Scuola Grande di San Marco (see p. 261).

THE STANDARD *BARBACANE*

Calle della Madonna 574

9

> *A standard measure for barbacani throughout the city*

Fixed into the wall between the last two buildings before the alleyway leads out onto Riva del Vin is a feature that is easy to overlook: a *barbacane* in Istrian stone bearing an inscription on both sides, PER LA IVRIDICIOM DE BARBACANI. Indeed, this was the "standard measure" for the projecting girders whose size was rigorously controlled by the Venetian authorities.

WHAT IS A *BARBACANE*?

The *barbacani* were the projecting wooden beams that made it possible to increase the floor space on the first floor of a building without obstructing the narrow streets of Venice. Thanks to these projecting beams, every floor above ground level could be extended without causing any problems to the flow of pedestrian traffic in the *calle* beneath.

As is clear from its similarity with the English "barbican", the word *barbacane* also figured in military architecture. In the Middle Ages, it referred to the circular fortifications that served as a primary defence for fortresses and castles. The term might also be used for the walls with narrow slits, from where archers and others could protect gateways, passages or posterns. Similarly, it could refer to the spurs of masonry that sometimes linked the arcade supporting a covered walkway. Ultimately, the word came to be used for any sort of reinforcing structure external to the walls of a house.

The etymology of the term is uncertain. Some claim it is of Eastern origin, perhaps deriving from the Arabic *b-al-baqara* (cattle gateway), a structure serving to protect the enclosure where livestock were kept near ramparts. In Constantinople, there were *barbacani* just like those found in Venice, as shown in an 1878 drawing by Cesare Biseo, the illustrator of a work on the Ottoman capital by author Edmondo De Amicis.

Barbacani can be seen throughout Venice. The best-preserved ones are near the Rialto Bridge and in the Calle del Paradiso near Campo Santa Maria Formosa.

HIGH-RELIEF OF FOUR CROWNED SAINTS

Former *Scuola* of Stonemasons and Sculptors

Just to the left of the façade of the former church of Sant'Aponàl, the house at number 1252 has a high-relief at the second floor which depicts Four Crowned Saints. This house used to be the premises of the *Scuola dei Tagliapietra*, founded in 1515, and the four figures are the patron saints of these craftsmen (see below).

WHY DO THE SCULPTORS AND STONEMASONS HAVE FOUR CROWNED PATRON SAINTS?

Legend has it that Claudius, Castorius, Symphorien and Nicostratus were all Roman sculptors who converted to Christianity. Having refused to carve a statue of the pagan god Aesculapius for Emperor Diocletian, they were put to death in 304 in Pannonia (modern-day Bosnia) by being enclosed in lead coffins and then thrown into a river. Simplicius, another Christian sculptor, was then discovered recovering their bodies from the river, an act for which he himself suffered martyrdom and why he thus sometimes figures along with the other Four Crowned Saints.

Sometimes these four are confused with the saints Secondus, Carpophorus, Victorin and Severinus – four Roman soldiers who are said to have suffered martyrdom around AD 289 for having refused to worship a statue of Aesculapius. However, the existence of these four has been questioned.

The group name of The Four Crowned Saints was coined at a time when the names of the martyrs were unknown.

They became the patron saints of *tagliapietra* (stonemasons and sculptors) and their feast day is 8 November.

THE CHAPTER ROOM OF THE FORMER *SCUOLA* OF WINE MERCHANTS

Church of San Silvestro

• Open daily 9am to 12pm and 2pm to 5pm
• Access to the Chapter Room upon request

If the keyholder is available, a simple request will gain you admission to the pretty Chapter Room of the former *scuola* of wine merchants. Built between 1573 and 1581 by Chiona Lombardo, it is on the first floor at the right side of the church, which itself dates from much later. The present structure was entirely rebuilt in 1837-1843 and the façade dates from 1909. Other traces of the activities of wine merchants in this area are the placename Riva del Vin, the high-relief of a barrel, and the "barrel" doorway (p. 133).

THE FREEMASONS IN VENICE

The "speculative" Freemasonry* of the 18th century was defined in the following terms by one of its founders, Wilmshurst: "It is a sacramental system which, like all sacramental systems has a visible external aspect – ceremonial, doctrines and symbols – and an inner, spiritual and mental, aspect, which is hidden behind the ceremonies, doctrines and symbols. This latter is only accessible to the Freemason who has already learnt to use his spiritual imagination, who is capable of appreciating the reality which is veiled behind the exterior symbol." Frosini would claim that the original "operative" Freemasonry was already present in Venice in the 15th-16th centuries. In 1515, the premises of this association were moved to Sant'Aponàl, thanks to Pietro Lombardo, who had bought a plot of land at the base of the bell-tower there. On the façade of number 1252, you can still see a high-relief of the "Four Crowned Saints" with the inscription MCCLII SCOLA DEI TAGLIAPIERA (see p. 140). This guild of free stonemasons remained active in Venice right up to 1686, when Freemasonry was banned. It was only after 1729, when the Grand Master of the London Lodge visited Venice and lived for some time in a house near Madonna dell'Orto, that Freemasonry again became active, but this time in its new speculative form. Later, Marconis de Nègre, son of an officer of the French fleet in Egypt, founded the Société des Sages de la Lumières, which was behind the expansion of Freemasonry in 18th-century Venice. Aiming to make of Venice a model of social and moral perfection – the sort of model described in the poem La Venetia Edificata by the philosopher and Freemason Giulio Strozzi (see opposite) – the Freemasons saw literature and the fine arts as a means to achieve far-ranging reforms of the city's urban and social fabric. In clear opposition to these ideas, Freemasonry also resorted to practices that seemed to herald the Carbonari, a movement that emerged under General Pepe in early 19th-century Italy and was responsible for armed actions that spread terror throughout the Venetian Republic and the entire Italian peninsula.** It was partly for this reason that Freemasonry was always kept under careful surveillance by the Venetian authorities. Nevertheless, in 1778, there were five lodges active within Venetian dominions (two in Venice and one each in Brescia, Vicenza and Padua). Certain of these masons kept their distance from the political upheavals of the day, dedicating themselves solely to spiritual activities. However, this did not spare them eager surveillance by the Catholic Church, which saw Freemasonry as a threat to its traditions and teachings. According to the Inventario del 7 Maggio 1785, published in 1988 by Rossi Osmida, the main lodge in Venice was called Fedeltà and was founded in 1780. Its premises were in the Palazzo Contarini on Rio Marin (Santa Croce 803) and the lodge was known for its studies of alchemy and the observation of the Rectified Scottish Rite. It also showed some sympathy for the Rites of Memphis and Misraim, which were inspired by the Egyptian tradition. The lodge itself had been founded by Domenico Gasperoni and the Venetian Michele Sessa. Known as Ecques Michael a Leone, the latter became the "Venerable" or "Supreme Master" of the lodge by authorisation of the Great Lodge of

Verona in 1778. The *Fedeltà* probably remained active right up to the end of the 19th century. Famous members of this lodge included Giuliano de Lorenzo, Francesco Milizia and his pupil Tommaso Temanza (1705-1789, architect of the church of La Maddalena; see p. 237). The "Union" Lodge was housed in Corte da Mosto at San Marcuola. Another famous Freemason in Venice was Casanova.

** "Operative" Freemasonry was the descendant of the *Colegium Fabrorum*, the guild of architects and craftsmen in ancient Rome. It became famous through the work of the monk-builders of the Middle Ages and continued in existence up to the beginning of the 17th century. Modern "speculative" Freemasonry was founded in France in 1717, at Clermont-Ferrand, and is still known for its philosophical studies and its secret rituals.

** The "good cousins *Carbonari*" met secretly in the isolated cabins of charcoal-burners (*carbonari*), hence their name.

THE HIGH-RELIEF OF A SLEEPING POPE ⓬

Sotoportego della Madonna

> ### *The false legend of a pope forced to sleep in the street*

Just a short way from Campo Sant'Aponàl, the entrance to Sotoportego della Madonna (at the corner of Calle Madonna and Calle del Perdon) has a text engraved in the wood under the name of the *sotoportego*; in the middle is a small carved image that was inspired by a very curious anecdote.

Having come to Venice to sign a peace treaty with Emperor Frederick Barbarossa, Pope Alexander III (see p. 66) was, according to legend, forced to spend the night here, out in the street. He was said to have feared that, if he slept at his official residence, he would fall victim to a plot hatched by the emperor. His official residence was the patriarchal Palazzo of San Silvestro not far from here, a fresco from which can still be seen in the *sotoportego* that leads to the San Silvestro vaporetto stop. There is, however, another version of the story, which says the pope's concern for his safety led him to spend the night on the other side of the Grand Canal, at San Salvador. Some sources argue that he did risk the night in the patriarchal palace, whilst others suggest he may have slept near here, but not in the street. Documents reveal that the Templars (who apparently formed the pope's personal guard – see p. 243) owned a "Casa della Madonna" that stood on the site of the building now to the left of the

sotoportego, and that the pope slept here.

What is surprising is that there are neo-Templar inscriptions on the walls within the *sotoportego* itself (see opposite), and a small sculpture of a sleeping pope has been placed behind the grille in front of the altar located within the *sotoportego*.

Those who say a single "Our Father" or "Hail Mary" at this spot are, as a result of this episode, said to receive a perpetual indulgence.

NEO-TEMPLAR INSCRIPTIONS IN SOTOPORTEGO DELLA MADONNA

If you look up in Sotoportego della Madonna, you will find some curious inscriptions tucked away just below the ceiling; they include the famous motto *Non nobis domine, non nobis, Sed nomini tuo gloriam nos perituri mortem salutamos* (see p. 242). If you look even more carefully, you can see a depiction of a small Knight Templar hidden behind the bouquet of flowers on the "sleeping-pope" altar. These inscriptions do not date from the time of the Templars; they were probably the fruit of some neo-Templar revival associated with the Casa della Madonna that had once belonged to the Knights. The present house itself seems to date from the 1830s and has no extant traces of the era of the Templars.

THE VENETIAN CROSS

The cross seen at the entrance to Sotoportego della Madonna is not the Templars' Cross but a Venetian Cross (see p. 82). Others can also be seen at the entrance to Campo San Polo (at the corner of Calle Bernardo) and at the end of Calle del Perdon, a few metres from the *sotoportego*.

INDULGENCES: "AS SOON AS THE MONEY CLINKS IN THE COLLECTION-BOX, THE SOUL FLIES OUT OF PURGATORY"

In Roman Catholic doctrine, sins are erased by the sacrament of penance. But the confessional does not remove the pain of Purgatory, a place from which sinners hope to be liberated as quickly as possible. The length of time spent in Purgatory can be reduced or even written off completely by the granting of indulgences. These can be partial or full, depending on whether they free the penitent partially or totally from the duration of punishment for the sin in question. An indulgence is obtained in exchange for an act of piety (such as pilgrimage, prayer, mortification), carried out to this end in a spirit of repentance. Partial indulgences were traditionally counted in days, months or years. Contrary to what you might think, they do not correspond to an equivalent amount of direct remission from Purgatory, but indicate the remission corresponding to a particular penance. This practice, handed down from Roman law, goes back to the 3rd century, when it was important to bring back into the fold those Christians who had denied their religion because of persecution. "Simony" is a corruption of the practice of indulgence: the faithful made a bargain with the priest through an act of charity, which often took the form of a cash donation... A notorious example dates from 1515: that year, the Dominican friar Johann Tetzel was responsible for the sale of indulgences in the name of the Archbishop of Mainz, Albrecht von Brandenburg, who deducted 50% of the money to cover his household expenses. The hugely cynical motto of the enterprising monk, who beat a drum to attract the crowds, was "As soon as the money clinks in the collection-box, the soul flies out of Purgatory". It was against this background of scandal that Martin Luther intervened on 31 October 1517, the eve of All Saint's Day, posting his Ninety-five Theses denouncing the practice. The dispute over indulgences became one of the main causes of the schism between Protestants and Catholics.

In 1967, Pope Paul VI suppressed the references to a fixed number of days or years, but the indulgence itself, although perhaps less well known today, is still practised: during the millennium Jubilee celebrations, for example, indulgences were granted by Pope John Paul II. Protestants objected in vain. Five centuries may have gone by, but history repeats itself ...

Simony is the term used by Christians to refer to the buying or selling of pardons and other spiritual privileges. The practice owes its name to a certain Simon Magus, who practiced sorcery and wished to buy Saint Peter's ability to work miracles (Acts 8: 9-21), earning him the apostle's condemnation: "May your silver perish with you, because you have thought that the gift of God may be purchased with money!"

SOULS IN PURGATORY

While you can shorten your own stay in Purgatory (see above), it is also possible to alleviate the pain of souls already there, in what is known as the communion of saints.

When a living Christian prays for a soul in Purgatory, that soul sees its time reduced. Equally, a soul in Purgatory can intervene on behalf of a living person...

PROSTITUTION IN VENICE, A CITY THAT IN THE 16TH CENTURY WAS SERVED BY MORE THAN 11,000 PROSTITUTES

When Venice's power was at its height, a district in the area behind the Rialto was entirely given over to a flourishing sex trade that was an important source of revenue. Traces of this can still be found today near the Antiche Carampane restaurant (the name literally means "Old Whores"). Just alongside is *Ponte delle Tette*, the bridge where prostitutes were allowed to display their naked breasts (*tette*) in order to attract clients. Tradition has it that this custom was actually imposed by the government itself. Concerned about the increasing spread of homosexuality within the city, the authorities had resigned themselves to the lesser evil of fornication rather than have their citizens engage in what was then considered a "crime against nature".

In fact, homosexuality was so widespread in Renaissance Venice that the city's prostitutes had appealed to the Patriarch himself to take measures against it. Their business was suffering as men looked elsewhere for the sexual release they were supposed to get from prostitutes. However, another explanation for business being so bad may well be that there were just too many prostitutes. A census carried out at the time estimated that, in 1509, the city had no fewer than 11,164 of them. One inhabitant in five (or ten, according to other sources) was engaged in "the oldest profession in the world".

Just a short walk from Ponte delle Tette, the Antiche Carampane restaurant is very probably the best restaurant in Venice.

WHY WERE VENETIAN PROSTITUTES CALLED *CARAMPANE*?

Up to 1358, prostitutes were contained within an area known as Il Castelletto, a group of houses owned by the Venier and Morosini families and located near the Rialto church of San Matteo. In the evening, upon the third strike of the bell of St. Mark's, the prostitutes had to shut themselves indoors and on no account show themselves during the various parish festivities. Over time, they spread throughout the city, however, plying their trade in various places – particularly near churches.

Angered by this growing lack of respect, in 1421, the city decided once again to group the prostitutes together – this time in the houses the State had inherited from the Rampani family, a rich and ancient family whose last scion had died in 1319. As was the custom in Venice, the original family *palazzo* was known as Ca' Rampani, so the term "*carampane*" was soon coined for the courtesans who lived there.

Customers would come from far and wide to enjoy a service that was strictly controlled within set boundaries. For example, prostitutes were subject to an evening curfew, and any caught breaking that rule were punished with ten lashes. Similarly, they were forbidden to try and entice clients in the period around Christmas, Easter or other major religious holidays; the punishment for the transgression of that rule was fifteen lashes of the whip. Furthermore, prostitutes were not allowed to go into bars and restaurants, and were only allowed to walk around the city on Saturday (wearing a yellow scarf around their neck).

In the 17th century, young prostitutes again spread throughout the city, so that the Ca' Rampani district was populated only by the older women (who were now banned from the public streets because the very sight of them had become offensive). As for the younger prostitutes, the legal restrictions remained severe. For example, a law of 13 August 1644 banned them from living on the Grand Canal or in premises where the rent was above 100 ducats, from travelling in a boat powered by two or more oars, from entering a church during religious services and festivities, from wearing the white mantle associated with young virgins, or from adorning themselves with gold, jewellery or pearls. And just like their pimps, prostitutes could not give evidence in criminal trials nor bring legal action against anyone who tried to default on payment for their services.

Another reminder of the sex trade is **Traghetto del Buso**, which indicates the place where gondoliers ferried customers across to the prostitutes from the Fondaco dei Tedeschi side of the Grand Canal near the foot of the Rialto Bridge. *Buso* in Venetian means "hole" ... so you can imagine what it was used to refer to in vulgar parlance. However, another source has it that the name comes from the fact that, after one of the periodic bans on their activities, large numbers of prostitutes took this ferry when they were finally allowed back to work. In his 1697 book *Voyage d'Italie en Angleterre*, Vincenzo Coronelli also mentions a *Traghetto dei Ruffiani* (pimps), later "del Buso". It would seem that the real reason for the name, however, was that the coin used to pay the fare had a hole in it.

PLAQUE COMMEMORATING THE SITE OF ALDO MANUZIO'S PRINT SHOP

San Polo 2311
Rio Terà Secondo

Aldo Manuzio, the inventor of italic script

The plaque at number 2311 reads "*MANUCIA GENS ERUDITOR NEM IGNOTA HOC LOCI ARTE TIPOGRAPHICA EXCELLUIT*," commemorating the fact that these are said to be the premises where Aldo Manuzio (1449-1515) set up his print shop. The inscription also recalls the glorious tradition of printing that quickly became established in Venice. Soon after Johannes Gutenberg's discovery of movable type around 1440, the city rapidly understood the importance of the cultural revolution that was taking place. For example, Giovanni da Spina obtained the first authorisation for a printshop in 1468, there producing the first book ever printed in Venice, *The Letters of Cicero*. However, one of the most famous printers in Venice would be Aldo Manuzio (also known in English by his Latin name Aldus Manutius), who opened his print shop in 1494. Influenced by the ideas of Pico della Mirandola, one of Manutius' ambitions was to preserve all the best texts that were threatened by the Roman Inquisition and its Index. In doing so, he provided important help to Renaissance humanists intent on restoring Classical learning, thus initiating a cultural revolution that would lay the basis for a new society. In order to facilitate the spread of his publications, Manutius produced books that were smaller, cheaper and easier to transport. In 1501, he also had the brilliant idea of producing slightly sloping characters, so that more letters would fit into the same space. He thus created what we now call italic script.

One of his most famous publications was *Hypnerotomachia Poliphili* (Poliphilo's Dream). Attributed to Francesco Colonna and dated 1499, it is often considered one of the most beautifully produced books of the entire Renaissance. Almost flawless in layout, it includes a large number of engravings (see p. 329).

A plaque has also been placed on Aldo Manuzio's house in what is now Campo Manin (the former Campo San Paternian, see p. 33). This house also served as the premises of the *Accademia Filellenica Aldina*, a lively cradle of humanist thought and a worthy successor to the Florentine Academy founded by Marsilio Ficino and Pico della Mirandola.

MANVCIA·GENS·ERVDITOR·NEM·IGNOTA·

HOC·LOCI·ARTE·TIPOGRAPHICA·EXCELLVIT

SIGHTS NEARBY

THE PAVING STONE OF THE "COLUMN OF INFAMY"   **14**

Campo San Agostino

In the pavement of the *campo*, at number 2304B (on the corner of Calle Chiesa), is a small paving stone with the cryptic inscription LOC. COL.BAI. THE.MCCCX. It refers to the 1310 conspiracy led by Bajamonte Tiepolo, an attempt to overthrow the Venetian Republic that resulted in the burning of the Rialto Bridge and in Tiepolo ultimately being exiled to Istria. The conspirator's house was razed to the ground, and its place taken by a column recording his infamy (this small paving stone commemorates its position). After having decorated the garden of a villa on Lake Como, the column was brought to Venice by the villa's last owner, Duchess Josephine Melzi-d'Eril Barbo. Today, the column is part of the reserve collection of the Doge's Palace. Tradition has it that it was after the Tiepolo conspiracy that the Council of Ten was set up.

Other traces of this infamous conspiracy are still to be found in Venice (see p. 29, p. 61 and p. 120).

CA' SAN BOLDO

Rio Terà I
San Polo 2281
Reservations: 0421 66171 or info@adriabella.com
Tennis: €15 per hour
Grimani apartment: from €230 to €290 per night (3 nights minimum)
and from €1,400 to €1,750 per week

> *Sleep overlooking the only clay tennis court in Venice*

For those who do not live in the area it is extremely difficult to believe that there is a magnificent clay-surface tennis court right in the heart of the city. If you are staying in one of the three apartments opposite, when the court is not in use by club members you can have a game (supplement €15 per hour)! The sensation of knocking a ball about surrounded on all sides by the residences overlooking the court is quite unique and not only takes away the feeling of being a tourist but gives the very enjoyable impression of being in the countryside.

The owners, the Pasti family, have three apartments to let. The one known as Grimani (140 m², sleeps six) is particularly desirable: it has exclusive access to the small garden that separates the tennis court from the house. There are two outdoor tables (one in the sun, one in the shade), where you can have breakfast, lunch and dinner in an atmosphere that is unique for Venice. The three apartments – all with exposed-beam ceilings – are pleasantly furnished and have modern facilities. From the tennis court and apartments, there is also a stunning view of the truncated bell-tower of the old church of San Boldo, finally destroyed in 1826. What remains of the tower has been converted into residential accommodation.

THE ORIGIN OF THE NAME SAN STIN

Campo San Stin, just a short distance from the tennis court, takes its name from the diminutive form of San Stefanino (a small church here that was destroyed in 1810). Officially, the church was called Santo Stefano, but to avoid confusion with the much more imposing structure in the sestiere of San Marco, it became known locally as San Stefanino. However, the two churches were not dedicated to the same St. Stephen: the patron of the larger church was the first Christian martyr, while that of the church of Santa Croce was St. Stephen the Confessor.

THE INSCRIPTION *STATIONI DELLE SETTE CHIESE DI ROMA IN PERPETUO* ⑯

Church of San Polo
Campo San Polo

> ### A record of St. Philip Neri's Roman pilgrimage?

Just over the doorway into the church of San Polo there is this very discreet inscription within the wooden frame: *Stationi delle sette chiese di Roma in perpetuo*. This is probably a record of a pilgrimage that was first initiated by St. Philip Neri (1515-1595) and included the seven main churches of Rome: the four major basilicas (St. Peter's, St. John Lateran, Santa Maria Maggiore and St. Paul without the Walls), as well as San Lorenzo, Santa Croce in Gerusalemme and San Sebastiano (see our guide *Secret Rome*).

The tradition was that each route of this pilgrimage represented one of the seven "routes" Christ followed during his Passion: from the Last Supper to Gethsemane; from the Garden of Gethsemane to the House of Annas; from there to the House of Caiaphas; then on to the palace of Pontius Pilate; from there to the palace of Herod; from there back to the palace of Pontius Pilate; and from the palace to Calvary.

For those in Venice who could not make the pilgrimage to Rome, a Renaissance equivalent was established within the city, linking seven Venetian churches. Whilst there are few extant traces of this, it would seem that the pilgrimage churches included San Polo (standing in place of the Roman St. Paul's without the Walls; in 1805 the nave columns in this Venetian church were modelled on those of the basilica), Madonna della Fava (the church of the Congregation of St. Philip Neri in Venice), San Martino (see the sacristy paintings referring to St. Philip Neri), La Maddalena and the no longer extant church of L'Umilità on the Zattere (its oratory was dedicated to St. Philip Neri).

In the same way, the Franciscans of the 15th-16th centuries – a period when it was particularly dangerous and difficult to travel to the Holy Land – created places of pilgrimage where the scenes of Christ's Passion were reproduced. The three places they chose in Western Europe were: Monaione in Tuscany (see our guide *Secret Tuscany*), Varallo in Lombardy and Braga in Portugal.

ST. PHILIP NERI: A SAINT WHOSE HEART DOUBLED IN SIZE AS HE RECEIVED THE HOLY SPIRIT

Founder of the Congregation of the Oratory, also known as the Congregation of Filippinis after his forename, St. Philip Neri (1515-1595) was often referred to as the joyful saint because of his cheerful disposition. Inspired by the early Christian communities, he wanted to anchor an intense spiritual life in daily routine based on prayer (he was one of the first to gather around him laymen with whom he prayed), reading, meditating on the word of God, and praising the Lord, mainly through chant and music. According to him, music was a special way of reaching people's hearts and bringing them to God. Thus he became one of the most avid defenders of the rebirth of sacred music. In 1544, while the saint was praying in the catacombs of St. Sebastian over the tombs of the early martyrs, his heart was suddenly seized with immense joy and an intense light shone down on him. Raising his eyes, he saw a ball of fire which descended to his mouth and penetrated his chest. His heart, in contact with the flames, instantly dilated. The violence of the impact broke two of his ribs. The Holy Spirit had come to the saint, just as it had to the Apostles at Pentecost. In the 17th century, a scientific autopsy on his body confirmed that his was twice the size of any other human heart. Nothing was the same again for St. Philip. The beating of his

heart was so strong that it could be heard some distance away and the heat that constantly devoured him meant he could face the rigours of winter in his shirtsleeves. The symbol of the congregation today, a heart in flames, is based on this episode of his life. While looking after the sick, the poor and the infirm, he also took care to spend time with young people, wishing to stop them from falling into boredom and depression. He often gathered a group around him and while always reminding them that life was to be lived joyfully, when the din became too loud one day, he is supposed to have said "Quieten down a bit, my friends, if you can"! His great spiritual gifts even enabled him to bring a child back to life for a few moments.

SIGHTS NEARBY

BAS-RELIEF OF "A COLUMN AND A HALF"

The pharmacy in Campo San Polo has a fine late-19th-century interior and goes by the strange name of "Alla Colonne e mezza". It was originally called "Alle due Colonne"; however – given there was another pharmacy by this name at San Canciano (see p. 189) – an ordinance of 1586 required the name to be changed. So, the owners simply lopped the top off the second column on the shop sign carved on the right-hand side of the façade. The same symbol can also be seen inside, on the ceiling behind the counter.

THE LIONS ON THE SAN POLO BELL-TOWER

At the base of the San Polo bell-tower, which stands slightly beyond the present-day entrance to the church, are two curious carvings of lions. One is fighting a serpent (or a snake-headed dragon), whilst the other clasps a human head in its claws. Legend has it that these two sculptures refer to the punishment inflicted in 1432 on Francesco Bussone – known by the name of "Il Carmagnola" – who, suspected of having betrayed the Venetians, was imprisoned and then hanged. Initially in the service of the Duke of Milan, Francesco Bussone was at one point hailed as the "Liberator of the Milanese". However, when the duke, Filippo Maria Visconti, began to fear his power, Carmagnola was forced to flee to Venice in 1424. Leading the Venetian army, he won a great victory at Macalo (1427), but his generosity towards the prisoners taken made him suspect within the city. Some subsequent reversals of fortune, including a defeat in 1431, led to him being recalled to Venice in 1432. The day after his triumphal entry into the city, he was imprisoned; he later died on the scaffold.

Note that other sources claim that the figure depicted here is not Il Carmagnola but Doge Marino Falier, who betrayed the Republic in the 14th century.

THE MASCHERON OF HERCULES
Palazzo Maffetti-Tiepolo – Cannaregio 1957

Above the entrance to Palazzo Maffetti-Tiepolo is a discreet but pretty mascheron depicting Hercules ("Herakles" in Greek) with a lion's head. This recalls the first of his famous "Twelve Labours": the killing of the Nemean Lion. The son of Zeus (Jupiter), Hercules killed the supposedly invincible lion by throttling it. He then used the animal's hide as a cuirass and its head as a helmet, thus becoming invulnerable. The mascheron is hence a statement of the power of the building's owners. The present structure was rebuilt in the 18th century, probably by G. Massari.

Hercules and the Nemean Lion also figure in a high-relief at Palazzo Soranzo, a few metres to the left (number 2170).

THE BAS-RELIEF AT THE SCUOLA DEI CALEGHERI

⑳

Campo San Tomà

> **St. Mark:
> the patron saint
> of Venice and
> its shoemakers**

The former building of the *Scuola dei Calegheri* (shoemakers) dates from 1446 and has a very interesting bas-relief just above the main doorway that is often overlooked. Sculpted by Pietro Lombardo, it shows St. Mark healing the cobbler Anianus.

This episode in the life of Venice's patron saint – which took place in Alexandria (see below) – explains why he also became the patron saint of shoemakers.

Note that the Shoe Museum in Barcelona bears a bas-relief of the Lion of St. Mark on its façade, which may seem curiously out of place in the city of Barcelona (see our guide *Secret Barcelona*).

WHY IS ST. MARK THE PATRON SAINT OF SHOEMAKERS?

After preaching the Gospel in Italy, St. Mark moved to Egypt, where he became the first bishop of Alexandria. In that city, he founded the Orthodox Christian Church (the Church of the Roman Empire of the East and of the Greek part of the Roman world), ultimately becoming its pope. Captured, he suffered martyrdom in AD 67 because of the number of people he had converted to the faith. His body was then kept in a small chapel in the fishing port of Bucoles (near Alexandria), where he had been killed; from there, it was removed to Venice in a daring "snatch".

In AD 42, whilst he was in Alexandria, Mark miraculously cured a cobbler by the name of Anianus, who had been seriously injured when repairing the saint's shoes.

St. Crispin, a 3rd-century martyr, is another patron saint of shoemakers. He and Crispinian – both cobblers from Soissons – came to Rome towards the end of that century and were beheaded in AD 285 or 286.

Near Campo Santo Stefano is the former premises of the *Scuola* of German shoemakers (see p. 38). It has an interesting high-relief of a shoe dating from the 14th century.

The first floor inside has frescoes which are very badly damaged, works of little interest to the non-specialist.

THE SYMBOLS IN CANOVA'S FUNERAL MONUMENT ㉑

Basilica dei Frari
• Open Monday to Saturday from 9am to 6pm; Sunday from 1pm to 6pm

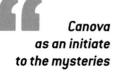

Canova as an initiate to the mysteries

Located within the Basilica of the Frari, the famous funeral tomb of the sculptor Antonio Canova (Possagno, 1 November 1757 – Venice, 13 October 1822) is rich in symbols that most people overlook.

Inspired by the art and symbolism of the Middle Ages, Canova here depicts such mythological figures as _Eros and Psyche_ (representing Spirit and Soul), _Perseus and the Medusa_ (representing the hero's victory over the trials of earthly life) and the _Three Graces_ (symbolising Faith, Hope and Charity – the three Cardinal Virtues of Christianity – but also perhaps the Three Masonic Lights: the Book of the Law, the Set Square and the Compass located on the Altar of Oaths in a Masonic Lodge).

It is said that Antonio Canova was initiated into Scottish-rite Freemasonry towards the end of the 18th century, prior to receiving commissions from figures who openly belonged to Christian Masonic circles. For example, he sculpted a portrait bust of George Washington in 1816, a work sadly destroyed in a fire shortly afterwards.

A man of sincere religious belief who had little interest in the mondaine delights to which he was so pressingly invited, Antonio Canova was viewed as an exemplary figure by his contemporaries – not only for his artistic excellence but also for his personal conduct and charity (for example, he worked extensively to encourage young artists). His death was mourned by Catholics and Freemasons, artists and humble folk alike.

The triangular form of the tomb clearly represents the Triangle of the Most Holy Trinity, as well as the Delta of the Great Architect of the Universe, of whom the Sun (or central Eye) is here indicated by the bust of Canova himself held aloft by two flying angels. For those initiated into the Primordial Tradition, this was clearly intended to signify that the master-artist had been a spiritual initiate and thus after death would find his way to the Eternal Orient (the Heavenly Jerusalem).

Beneath the central medallion is the doorway towards which the funeral cortege moves. The veiled figure of Death, carrying the Canopic vase, is followed by a half-naked male figure bearing a lit torch, the symbol of Immortality. Symbolically, in fact, Immortality comes after Death. Behind them are two women carrying a wreath of flowers; they represent Hope in the Charity of Immortal Life.

The cortege ends with two boys carrying lit torches; they symbolise that renewed Faith is ever young, the certainty produced by Faith.

To the left, on the first of the three steps that lead up to the doorway to the Afterlife, is a sleeping winged lion whose paws are crossed upon a closed book. This represents Power, Wisdom and Justice, symbolising the Father/Master/ Sovereign. In the Apocalypse, for example, it is the Winged Lion that opens the Book of Life after having broken the seven seals, thus becoming a symbol of Christ as described by the Evangelist Mark. The presence of the sleeping lion and closed book here means that Antonio Canova has closed his eyes forever, taking with him Wisdom and Faith as he moves towards the Throne of God.

On the second step is an angel with spread wings. Hanging his head, he looks towards the door of the tomb with an expression that is one of sadness and melancholy. His right hand resting on a club, he represents the Guardian Angel who has flown off through the doorway of Death. This makes him the heavenly witness that there is no Death without Immortality. One tip of his gown has slid towards the third step, on which is a laurel crown – the crown of victory, abandoned here by the man who enjoyed glory during his life but kept his distance from the vanities of the world. Without his tunic, the Angel is thus denuded, like the Bare Truth or "Isis Unveiled".

THE TRIPLE ENCLOSURE AT THE SCUOLA DI SAN ROCCO ㉒

Just a game or an esoteric symbol?

Just to the left of the main entrance of the magnificent Scuola di San Rocco, a curious symbol is carved into the stone ledge that many visitors use as a bench.

While some see this simply as the board game known as Nine Men's Morris, others – such as René Guénon and Paul Le Cour – have pointed out that this engraving has been found carved on vertical walls or reproduced on a very small scale, which would prevent it from being used as the basis for a game.

In Venice, for example, a similar engraving can be found on the first floor of the Fondaco dei Tedeschi (see p. 17).

Are these inscriptions meant to indicate that Venice was a special sort of holy place?

Nine Men's Morris, also known as Mills or Merrills, has been played since antiquity (in Rome, Greece and Egypt). Two players each have nine pieces ("men") and take turns placing them on one of the board's twenty-four intersections. The object of the game is to align three pieces belonging to the same player. Sometimes ordinary pebbles of different colours are used.

THE TRIPLE ENCLOSURE: AN ESOTERIC SYMBOL?

Composed of three interlocking squares with four horizontal lines that stop short of the central square, this design can be found carved in many places in Europe, and even in China and Sri Lanka.

In certain cases, it has been argued that this is an esoteric symbol referring to a spiritual quest. It is said to represent the three levels of the path followed by initiates, who pass through the physical, intellectual and spiritual worlds to finally achieve the divine.

For the druids, these triple enclosures could also have represented the three levels of their priestly hierarchy: druid, prophet and bard (teacher). Throughout medieval Europe, numerous castles were built with three rings of walls, in locations where powerful telluric energies marked the place as suitable for spiritual endeavour.

Having symbolised the triple enclosures of Solomon's Temple in Jerusalem (as described in the Book of Kings I, 7:12), this design may also represent the Heavenly Jerusalem with its twelve gates (four on each side) described in the Book of Revelations 21:11-22. The four lines forming a cross that links the three enclosures symbolise the means whereby teaching is propagated. It is also from the central point, the "fountain of tradition", that run the four rivers of *Pardes*, or paradise.

The grid is sometimes found in circular form. The circle initially would have corresponded to the beginning of the road while the square signified the culmination of the quest, hence the expression "squaring the circle" to symbolise the successful resolution of a problem.

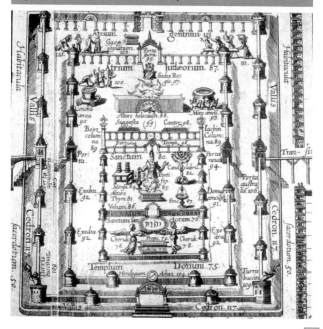

THE SECRETS OF THE SCUOLA GRANDE DI SAN ROCCO

Scuola Grande di San Rocco
Campo San Rocco
• Open daily from 9:30am to 5pm
• Tel: 041 5234864
• www.scuolagrandesanrocco.it • snrocco@libero.it

> **Is there a hidden message in Tintoretto's famous paintings?**

The members of the confraternity of the Scuola Grande di San Rocco commissioned their first paintings from Tintoretto (1518-1594) in 1564, ultimately amassing the magnificent group of works that today forms one of the most significant collections of Renaissance Venetian art. Three cycles of paintings were gradually installed in the different rooms of the Scuola: the history of Christ's Passion in the so-called *Albergo* in 1564-1567; scenes from the Old Testament and the Life of Christ in the Chapter Room (1576-1581; on the ceiling and walls respectively); and scenes from the Life of the Virgin and Christ's Childhood in the lower room (1582-1584).

Experts have until recently interpreted these works as simple illustrations of Holy Scripture, but now research has revealed that certain unusual iconographical features and previously inexplicable details in the paintings could have been inspired by the theological ideas of Guillaume Postel, a French linguist and prophet who was charged with heresy by the Inquisition in Venice in 1555 (see following double page). For example, in *The Adoration of the Magi* on the Scuola's ground floor there is a kneeling man dressed as a pilgrim who reveals a surprising resemblance to known depictions of Guillaume Postel himself.

Similarly, the Life of the Virgin and the scenes from Christ's Childhood can be read in a new key, taking on new meaning. *The Adoration of the Magi*, in particular, could be a depiction of the legend of Venice as a New Jerusalem, whilst the female saints depicted in atmospheric landscapes at the far end of the room could evoke the coming of a second Messiah, who, Postel argued, would be a woman, entrusted to complete Christ's work of redemption from the Original Sin brought into the world by Eve (see p. 166).

Whilst the decision to take Postel's ideas as the inspiration for these paintings must undoubtedly have come from those commissioning the work, there is nothing to rule out an actual meeting between Tintoretto and the French theologian when the latter was at the hospital of Santi Giovanni e Paolo in 1547-1548. That was, in fact, the period when Tintoretto was completing his first great masterpiece, *The Miracle of The Liberated Slave*, for the Scuola Grande di San Marco, which stands very close to that Ospedaletto.

GUILLAUME POSTEL AND THE PROPHECY OF A NEW FEMALE MESSIAH

Born around 1510 in Barenton, a small village in the diocese of Avranches (Normandy), Guillaume Postel studied oriental languages at the college of Sainte-Barbe in Paris. Having become one of the foremost experts in his field, he was appointed as *Lecture royal* to the French court of François I and made his first journey to the East in 1537. His actual itinerary is unknown, but we do know that he visited Egypt and spent some time in Constantinople perfecting his knowledge of Eastern languages. It was on his return trip that he "discovered" Venice. Desiring to join the Jesuits, he then went to Rome, but he was soon expelled from the Order for his unorthodox religious ideas. Having taken refuge in Venice, he remained there for two years (1547-1548), and it was at that city's Ospedaletto di SS Giovanni e Paolo that he met the holy woman Giovanna, whom he considered to be a new Messiah. He admired not only her great works of charity, but above all her extraordinary understanding of ancient Kabbalistic texts. Although she was barely literate, Postel claimed Giovanna could unveil the secrets of the *Zohar*, which the theologian was then translating into Latin. Endowed with supernatural powers, the woman could also see through solid objects and was able to live almost totally without drink or food.

According to Postel, Giovanna's mission on Earth was to complete the work which Christ had begun. Through his sacrifice, the Son of God had freed men of Original Sin; now a new female Messiah would do the same for women. Thus, humanity would recover its original purity and the world would see an end to the religious wars that were tearing Europe apart. Peace and prosperity would reign, and humankind would enter an age of Universal Concord.

In 1555, Postel published two small works in Italian that summarised his views: *Il Libro de la Divina Ordinatione* and *Prime Nove del altro mondo*. These two works were immediately added to the Index of banned books, and when Postel applied to the Congregation of the Holy Office for an explanation he was imprisoned. The Venice Inquisition then sent him before a tribunal in Rome, which judged him *amens* – that is, mad – so his death sentence was commuted to life imprisonment.

Following the death of Pope Paul IV in 1559, a popular uprising enabled Postel to escape. He returned to France, where an equally cruel fate awaited him. Due to the religious conflicts in Paris that were then spreading throughout the rest of the country, the king decided to confine the theologian to the monastery of Saint-Martin-des-Champs, where he died some twenty years later (1581).

Profoundly influenced by the Jewish Kabbalah, Postel's ideas are very complex, and his writings abound with so many metaphors that they are difficult to interpret. For example, when he speaks of Madre Giovanna as nourishing herself with a little water mixed with wine he is probably referring to the symbolic significance of these substances. Water, wheat and the colour white are associated with the male principle, and wine, blood and the colour red with the female. Through nourishing herself physically – but primarily spiritually – with a mixture of the two, for the theologian Madre Giovanna symbolised the absolute perfection that results from the union of opposites, of the male and female principle.

THE PAINTINGS OF THE TWO MARYS

Lower room of the Scuola Grande di San Rocco
Campo San Rocco
• Open daily from 9:30am to 5pm
• Tel: 041 5234864
• www.scuolagrandesanrocco.it • snrocco@libero.it

The two Marys: the prophecy of a female redeemer

Traditionally, the two paintings to either side of the altar in the lower room are interpreted as depicting St. Mary Magdalene and St. Mary of Egypt. However, an analysis on the basis of the theories of Guillaume Postel suggests a very different interpretation.

The first thing to note is that the woman in the two paintings is the same. Wearing the same clothes and with the same hairstyle, the female figure is simply depicted once from the front and once from the back. Furthermore, her appearance is very similar to that of the Virgin in *The Adoration of the Magi* and *The Annunciation* in the same room. A large part of both paintings is occupied by a tree; that on the right is a palm tree, while that on the left is difficult to identify. In his *Prime nove del altro mondo*, Postel actually refers to two trees as existing in the Earthly Paradise, one with its branches reaching towards Heaven and its roots stretching into the ground, and the other – standing just above it – with its branches reaching downwards and its roots growing up towards the sky. According to the theologian, these two trees symbolise respectively the female and male parts of the godhead. He also says that the trunk of the tree representing the female principle in God opens up in the middle to then come together again – this re-conjunction corresponding to the work of the Holy Spirit. In the two paintings under consideration, the tree fits this description perfectly. Its fine roots are clearly visible, whilst its foliage seems to reach from beyond the edge of the canvas (a feature that suggests the presence of another, inverted, tree), and in the middle is a small white mark that evokes the dove, the symbol of the Holy Spirit.

Postel also specifies that the Mother of the World – that is, the female Messiah whom the world is awaiting – "finds her seat" at the root of these trees. Thus, the saint depicted sitting at the foot of the tree could be a reference to this second Messiah.

In the same book, Postel refers to the prophecy regarding the marriage of Tamar, whose name is the Hebrew word for "palm tree". This tree, in fact, has the peculiar characteristic that it only bears fruit in the presence of male and female plants of the same species. On the one hand, therefore, it is a metaphor for the double (male and female) nature of the godhead, and on the other hand, it symbolises the imminent arrival of the female Messiah. Furthermore, the small wooden bridge that Tintoretto painted between the saint and the palm tree could be a perfect visual allusion to the marriage of Tamar, which is supposed to be essential for the coming of the Age of Universal Concord.

THE CEILING OF THE CHAPTER ROOM ㉕

Scuola Grande di San Rocco
Campo San Rocco
• Open daily from 9:30am to 5pm
• Tel: 041 5234864
• www.scuolagrandesanrocco.it • snrocco@libero.it

A path of initiation within a Christian Kabbalah?

Known as the Chapter Room, this was where the ruling council of the confraternity held its meetings. Its ceiling is decorated with 33 paintings representing scenes from the Old Testament which were painted by Tintoretto from 1576 to 1581.

Whilst some experts draw parallels between these Old Testament scenes and those from the Life of Christ depicted on the walls, the ideas of Guillaume Postel again suggest a very different reading of the ceiling iconography. For example, it is striking how the Chapter Room ceiling reflects the classic form of

the sephirot Tree of Life as described in the Christian Kabbalah in which Postel was so well-versed (see following double page).

Following this approach, the painting of *The Passover* would correspond in location to the sephirot Kether, which the *Zohar* describes as "the blood of the Passover and the blood of circumcision" or as "a point of darkness from which emanates light". The coincidence is all the more striking when one notes that on the table in Tintoretto's painting there is a strange black object from which flows a powerful light that illuminates the figures.

Whilst *The Collection of Manna* – "the corn of heaven" (Psalms 78:24) – naturally refers to the Eucharist, the entire meaning of the scene can be grasped from the description given in the *Zohar*: the manna is the dew cast by Kether, whose light illuminates the entire universe. Below this, *The Sacrifice of Isaac* is in a position that corresponds to that of the Tipharet, which the *Zohar* associates with that sephirot. The magnificent painting of *The Bronze Serpent* is located on the "path" traditionally designated by the Hebrew letter Teth, which means "serpent".

At the far end, *The Temptation of Adam and Eve* ends this representation of the sephirot and is located in the position of the Malkout, which the *Zohar* describes as a "field of apples" – and which Blaise de Vigenère, a friend of Postel's, identified as the place where "out of curiosity, Adam desired to taste of the fruit of knowledge, of good and evil".

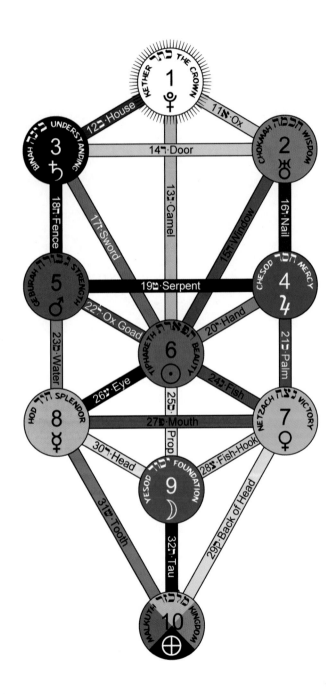

WHAT IS THE KABBALAH?

The origin of the Kabbalah (*Tradition* in Hebrew) goes back to the dawn of time. After their flight from Egypt, led by Moses, the Hebrew people are believed to have inherited this secret, esoteric knowledge from Egyptian sages and to have adapted it to their monotheistic beliefs.

Since the Pharisees and the Sadducees had strayed from the correct understanding of the Pentateuch compiled in the Talmud, a new current of thought, that of the Essenes, appeared. They became the faithful keepers of the Kabbalah's wisdom until the arrival of Jesus Christ, who immediately incorporated it into his philosophy. After Christ, the Christian gnostics of Alexandria assimilated the Judaic Kabbalah to adapt it to their own concept of the universe and of man. The Judaeo-Christian Kabbalah was born.

In the 12th century, in his great work *Sepher ha-Zohar* (*Book of Splendour*), Rabbi Moses de León retranscribed the idea of the *Kabbalah*. Written in León but conceived in Lisbon, this work, along with the *Sepher ha-Yetzirah* (*Book of Creation*) dating from the 3rd century AD, forms the Kabbalistic system. Its origins go back to the *Maaseh Merkavah*, the first mystic Jewish system that interpreted the sacred texts of the Torah in the 1st century AD and created a new doctrine that, at first, was only transmitted orally (*shebeal pe*) by its followers (*iordei merkavah*).

In the *Sepher ha-Yetzirah*, which discusses the Universe and the laws that rule it, the patriarch Abraham reveals the understanding of Nature and its manifestations as emanations of God. The various levels of creation form ten interconnected spheres (*sephirot*) representing the paths of Kabbalistic spiritual realisation, which thus form the Tree of Life (*Otz Chaim*).

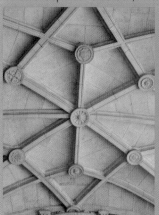

The Spirit becoming the Word or Gospel is the first sphere and the breath that results from it, the second. The breath, by combining letters, gives birth to the other spheres. The third is that of water, which produces the Earth and matter. The fourth sphere is that of fire, which nourishes life. The last six spheres correspond to the four cardinal directions and the two poles.

HERMES TRISMEGISTUS AND HERMETISM: ATTRACTING CELESTIAL ENERGY TO EARTH BY REPRODUCING THE COSMIC ORDER

Hermes Trismegistus, which in Latin means "thrice-great Hermes", is the name given by the neo-Platonists, alchemists, and hermetists to the Egyptian god *Thot*, *Hermes* to the Greeks. In the Old Testament, he is also identified with the patriarch Enoch. In their respective cultures, all three were considered to be the creators of phonetic writing, theurgical magic, and messianic prophetism.

Thot was connected to the lunar cycles whose phases expressed the harmony of the universe. Egyptian writings refer to him as "twice great" because he was the god of the Word and of Wisdom. In the syncretic atmosphere of the Roman Empire, the epithet of the Egyptian god *Thot* was given to the Greek god *Hermes*, but this time was "thrice great" (*trismegistus*) for the Word, Wisdom and his duty as Messenger of all the gods of the Elysium or of Olympus. The Romans associated him with *Mercury*, the planet that mediates between the Earth and the Sun, which is a function that Kabbalistic Jews called *Metraton*, the "perpendicular measure between the Earth and the Sun".

In Hellenic Egypt, *Hermes* was the "scribe and messenger of the gods" and was believed to be the author of a collection of sacred texts, called *hermetic*, that contained teachings about art, science, religion and philosophy – the *Corpus Hermeticum* – the objective of which was the deification of humanity through knowledge of God. These texts, which were probably written by a group belonging to the *Hermetic School* of ancient Egypt, thus express the knowledge accumulated over time by attributing it to the god of Wisdom, who is in all points similar to the Hindu god *Ganesh*.

The *Corpus Hermeticum*, which probably dates from the 1st to the 3rd centuries AD, represented the source of inspiration of hermetic and neo-Platonic thought during the Renaissance. Even though Swiss scholar Casaubon had apparently proved the contrary in the 17th century, people

continued to believe that the text dated back to Egyptian antiquity before Moses and that it announced the coming of Christianity.

According to Clement of Alexandria, it contained 42 books divided into six volumes. The first treated the education of priests; the second, the rites of the temple; the third, geology, geography, botany and agriculture; the fourth, astronomy and astrology, mathematics and architecture; the fifth contained hymns to the glory of the gods and a guide of political action for kings; the sixth was a medical text.

It is generally believed that Hermes Trismegistus invented a card game full of esoteric symbols, of which the first 22 were made of blades of gold and the 56 others of blades of silver – the *tarot* or "Book of Thot". Hermes is also attributed with writing the *Book of the Dead* or "Book of the Exit towards the Light", as well as the famous alchemy text *The Emerald Table*, works that had a strong influence on the alchemy and magic practised in medieval Europe.

In medieval Europe, especially between the 5th and 14th centuries, hermetism was also a School of Hermeneutics that interpreted certain poems of antiquity and various enigmatic myths and works of art as allegorical treaties of alchemy or hermetic science. For this reason, the term *hermetism* still designates the esoteric nature of a text, work, word or action, in that they possess an occult meaning that requires a hermeneutic, or in other words a philosophical science, to correctly interpret the hidden meaning of the object of study.

Hermetic principles were adopted and applied by the Roman *Colegium Fabrorum*, associations of the architects of civil, military and religious constructions. This knowledge was transmitted in the 12th century to the Christian *builder-monks*, the builders of the grand Roman and Gothic edifices of Europe, who executed their work according to the principles of sacred architecture, true to the model of sacred geometry. It is the direct legacy of volumes three and four of the *Corpus Hermeticum*, according to which cities and buildings were constructed in interrelation with specific planets and constellations, so that the design of the Heavens could be reproduced on Earth, thus favouring cosmic or sidereal energies. All of this was done with the purpose of achieving the hermetic principle that states: "Everything above is like everything below".

During the European Renaissance (16th and 17th centuries), hermetism was replaced by humanism. Forms were rationalised and the transcendental ignored. It was the end of the traditional society and the beginning of a profane, Baroque and pre-modernist society, paving the way for the arrival of the materialism and atheism that dominates the modern world. There were, however, some exceptions to this predominant rule in Europe. In Portugal, in the 16th century, the *Master Builders*, the heirs of the builder-monks, founded the Manueline style according to the hermetic rules of sacred architecture. The influence of the *Free Builders* continued into the 18th century and their greatest work was the restoration of Lisbon after the earthquake of 1755. That is why Pombal's Lisbon is designed and constructed according to the geometric and architectural measures of the Tradition handed down by Hermes Trismegistus (see *Secret Lisbon*).

HIGH-RELIEF OF *LA DONNA ONESTA* 26
San Polo 2935

> *The legend of the honest woman*

There are various stories concerning the sculpture of a woman's head still to be seen on the house located at number 2935.

The most interesting story claims that Santina, the charming wife of a bladesmith, lived here. Marchetto Rizzo, a young nobleman who had become obsessed with her, decided to have a dagger made by her husband in order to have an excuse to see the woman again. One day, after having made sure that the husband was absent, he came to the house and raped the woman, who – to preserve her honour – then took the dagger on which her husband had been working and killed herself. Another version of the same history has it that Zuane, a friend of Santina's husband, noticed what the young nobleman was planning and tried to save his friend's wife. In the effort, he did not kill the nobleman, but he was banished from the city for six months on 14 October 1490, for having violated his social rank.

Yet another version says that the name simply comes from that of another woman living in the area, or even from that of a local prostitute whose rates were so reasonable that they were described as "honest".

SIGHTS NEARBY 27

AN INDISCREET OPENING IN THE CASA GOLDONI
The famous Casa Goldoni still bears evidence of the Venetian mania of being able to spy on others without being seen. In the floor of the *portego* (main hall) on the first floor is a twenty-centimetre square floor tile worked in such a way that it enabled the owner of the house to see who was arriving at the *porta d'acqua* (watergate) below.

Similar contrivances can be seen in the Casino Venier (see p. 25), though there you had to lift a slab in the floor in order to see into the street below. The former Casino dei Nobili, near Campo San Barnaba, also has a trace of this device, which is no longer functional.

A modern-day version of these can still be seen by glancing up to the first-floor windows of certain buildings. Small mirrors are angled in such a way that those inside can see down into the street below.

THE CHAPEL OF THE HOLY NAIL ㉘

Church of San Pantaleon
Campo San Pantaleon
• Open daily except Sundays and holy days from 4pm to 6pm
• Mass at 6:30pm

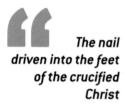

The nail driven into the feet of the crucified Christ

Contrary to first impressions, the chapel of the Holy Nail in the church of San Pantaleon is not always closed to the public. You simply have to apply to the church personnel and they will open the chapel for you.

The superb 15th-century altar (note the beautiful bas-relief of *The Entombment of Christ*) contains the nail that is probably one of the most precious holy relics in Venice. It is said to have been an (indirect) gift from St. Louis, the French king Louis IX, who in the spring of 1270 came to the city to try and obtain its adherence to a new crusade. Before leaving, he visited the convent of the Poor Clares in Santa Chiara and gave the Mother Superior there a small chest, telling her to keep it safe and only surrender its contents to a person in possession of a ring similar to the one he left along with the chest. As for St. Louis himself, he never came back from the crusades, dying on 25 August that year during an epidemic in Tunis.

A long time afterwards, when no one had come to collect the chest, the nuns – following the convent's miraculous escape from the disastrous effects of a particularly severe *acqua alta* – decided to open it. Along with the nail, there were various other holy relics, a few gold French coins and a text explaining how the king had come into possession of the Holy Nail. According to a tradition that is not universally accepted, it had been St. Helena, the mother of Constantine (the first Roman emperor to convert to Christianity), who had discovered the True Cross, together with the nails used at the Crucifixion. Having been brought to Rome by her son, the relics were then taken to Byzantium when Constantine there founded a new city that would become Constantinople. After the fall of that city to the crusaders themselves (in 1203), the holy relics of the Passion were divided between the Venetians and the French.

A further legend has it that the nail had performed a miracle, quelling a fierce storm at sea after St. Helena placed it within the waters of the Adriatic.

Following the fall of the Venetian Republic to Napoleon's army, when the convent of the Poor Clares was suppressed in 1810, the Mother Superior of the day, Sister Maria Lucarelli, came to live within the parish of San Pantaleon. Later, in agreement with the other nuns, she entrusted the precious relic to that church on 30 May 1830, and the nail was placed in its present location in a ceremony held on Good Friday, 1836.

In theory, since that date it has been on public exhibition to the faithful one day a year. However, in spite of the importance of the relic, for some reason this has not been the case for several years now.

SIGHTS NEARBY

GIOVANNI DI ALEMAGNA'S *IL PARADISO*

San Pantaleon's Chapel of the Holy Nail (see opposite) contains other treasures besides that holy relic.

Just to the right as you enter is a superb but often ignored painting, *Il Paradiso*

by Giovanni di Alemagna, a gifted pupil of Vivarini's, which was probably painted in 1444. Properly speaking, the work in fact depicts the Coronation of the Virgin, but its more usual name comes from the fact that it shows a large number of the heavenly hierarchies of angels. In both draughtsmanship and palette, the work is a real masterpiece of 15th-century Venetian painting. Opposite, note two fine paintings in the style of Paolo Veneziano. Facing the entrance is the beautiful 15th-century altar with Marino Cedrini's fine bas-relief of *The Entombment of Christ*.

A DECEPTIVE FAÇADE

Contrary to expectations, the façade of San Pantaleon is not particularly old. As is the case with San Marcuola and San Lorenzo (in Florence), the present state of the façade is simply due to the fact that it was never completed for lack of funds. Note the projecting parts of the brick frontage, which were intended to support the weight of the marble facing that was never added. If it had been completed according to plan, the church façade would have looked rather like those of San Moise, Santa Maria del Giglio, Santa Maria degli Scalzi or the Church of the Gesuiti – all of which were completed around the same period. On a foundation dating from the 11th century, San Pantaleon was totally rebuilt in the years following 1686.

THE LARGEST PAINTING IN THE WORLD

The church of San Pantaleon contains what is apparently the largest canvas in the world, *The Martyrdom and Ascension into Glory of San Pantaleon*, painted by Giovanni Antonio Fumiani in 1684-1704. Contrary to traditional claims, the decoration on the ceiling of the nave is a painted canvas and not a fresco. Look at the ceiling around the choir and you will see the feet of a winged angel clearly projecting. The same scene of the martyrdom of San Pantaleon is also depicted in the right aisle. All in all, the nave painting comprises 40 different canvas panels, which were painted separately then assembled in the church.

THE MEDALLION OF A BYZANTINE EMPEROR

Campiello Angaran
San Polo 3717

A very discreet medallion

Just a few steps from the church of San Pantaleon, the small Campiello Angaran is slightly off the beaten track. On the façade of the house at number 3717 is a fine marble medallion depicting an emperor in Byzantine costume.

Legend has it that when, in 1256, the Venetian general Lorenzo Tiepolo was sent to fight the Genoese at St. John d'Acre, a number of his friends and relatives did not believe him up to the task. As a result they told him that, should he be successful, he had to bring back material proof of the fact. Thus, when Tiepolo won the battle he is said to have sent this medallion, which he took at the Fort of Montjoie, back to Venice.

Whilst this story is open to doubt, there are some that argue that the medallion was originally placed in the pavement between the church of San Pantaleon and this house (home to one of those who had doubted Tiepolo) so that, every time he went to mass, the occupant would pass the visible proof of the general's valour.

Other, probably inaccurate, sources claim the medallion is from the 9th century and depicts Emperor Leo VI "the Wise", who reigned from 886 to 911.

Other sources dismiss all these stories as just legends, claiming the piece dates from the turn of the 13th century. Another very similar medallion can be seen in the Dumbarton Collection (Washington).

WHEN A HOUSEHOLDER TURNS DOWN A MUSEUM...

In 1972, the medallion was exhibited at the Museo Corror in the city, and the museum asked to be granted permanent custody. We have one of the owners of the houses to thank for rejecting the proposal. The fact that you can come across such an unexpected artistic treasure simply by turning a corner is one of the inestimable charms of Venice.

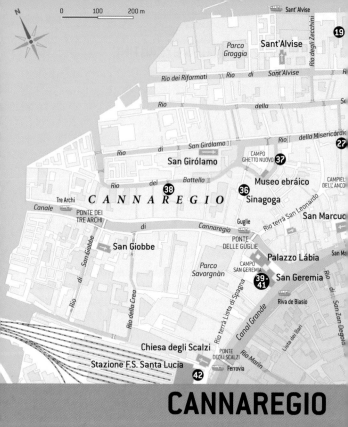

CANNAREGIO

There is another Man of the Forests on the façade of the Brass house (Dorsoduro 1083), near the church of San Trovaso.

Assimilated by Christianity, Silvanus would be the origin of the figures of St. Silvanus and St. Sylvester. Like other saints subsequently withdrawn from the Roman Church's calendar – for example, George, Christopher and Philomena – they did not actually exist.

THE SCULPTURE OF *HOMO SILVANUS* ❶

Palazzo Bembo-Boldù
Cannaregio 5999

A reminder of Ancient Rome's "Man of the Forests"

Standing just a few steps from the church of Santa Maria dei Miracoli, the façade of Palazzo Bembo-Boldù is decorated with a very distinctive sculpture: a life-size figure of a hairy man holding a round shield adorned with the Sun. This pelt-covered figure is a rare depiction of *Homo Silvanus*, the "Man of the Forests", a primitive who, like Adam, did not know sin because he lived in remote forests during the earliest ages of the world. Symbolising the innocence of feelings, this was a figure who rejected a world of falsity, lies and cruelty (of which he may perhaps have been the victim). At the same time, however, this "Man of the Forests" also embodied the dark and violent side of each of us, symbolising that psychological and sexual perversion which, in Christian iconography, is depicted by the satyr.

Here, this idealisation of Primordial Man is associated with the Sun, the "king" which nourishes the natural world. As such, he reminds us of the "savage" purity of humankind in the Garden of Eden (the original Paradise).

In Ancient Rome, Silvanus was the god of forests (*silvae*). He was said to be one of the sons of Saturn or of Faunus (Saturn's grandson), with whom he was often identified. Just like Faunus – the god of shepherds – Silvanus was a purely Roman god. The guardian of the forests, he was also apparently the first to permit a separation of the countryside into private property. In this sense, he evokes the establishment of the first rural communities, where religion was based upon the cycle of the seasons (determined by Saturn, the god of Time). Traces of this ancestral paganism can still be found in various practices of "popular religion" throughout Europe.

Whilst an image of Silvanus was to be found in the temple of Saturn in Rome, the city also had two sanctuaries dedicated specially to a god whose worship, Dillaway argues, was first introduced into Italy by the Pelsagians. Silvanus sometimes appeared naked, sometimes in a knee-length rustic garment. According to Murray, he was depicted as a young man playing a shepherd's flute (like all the other gods of pastoral activity, he was a musician) and holding the branch of a tree. This latter attribute recalled his status as God of the Forests, but also his love for the beautiful youth Cyparissus, who had been changed into a cypress tree, a symbol of the power of Death. According to Dillaway, however, the god was depicted as a small-sized figure with a human face but goat's feet – but again with a branch of cypress in his hand (as mentioned by Virgil).

SIGHTS NEARBY

THE EXECUTIONER'S HOUSE

Calle della Testa
Cannaregio 6216

Attached to the wall of the relatively modern building at number 6126 is a strange-looking head that stares out at the few passers-by who venture into this part of the neighbourhood. According to popular legend, the head marks the site of the home of one of 15th-century Venice's executioners. At the time, it was attached to his house, and, through its mouth, the State "posted" messages giving the date of forthcoming executions for which the man's services would be required.

THE OTHER EXECUTIONERS' HOUSES IN VENICE

The free-standing building in Campo Santa Margherita, once also the premises of the *Scuola dei Varotari* (Guild of Furriers).

The low house overlooking the Grand Canal, between the Fondaco dei Turchi and Riva de Biasio.

SESTIERE: A RARE CASE OF ETYMOLOGICAL PRECISION

The districts in Venice are known as *sestieri*; the term is derived from the word for "six", the city being divided into six sections. Thus, it is far more precise than the use of the term "quarter" – as in the expression "residential quarter", etc. – which originated in the fact that a Roman city actually was divided into four "quarters", created by the intersection of a north-south and east-west road (the *cardo* and *decumanus* respectively).

THE OBELISKS ON VENETIAN *PALAZZI*

These obelisks indicated that the owner of the building had served as an admiral with the Venetian fleet. The one exception is Palazzo Papadopoli – on the Grand Canal, near San Silvestro – where they simply replaced the old chimneys.

ETERNA
MEMORIA
DELL ANNO
1854 DEL
CIACCIO
VEDUTO IN
VENEZIA
HE RES
MILE DIRA
MENTE NOV
ANOI
ANFA V
IN TER LUI
SIAN HE
MAVI

SIGHTS NEARBY

GRAFFITI RECORDING A "GREAT FREEZE" ON THE LAGOON
Sotoportego del Traghetto

Located not far from the church of San Canciano, the quiet Rio dei Santi Apostoli was a busy shipping channel within the city. Boats from Istria and from islands such as Torcello and Mazzorbo passed here. The very name of these arcades (Sotoportego del Traghetto) comes from the fact that the waterway was used by the *traghetto* (ferry) to Murano. Previously, the space was not divided up by the various grilles present today. The entire arcade was used by passengers, who waited here for the boats to the various destinations.

Among the graffiti scratched on the columns is one that records the "great freeze" of the lagoon that had such spectacular effects. It reads:

Eterna memoria dell'anno 1864 / Del giaccio veduto in Venezia / Che se sta sule Fondamenta Nove / a San Cristoforo andava la gente / In procision che formava un liston / Vincenzo Bianchi / A 1864

Thus, in the winter of 1864, people could walk across the ice as far as the island of San Michele (which is in fact two islands, one of which is called San Cristoforo della Pace).

WHAT IS A *LISTON*?
The word used in the graffiti is a Venetian term for a sort of paved avenue through the centre of a large public square (such as St. Mark's or Campo Santo Stefano), along which people promenaded at certain hours of the days. *Fare il liston* thus meant to "take a stroll", given that it was more pleasant to walk on the paving stones than on the bare earth and grass that then covered most of the Venetian *campi* (the term *campo* actually means "field").

THE FROZEN LAGOON
Over the centuries, the harsh winters of 1789, 1864 and 1929 have remained famous. The ice that formed on the water of the lagoon was so thick that it could bear the weight of sledges.

THE *TERIACA* HOLE
Outside the pharmacy "Alle Due Colonne", you can still see a hole in the paving, into which the mortar used to pound up the ingredients of *Teriaca Fina* (see p. 44), a famous medicine produced in the old *spezieria*, was fitted.

GOOD LUCK ANCHORS
On the wall of the building at the corner of Sotoportego del Traghetto are two small anchors referred to as *le ancorate*. Venetians often tap them against the wall when they pass. For some reason, this is said to bring good luck.

THE SECRET GARDEN OF CA' MOROSINI DEL GIARDIN

6

Calle Valmarana 4629/B
• To visit the garden, ring the bell and ask the porter, or contact Signora Mariagrazia Dammicco at Wigwam Club Giardini Storici Venezia
• Tel. 328 8416748 – 320 4678502
• giardinistorici.ve@wigwam.it • www.giardini-venezia.it

Where a fruit garden merges with a botanical garden

Between Calle Valmarana and Rio dei Santi Apostoli are the walls enclosing the garden of Ca' Morosini, a place rich in history. From the outside, all you glimpse are a few branches above the walls, but this vast area alongside the canal contains a large vegetable garden and orchard (with pomegranate, medlar, fig, apricot and persimmon trees), as well as a botanical garden with a whole range of scented flowers. The place is splendid in springtime when the twin arbours flower, one of white wisteria, the other of rose, passionflowers and fox grape.

The parterres are laid out in two geometrical sections. At the height of summer, they are a spectacular explosion of colour: petunias, hibiscus, hydrangeas, dahlias, hollyhocks, gillyflowers, carnations and snapdragons, amongst flowers traditionally associated with the Virgin (roses and irises) and plants that are usually found within monastery grounds (olive trees and cypress).

Jacopo de Barbari's bird's-eye view of the city shows that this vast area was already cultivated as a garden at the beginning of the 16th century. The owners, the Erizzo family, also had a *casino* built that gave onto the canal behind. This pavilion with three arcades flanked by two towers was attributed to Palladio and apparently had frescoes by Paolo Veronese. In fact, the garden became so famous that, over the years, the Morosini, who bought this and other properties during the 17th century, would become known as the Morosini del Giardin.

The entire complex was redesigned once again in the 17th century, perhaps by Longhena. In the 19th century, the brick paving was torn up and some of the buildings demolished. This explains why there are only some parts of the original layout – for example, the white-stone frame of a 16th-century wall (on the Campiello Valmarana side) and two bricked-in 17th-century gateways (surmounted by mascherons) that gave onto Calle della Posta.

Today, the garden belongs to a community of Dominican nuns, who dedicate great passion and care to the upkeep of a garden laid out in the space remaining after the demolition work carried out in the 19th century.

The Jesuits, who were learned in the esoteric and Gnostic traditions of Christianity, also had relations with the Jews of the nearby Ghetto, where the tradition of the Kabbalah was extensively studied.

STATUES OF THE ARCHANGELS SEALTIEL, URIEL AND BARAQUIEL

❼

Church of I Gesuiti (or Santa Maria Assunta)
• Open daily from 10am to 12pm and 3:30pm to 5:30pm

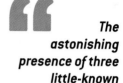

The astonishing presence of three little-known archangels

At the transept crossing in the church of I Gesuiti, the statues of four archangels sculpted by Giuseppe Torretti (*c.*1660-1743) are enthroned within specially created niches. Whilst the archangels Gabriel, Raphael and Michael are well-known, the forth – Sealtiel – is much less so. In the choir beyond, there are also statues of two other little-known archangels: Uriel and Baraquiel.

Michael (prince of the celestial militia), Gabriel (protector of travellers; his name means "God heals"), Raphael (celestial messenger*; his name means "The Power of God"), Baraquiel, Sealtiel, Uriel and Oriphiel (or Jehudiel, absent here) are the seven archangels of the Gnostic tradition and the Jewish Kabbalah. In the latter, the last four are named Samael, Zadkiel, Anael and Kassiel.

Only Michael, Gabriel and Raphael are actually named in the Bible. However, all seven archangels are mentioned in the Book of Tobit: "I am Raphael, one of the seven holy angels, which present the prayers of the saints, and go in before the glory of the Holy One" (Tobit, 12.15).

Judaeo-Christian tradition also associates each of the archangels with one of the planets:

Sun – Michael	Moon – Gabriel
Mars – Samael (Baraquiel)	Mercury – Raphael
Jupiter – Zadkiel (Sealtiel)	Venus – Anael (Uriel)
Saturn – Kassiel (Oriphiel/Jehudiel)	

Previously also called Sakiel, Sealtiel's name means "the roof or head of God" in Hebrew. Hence, he is the archangel that "contemplates" the Divinity. However, he is also the angel that possesses the horn of plenty, and is therefore invoked here so that his intervention in the court of heavenly justice may supply the material needs of the Company of Jesus (the other name for the Jesuits).

Uriel ("Flame of God" in Hebrew) is identified as the keeper of the gates of the original Paradise (Eden); he carries a sword of flame. He is also the angel that will open the gates of Hell on Judgement Day (according to the Apocalypse). His presence here serves to protect the church – and, by extension, Venice – by separating Good from Evil, and Light from Darkness.

Baraquiel ("Blessing of God" in Hebrew) maintains mankind in a state of Grace. By keeping man on the right path and protecting him from the enemies of the Faith, he guarantees final beatitude after death. He is the archangel of divine goodness.

*In the Muslim religion, this is the angel who, by the name of Djibril, reveals the verses of the Koran to Muhammad.

THE HIERARCHIES OF ANGELS

In the Judaeo-Christian tradition, the celestial powers that created the Universe, Earth and Man are organised into nine choirs called the *Celestial Militia*, composed of archangels, angels, saints and prophets, who are all under the authority of the Archangel Michael, the closest to the throne of God.

Various Church authorities have discussed this matter (St. Ambrose, St. Jerome, Pope Gregory the Great), as have such Jewish authorities as Moses de Leon and Moses Maimonides. The question is also examined in Hebrew theological texts such as the *Sefer Hazohar*, *Maseket-Atziluth* and *Berith-Menusha*. However, the most widely accepted version is that given by the figure known as Dionysius the pseudo-Areopagite, a 6th-century writer who was for a long time confused with Dionysius of Athens, a martyr whose conversion by St. Paul is recorded in the Acts of the Apostles. The writings of the later writer (or group of writers) included *The Celestial Hierarchy* and *The Ecclesiastical Hierarchy*. It was only when the distinction between the two "Dionysius" was accepted that their author was referred to as the "pseudo-Areopagite".

St. Thomas Aquinas, however, accepted the writings as genuine, and in his *Summa Theologica* he talks of three Orders of Heavenly Powers, each divided into three choirs, making a total of nine. They are divided as follows:

First Order (God the Father): present at the genesis of the world, its three choirs preserve the harmony of creation and manifest/perform God's will. They comprise:

Thrones

Cherubim

Seraphim

Second Order (God the Son): its three choirs represent the Power of God in the genesis of the planets, which they govern, and of the Earth in particular. They carry out the orders of the Powers of the first Order and exercise command over the third Order. They comprise:

Powers

Dominions

Virtues

Third Order (God the Holy Spirit): present in the genesis of mankind, these three choirs protect and guide humanity. They carry man's virtuous thoughts and prayers up to God. They comprise:

Principalities (*Arqueus*)

Archangels

Angels

This last Order brings together all the qualities of the previous ones. As the closest to mankind, it is they that humans address, and it is they who are most frequently depicted in works of art. If angels are God's messengers, archangels are those who announce the most important events.

THE SACRISTY OF THE JESUIT CHURCH

Church of I Gesuiti (or Santa Maria Assunta)
• Open daily from 10am to 12pm and from 4pm to 6pm

**Just push
the door**

The magnificent church of I Gesuiti has a remarkable interior in polychrome marble "damasking". However, in spite of its beauty, it receives comparatively few visitors, and even less of them make their way into the charming sacristy. Though a small notice on the closed door makes it clear that the place is open to visitors, only rarely do people take up the invitation. Perhaps the fact that you almost always have the place to yourself adds to the charm.

With a delightful ceiling in painted wood, the sacristy is primarily dedicated to the history of the Order of *I Crociferi* and to the often forgotten history of St. Helena's discovery of the True Cross (see p. 121).

THE JESUITS: EXPELLED FROM VENICE IN 1606, THEN – IN EXCHANGE FOR THE PROPERTY OF THE ORDER OF *I CROCIFERI* –READMITTED IN 1657 DURING THE COSTLY WAR OF CANDIA

The church of I Gesuiti was built on the site of the old church and monastery of the Order of *I Crociferi* (see opposite). The dissolute morals of the monks ultimately led Pope Alexander VII to dissolve their foundation in 1656, and their property was transferred to the Venetian State. The dissolution came at just the right time for Venice, which was engaged in a full-scale war for the control of Candia (Crete) and had difficulty meeting the costs of the campaign. However, this timely decision was not entirely coincidental. In exchange for the property of *I Crociferi*, the papacy negotiated with Venice for the readmission of the Jesuits into its territory. The latter had, in fact, been expelled in 1606 for having supported the pope rather than Venice in a dispute regarding two priests. It may not seem to have been a very important dispute, but Venice placed great importance on its independence from the papacy.

And even after 1657, when the Jesuits made their official return to Venice by re-purchasing the old monastery of *I Crociferi*, the authorisation for their presence in the city still had to be renewed every three years.

THE GRILLE OF THE ORATORIO DEI CROCIFERI

Cannaregio 4905
Campo dei Gesuiti
• Open April-October including Fridays and Saturdays, from 3:30pm to 6:30pm
• Tel: 041 27190 12

An unknown gem

The Oratorio dei Crociferi is one of the unknown marvels of the city of Venice. Decorated by Jacopo Palma Il Giovane in the years 1583-1592, it now houses eight wonderful canvases by this Venetian master. They depict episodes from the history of this Order of crusader monks, with particular reference to its two main benefactors: the doges Renier Zen and Pasquale Cicogna.

The oratory is the old chapel of a hospital/hospice founded in the 12th

century by the crusader monks for pilgrims and crusaders on their way to the Holy Land. In the 14th century, it became a hospice for poor women and widows, a role it still has today. The twelve rooms are linked directly with the oratory. Above the entrance, note the grille which allowed those suffering from infectious diseases to hear mass without infecting the rest of the congregation.

AN ALTARPIECE STOLEN, RE-COPIED AND THEN STOLEN AGAIN
The painting on the high altar is a rarity because it replaces not only Palma Il Giovane's original of *The Adoration of the Magi* (which was stolen shortly after the oratory opened), but also the replacement for that work, which was painted by Paris Bordone and then also stolen. When asked to make a copy of his copy, the artist refused, producing instead the *Virgin in Glory adored by Venice* which can still be seen here.

"ANTONIO MARIA TRAVERSI" MUSEUM OF PHYSICAL SCIENCES

⑩

Fondamenta Santa Caterina 4942
• Visits by appointment: Tel. 041 5224845
• museo.traversi@liceofoscarini.it
• http://museo.liceofoscarini.it/virtuale/index.html

A 19th-century physics laboratory

Even most Venetians are unaware of the existence of the "Antonio Maria Traversi" Museum of Physical Sciences, which is tucked away in the heart of the Marco-Foscarini high school.

The collection comprises more than 200 scientific instruments, for use in both research and teaching, that were part of the school's physics laboratory in the 19th century.

Occupying the former monastery of Santa Caterina, the school was founded in 1807 by Napoleonic decree and its first headmaster was monk Antonio Maria Traversi, a celebrated physicist and passionate researcher who would bequeath his collection of scientific instruments to the institution he had headed. This formed the initial core of the physics laboratory, which was then located in what is the present-day conference room.

Other equipment was later bought and skilful craftsmen were commissioned to produce precision instruments that could be used in both research and teaching. The Austrian government adopted a policy of enlightened support towards the school, trying whenever possible to satisfy the teachers' requests in order to add to the rich collection of instruments that already existed.

The equipment is divided into various sections: Measurement, Mechanics, Fluid Mechanics, Thermodynamics, Optics, Acoustics and Electromagnetism. A number of them are one-off pieces or prototypes of more accurate and modern versions that were produced later. Some are works of very refined craftsmanship, involving decorative additions and the use of precious materials. One of the most remarkable instruments is Father Cannini's superb navigational compass (18th century), a veritable collector's piece that has a wind rose and allegorical depictions of four continents (there is no Australasia). Together with this assortment of instruments, ranging in date from the second half of the 17th century to the beginning of the 20th, the collection also contains texts and documents.

For small groups, the school supplies guides from amongst its own students; a special training course enables them to give a thorough account of everything that is on display. Visitors also get the chance to see some of the instruments in use; the young guides are delighted to carry out simple but significant procedures using the equipment. There is also a website where you can see all the instruments within a sort of virtual museum.

THE EYES OF ST. LUCY

Painting by Giambattista Tiepolo: *The Last Communion of St. Lucy*
Cappella Corner
Church of Santi Apostoli
Cannaregio
• Vaporetto stop: Ca d'Oro or Rialto

**Served up
on a platter**

L ocated in Cappella Corner in the church of Santi Apostoli, Tiepolo's *The Last Communion of St. Lucy* is not a very well-known work. In the bottom right of the painting, note the saint's two eyes, placed in a rather startling manner on a platter, alongside a knife.

The image refers to the martyrdom of St. Lucy (see below). Legend has it that she was blinded before being beheaded. The painting itself depicts the saint taking Holy Communion before her death. Certain sources have it that the saint replaced the eyes in her head after it was severed by the axe.

ST. LUCY

Born in Syracuse around the year 300, Lucy was a Sicilian noblewoman who pledged herself to God, taking a vow of celibacy and poverty. Upon seeing that she was "throwing away" her fortune in charity to the poor, the man to whom she was promised in marriage denounced her to the Consul of Syracuse, Pascasius, accusing her of being a Christian (an infraction of Imperial law). Having tried in vain to get her to renounce her faith, the Consul then tried to punish her by committing her to a brothel where she would be raped. Filled with the Holy Sprit, the saint suddenly became an immovable mass: dozens of men, then oxen, could not move her body one inch. Finally, after having her sprinkled with urine (said to drive out evil spells), then with boiling oil mixed with pitch and resin, the Consul had the saint's throat cut and, according to certain sources, her eyes put out. Miraculously, however, Lucy could still speak after her throat had been cut, continuing to invoke the name of God.

St. Lucy is the patron saint of opticians and of those suffering from eye diseases.

Certain sources claim, however, that the saint never actually existed.

Bassano's painting *The Martyrdom of St. Lucy* in San Giorgio Maggiore depicts the scene when a huge number of oxen and men are trying in vain to drag Lucy towards the place of her martyrdom.

Officially, St. Lucy's body now rests in Venice, in the Church of Santi Geremia e Lucia.

THE FORMER CASINO SAGREDO

Hotel Ca'Sagredo
Campo Santa Sofia, 4198
• info@casagredo.com
• www.casagredohotel.com
• Tel. : 041 2413111

> **Two superb bedrooms from an 18th-century casino**

The Hotel Ca'Sagredo has two magnificent bedrooms that, curiously enough, the hotel does not do much to promote. Rooms 305 and 306 in effect incorporate the six rooms that made up the old gaming hall of Palazzo Sagredo (for more information on the old gaming *casini*, see p. 27).

Decorated by Carpoforo Mazzetti and Abbondio Stazio in 1781, these two rooms are little gems of fresco and stucco-work. Unfortunately, the old alcove (private room) of the *casino* is now in the Metropolitan Museum of Art (New York).

The small salon in room 306, however, maintains its air of delicate refinement, with the small animals in stucco glancing out of the corner of their eye at the occupants of the room. The small salon in room 305 offers a superb and unusual view of the hotel's "Giants' Staircase". Note also the door to the secret passageway, concealed between the frescoes on one wall. It leads to the still existing ballroom of the *casino*, and allowed the host's guests to retire discreetly to this more private space.

Even if you do not stay at the hotel, the place is worth a visit. It is an opportunity to see a very well-restored private palazzo that has maintained its spacious interiors decorated with frescoes by such artists as Tiepolo, Longhi and Ricci.

Located just opposite the Rialto market, the hotel also has a terrace restaurant. Unfortunately, the food is not as striking as the location.

When you enter, ask permission to use the monumental main staircase. Designed by Tirali in the 17th century, this by itself is worth a visit – especially for Longhi's spectacular frescoes of *The Fall of the Giants* (1734).

On the first-floor *piano nobile*, take the first door on your left to get a good view of the magnificent old ballroom and the Tiepolo painting that decorates the ceiling of one of the two rooms in the restaurant.

ARTISTIC OVERFLOW PIPES

Ca' d'Oro, Cannaregio 3933; visible from Calle Ca' d'Oro
Ca' Cappello, Castello 6391; visible from Ponte Cappello
Castello 5507, in Corte Licini

> *A refined touch of urban decor*

The refinements of Venetian art can sometimes appear in unexpected details of urban decor. For example, in certain patrician *palazzi* (see addresses above) the hollowed stone "tubes" (*fossa*) which serve as overflow pipes for rainwater are, in some cases, decorated as if they were veritable works of art.

In Ca' d'Oro, at the junction of two roof cornices, the half-pipe ends in a capital enveloped in foliage. Above it is another capital sculpted in the form of a seated atlas surrounded by plant-motif decoration; it was supposed to be supporting the cornice alongside the *palazzo*.

At Ca' Cappello, the *fossa* or overflow pipe has a Gothic capital of rather simpler form, but which is still an interesting functional part of the roofing.

Less important buildings rarely have details of this kind that are visible from the outside. However, sometimes the idea of such decoration was "borrowed' from more patrician *palazzi*. One example of this is a small building in Corte Licini behind the church of Madonna de la Fava (Castello 5507). Here, the main interest is both the pipe itself and the way its upper end is finished (though the forms used are simpler than those in the above-mentioned *palazzi*).

The water from such drainage pipes might feed into water wells, which stood not only in the public squares (*campi*), but also within private courtyards or even inside the housing itself.

THE RAT GRAFFITI
Fondamenta del Traghetto

Five rats for every Venetian!

On the shaft of a thick column that stands at the end of Calle del Traghetto, just opposite the church of San Felice on the Grand Canal, there is a graffiti drawing of a rat with a long tail. If the accompanying date (1644) is to be trusted, it has been there for more than three and a half centuries. Perhaps the artist simply wanted to remind people that the history of Venice is also the history of its rats. According to recent estimates, there are five rats for every single Venetian in the city.

Thanks to their amazing ability to adapt to the circumstances, the common rat (*Rattus rattus*), the *pategana* or sewer rat (*Rattus norvegicus*), and the coypu (*Myocastor coypus*) have all adjusted perfectly to the very special urban environment of Venice. They have also flourished because of the progressive disappearance of the once sizeable colonies of cats in the city, which have fallen victim to excessive programmes of systematic sterilisation. It is said that the rats that arrived in Europe from distant lands where the plague was endemic were the main cause of the arrival of the Black Death.

SIGHTS NEARBY

GERMAN PROTESTANT CHURCH – FORMER SCUOLA DELL'ANGELO CUSTODE
Open every other Sunday, at 5pm or 10:30am
A timetable of services and the month's events is pinned to the door.

Built in the 18th century by Andrea Tirali, the former Scuola dell'Angelo Custode (Guardian Angel) stands just opposite the church of Santi Apostoli. Since the suppression of the Fondaco dei Tedeschi in 1812, it has housed the German Evangelist Church. Twice a month the church opens its doors for a public service to which one and all are warmly welcome. This also gives you a chance to see (in the chapel on the first floor) a magnificent painting by Sebastian Ricci, *The Virgin in Glory with the Angel Raphael*. The service is a journey back in time and history, well off the usual tourist track. Even when unlocked, the door of the chapel may seem closed (just push to enter), which naturally discourages the idly curious.

THE GARDEN OF THE CASINO DEGLI SPIRITI ⓰

Piccola Casa della Providenza Cottolengo, Fondamenta Contarini 3539
• Ring at the Porter's Lodge to ask the nuns if you can visit the garden, or contact Ms Mariagrazia Dammicco at the Wigwam Club Giardini Storici, Venice: Tel/Fax 041 610791
• giardinistorici.ve@wigwam.it • www.giardini-venezia.it

> *Spirits of a chosen few or a gang of forgers?*

Built for the cardinal and man-of-letters Gasparo Contarini in the first half of the 16th century, Palazzo Contarini dal Zaffo contains one of the finest Renaissance gardens. Nowadays, the property is shared and run by two religious institutions: the Piccola Casa della Providenza Cottolengo and the Casa Cardinal Piazza. The garden of the Istituto Cottolengo extends over a fairly vast area and overlooks the north of the lagoon, near the water-basin of the Sacca della Misericórdia. It also contains a small building known as the *Casino degli Spiriti* (Summerhouse of the Spirits). And what a charming summerhouse it is! In its day, it was a place where men-of-letters, scholars and artists such as Titian, Sansovino and Aretino used to gather. The interior was even decorated by Guarana, Tiepolo and Fossati, but no trace of their work remains today. However, it is still an ideal space for creative reflection, to feel the inspiration of "the spirits of the chosen few" engaged in conversation and discussion. From the 16th to the 18th centuries, the *palazzo* and its wonderful garden were admired by numerous visitors, enchanted by the views over the lagoon and the *stanze di verzura* (literally "rooms of greenery") which used to exist here. In effect, the rich collection of statues, columns and fountains must have made this place both magnificent and theatrical – well suited to the numerous parties and other entertainments held here. In the 19th century, the layout of the garden was changed entirely to make room for a wood store. Once abandoned, the Casino degli Spiriti soon acquired a certain air of mystery thanks to its isolated position within the lagoon. The sound of the wind and the lapping water caused lugubrious legends to spread, with people imagining ghosts bemoaning their fate within the walls of the garden or wandering forever over the still waters of the lagoon. More prosaically, a group of forgers took advantage of the legends that kept people away from the place and chose this as the site for their clandestine "mint". After a remarkable project of restoration, the garden has to a large extent returned to its original layout, with its refinement being praised by such writers as D'Annunzio and Brodsky. Today, the silence and beauty of this legendary place once more evokes thoughts of the charming old summerhouse where the select few used to meet, inviting us to indulge in the pleasures of contemplation.

The chapel in the Istituto Cottolengo occupies what was once one of the main salons of the *palazzo*; there is still evidence of where the fireplace used to be. On the ceiling are frescoes (by Tiepolo's studio) celebrating the glories of the Contarini family.

THE GARDEN OF CARDINAL PIAZZA'S HOUSE ⓱

Fondamenta Contarini 3539/A
• Ring at the door to ask the nuns for permission to visit the garden.
Or contact Ms Mariagrazia Dammicco at Wigwam Club Giardini Storici,
Venice: Tel/Fax 041 610791
• giardinistorici.ve@wigwam.it • www.giardini-venezia.it

> **The garden with skeletons as waiters**

S trolling along the Fondamenta Contarini towards Sacca della Misericórdia, a rich garden can be glimpsed through wrought iron railings. It belongs to the *Casa Cardinale Piazza,* where the Servants of the Sacred Heart of Jesus run an Old People's Home and a Youth Hostel. The nuns are happy to allow you to visit the garden (just ring at the door).

Inside, you will find a vast space full of age-old shrubs and plants. One of the ancient north-facing walls enclosing the garden is lined with niches that once held fountains and statues, making it an ideal backdrop for theatrical performances. The place also includes part of the garden of Palazzo Contarini dal Zaffo, recently shared with the Piccola Casa della Providenza (see p. 209), and part of the garden of Palazzo Minelli-Spada alongside. The Minelli family were rich *luganegher* ("grocers" in Venetian) from Bergamo. Originally sellers of sausages and cheeses, they acquired an aristocratic title in the 17th century after paying 100,000 ducats.

In the past, this garden was famous for its various buildings and structures and for the beauty of the setting it formed. An avenue lined by laurel trees and a bower of scented rose bushes lead through the garden to the two water gates giving onto the lagoon to the north.

After a long period of neglect, the garden was refurbished in the late 19th century by its new owners, an English couple by the name of Johnston. After having been restored to the serene harmony and refined layout that it had lost over the years, it became the setting for various social events. In the 1950s, for example – at the height of the period associated with *La Dolce Vita* – the eccentric owner of the day, a certain Mr. Eggs, held a party here that became legendary, with glimmering lamps and servants dressed as skeletons mingling silently with the guests.

Legend has it that it was in this romantic garden that the painter known as Morto da Feltre (literally "Death from Feltre", due to his cadaverous appearance) fell hopelessly in love with Giorgione's favourite model, Cecilia.

THE *ZATTIERI* (BOAT HAULERS)

In the vast expanse of water known as Sacca della Misericórdia, there is an enclosed mooring-area for boats guarded with watchtowers. It was here that, once upon a time, the *zatteroni* were moored. Under the expert guidance of the *zattieri*, these rafts were used to bring timber down from the Cadore area by river.

THE WORKSHOP
OF THE VALESE IRON FOUNDRY

Fondamenta Contarini 3535
• Visits by appointment: Tel/Fax 041 720234 • info@valese.it
• Window display: Calle Fiubera 793 (San Marco) • Tel: 041 5227282

*The magic
of molten metal*

Halfway along Fondamenta Contarini (not far from the *palazzo* of that name), a small door leads into a long, narrow alleyway. Having passed along it within what seems to be a labyrinth of high walls, you come to the superb workshop of the Fonderie Valese, where time seems to have stood still.

Founded in 1913, the workshop still uses the best-quality Fontainebleau sand, which – contained within a wooden form – receives the fine imprint of the object to be reproduced. Divided into two halves, just like the shells of a crustacean, the mould is opened and the original model removed. At this point a network of channels is created through which the molten metal flows over the sand, then sets to form the final shape. However, it is not uncommon for this foundry to use old moulds, a good number of them dating from the 18th century.

The sight of molten metal is always spectacular. And it is then followed by the emergence of objects in gold, silver, copper or tin, all of which have the appearance of jewels. The workshop's output includes: bulky light fittings, decorative components based on age-old designs or mythological themes, reproductions of the city's famous monuments, bronze fixtures for gondolas, and everyday objects such as bells, door-handles and doorknobs (which can be made to the client's own designs). And, of course, there are metal moulds for the making of glass – plus the traditional *musi da proton*, door-knockers in which the base is a lion's head and the knocker a ring clenched in its jaws.

THE OLD LIONS OF THE FILM FESTIVAL

Up to the 1950s, the awards handed out at the Venice Film Festival were very different to those used nowadays. To the winners in the various categories went lions in gold and silver plate (made to a design by Professor Soppelsa in Venice), but there were also other awards in the form of sea horses, dolphins and mermaids (all made in silver). Much lighter, the awards today are made in tin covered with gold or silver leaf. The days are long past when their predecessors – made with such skill at the Fonderie Valese – were the delight of the Festival winners. Over time, the Festival organisers have tightened the purse-strings, deciding to use a company that imitates the form of the statues but does not reproduce their quality.

Note the curious feature at the centre of the grotto/icehouse. The acoustics are so good that the sound runs around the space in a captivating manner, creating a surprising stereophonic effect.

THE OLD ICEHOUSE IN THE GARDEN OF PALAZZO RIZZO-PATAROL

⑲

Fondamenta de la Madonna dell'Orto 3499

A grotto hidden amidst greenery

The luxuriant garden of the Palazzo Rizzo-Patarol, now the Hotel des Doges, contains an old icehouse hidden away amidst the age-old shrubbery and the dense curtains of ivy and periwinkles. Concealed beneath a hump in the ground, this *grotin del giasso* is tangible proof of the "romantic" redesign of the garden in the 18th century.

Consisting of a brick cupola, the structure formed a sort of cellar for the storage of blocks of ice. It was used to keep food supplies for the palazzo kitchens at a time when there were no such things as refrigerators.

The Rizzo-Patarol garden was so highly regarded that, in 1815, Austrian Emperor Francis I visited it during his stay in Venice. The garden was created in 1700 by Lorenzo Patarol, a learned numismatist and botanist who also wrote a herbarium that is now in the Museo Correr. His particular fondness was for orange trees, jasmine, roses, lilies and halophile plants (that is, those that prosper in saline conditions). The garden was subsequently enhanced by his nephew, Francesco, who introduced various plants from the Botanical Garden in Padua.

CORTE CAVALLO: THE COURTYARD WHERE THE EQUESTRIAN MONUMENT TO BARTOLOMEO COLLEONI WAS CAST

Standing alongside Palazzo Rizzo-Patarol, Corte Cavallo gets its name from the fact that it was the site of the foundry that cast the famous equestrian monument to Bartolomeo Colleoni that stands in Campo Santi Giovanni e Paolo. The statue was modelled in wax by the Florentine Andrea Verrocchio (the teacher of Leonardo da Vinci), but he died before being able to complete the work. The casting, therefore, was entrusted to Alessandro Leopardi. Also responsible for the pedestal, he would subsequently be known as Alessandro del Cavallo (Alessandro of the Horse). The courtyard where he lived was also given the same name. At number 23494, you can still see what is left of Palazzo Leopardi, now incorporated in a wing of the Hotel des Doges. Highly irascible, Verrocchio was notorious for his biting comments. When he heard that a certain Vellano di Padova had been commissioned to do the face of the famous *condottiere* for the monument, he was so furious he lopped the head off the model of his horse and returned to Florence. The Venetian Republic threatened to sentence him to death for such an outrage, to which he is said to have replied, "Shame! That would stop me giving the horse an even better head!" Respecting such *sang-froid*, the Republic thereupon doubled the sculptor's fee and called him back to finish the job.

THE PLANT NURSERY AT THE MISERICÓRDIA ⑳

Fondamenta dell'Abbazia 3546
• Tel: 041 5244097
• E-mail: vivaio @lagunafiorita.191.it
• Visits during nursery opening hours: Monday to Friday, from 9am to
12:30pm and from 2:30pm to 5pm

The land behind the former monastery of Santa Maria della Misericórdia is today occupied by the only plant nursery in the old city centre. The three greenhouses are located within an enclosure where the remains of the old Valverde bell-tower are still visible. They afford a good view of the back of the abbey and of the Scuola Vecchia della Misericórdia.

Greenhouses, flowers and plants – in the heart of Cannaregio

The business of growing and selling the plants is run by the *Cooperativa Sociale Laguna Fiorita* and the place supplies all you need for plant care (pots, potting soil, fertilizers and anti-parasite products). Specialising in the creation and maintenance of gardens (such as the one alongside the Scuola Vecchia della Misericórdia), the co-operative also works on terraces and *altane* (the wooden roof platforms that are typical of Venice houses).

WHERE TINTORETTO PAINTED HIS FAMOUS *PARADISO*

The artist lived nearby (see p. 221), and he used the vast upper room of the Scuola Vecchia della Misericórdia when painting his mammoth *Paradiso*. Measuring 7x22 metres, the work had been commissioned by the Republic for the Sala del Maggior Consiglio in the Doge's Palace.

SIGHTS NEARBY

A FAÇADE CORNICE BECOME QUAYSTONE ㉑
Campo della Misericórdia and Fondamenta della Misericórdia
Cannaregio 3599
Cornice visible from the Ponte della Misericórdia

When you look down on the *fondamenta* (quay) from Ponte della

Misericórdia, you will notice that to the south and east of the Scuola Grande della Misericórdia there is a striking incongruity. The edging of the quay is, in fact, a façade cornice. This "recycling" of part of an (unknown) building dates from the 1610s.

THE DOUBLE GARDEN OF THE SCUOLA VECCHIA DELLA MISERICÓRDIA

Fondamenta dell'Abbazia 3553
• Visits only when the place happens to be open, otherwise by appointment; contact Ms Mariagrazia Dammicco at the Wigwam Club Giardini Storici, Venice: Tel/Fax 041 610791
• giardinistorici.ve@wigwam.it • www.giardini-venezia.it

The secret garden of La Misericórdia

Located on the site that once belonged to the Dominican friars of La Misericórdia, the garden of the Scuola Vecchia della Misericórdia (Ancient Confraternity of Misericórdia) extends over 2,300 m². You can glimpse this charming area through the railings that give onto the quayside (*fondamenta*) along Rio della Sensa; to be able to visit it, you need an appointment (see above).

A reminder of the luxuriant vegetation of the island of Valverde, this area of greenery combines the type of garden traditional to Venetian *palazzi* with that normally seen within the cloisters of a religious establishment. However, the entire complex of La Misericórdia has undergone numerous changes and alterations during the course of its history.

In the 17th century, when the Confraternity moved to its new premises (designed by Sansovino), the terrain was still occupied by a vegetable garden and a cemetery. Following the Napoleonic suppression of religious foundations (1808), the Scuola Vecchia was for a time used as a private theatre, with the outside space becoming an Italian garden, with hedges and borders laid out in geometrical designs. After further modifications, the complex – by then in a sad state of repair – was bought by the artist Italico Brass in 1920, who used it as his home and studio, and as a gallery for his rich art collection.

During extensive restoration work, the building received certain additions – for example, the small circular tower with its octagonal belvedere and *liago* (a sort of small covered balcony giving onto the garden). The owner also redeveloped the garden, which re-acquired its old splendour. In the raised part of the cemetery and old vegetable garden, cypresses and other scented shrubs were planted, while the part opposite the cloister once more became a *hortus conclusus* (enclosed garden), with geometric borders and low, topiary-work hedges shaped with architectural precision.

Having again been left empty for some years, the complex of the Scuola Vecchia della Misericórdia was bought by the State in 1974, which set up a Restoration Workshop there. Today, it belongs to the Venice City Museum Authority, both the building and gardens having been restored with great care.

Recent studies suggest that the real name of the painter was, in fact, Jacopo Comin. He was nicknamed Tintoretto because his father, Giovan Battista, had been a dyer. But it would seem that the name "Robusti" came from the fact that that same father had taken part in the stalwart defence of Padua against Imperial forces in 1509. The name was then passed on to Jacopo, the eldest of twenty-two children.

THE HIGH-RELIEF OF HERCULES AND HIS CLUB

Fondamenta dei Mori 3399

23

> ❝ **The legend of the witch and Tintoretto's daughter**

On the façade of the house where Tintoretto passed the last twenty years of his life (he died in 1594) is a high-relief, probably of Roman origin, showing Hercules holding a club. It is curious that this mythological character was used to decorate the artist's house. One reason for the choice of this symbol of virile strength may have been the painter's family name (Robusti), but there is a legend that gives another explanation.

In those days, it was customary for children to receive communion for ten days after they had first taken the sacrament. One day when Marietta, Tintoretto's oldest daughter, was going to the church of Madonna dell'Orto, an old woman came up to her and convinced her to collect the consecrated hosts she received at communion, telling her that if she did so she would become like the Virgin Mary. The girl obeyed, and every morning after receiving the host she hid it in her blouse rather than actually swallowing it. When she got home, she stored the hosts in a small box that she kept at the bottom of the garden, near the animals' water trough. Within a few days, however, the animals began to behave strangely. They kept kneeling down by the water trough and no one could make them stand up.

Marietta was frightened by what was happening, so she told her father everything. Aware of how old witches were said to use hosts in their magical rites, and often used their wiles to make the pure and innocent serve their purposes, the artist took protective measures. That afternoon he slipped into the church and replaced the hosts on the altar as if nothing had happened. Then, having procured a hefty stick, he went home. When the tenth day arrived, he told his daughter to call the old woman from the window, inviting her to come up.

As soon as the old woman crossed the threshold, blows rained down upon her, and, after a moment's surprise, she quickly changed into a cat that darted here and there, trying to climb the walls and escape. Finally, seeing that there was no way out, the animal gave a terrible howl and threw itself against a wall, bursting through it wrapped in a cloud of smoke. It was the hole made in the wall that Tintoretto is said to have had filled in with this sculpted relief of Hercules holding his club … a sort of warning set up to protect the house and its inhabitants. As for the witch, no more was heard of her.

ALCHEMICAL SYMBOLS AT PALAZZO LEZZE

Palazzo Lezze
Fondamenta della Misericórdia 3598

> **The "Philosopher's House" of Venice?**

Built between 1611 and 1617, Palazzo Lezze is attributed to the architect Baldassare Longhena, whose taste for the esoteric can also be seen at La Salute (page 327). On the façade to the right side of the building are a number of curious and discrete high-reliefs that are alchemical in theme. Indeed, Fulcanelli would describe this as Venice's "Philosopher's House".

The most clearly visible high-relief is almost on the corner of the building. It shows a king crowned with flames and flanked by two figures borne on pelicans and surmounted by the Sun and Moon, respectively. The king is the alchemical symbol for Philosophical Gold, the Solar Conscience which is symbolised by philosophical Sulphur. The two side figures represent Mercury and Salt (associated with the Sun and Moon, respectively), not in the sense of ordinary substances but rather as quintessences; they also refer to the *Solve-Coagula* (dissolutions-evaporations) that were a part of alchemy. This latter is what is symbolised by the pelican seen at the base of the entire image.

The next high-relief to the right is behind a grille and rather difficult to see. It depicts a crouched figure of indeterminate sex holding a bush in each hand. To either side is an imaginary creature – rather like a lizard with a human head – which rests upon a double-headed gryphon. The human figure symbolises the alchemical *rebis*, an hermaphrodite figure that recalls the human perfection which results from the synthesis of Mercury and Sulphur. One a fixed, and the

other a volatile substance, they are represented here by the lizards alongside. The gryphon takes up the symbolism of this synthesis and suggests the "vase" which symbolises the profundity of alchemical learning.

Higher up is a high-relief of an angel with, in each hand, a bunch of ears of corn that are being pecked at by birds on each side (similar to phoenixes). Below, again to each side, are two pelicans resting on fish, each with a snake in its beak.

The angel symbolises sublimation, or the ascension of the principle of evaporation in alchemy. The birds pecking at the corn are an allusion to the Divine Grace of Charity, the main virtue in alchemy and the equivalent of God's love for humanity. The pelican itself is the symbol of the alchemical art and it is "pecking" at the serpents that represent the male and female energies which oppose each other during the course of the Great Work but ultimately blend together in androgyny (here evoked by the angel). This is why the crucified serpent – or the serpent "pecked by the beak" – represents the fixing of the volatile element. Finally, the fish represent the element of Water linked to the Salt of the Earth. This is the densest principle, and hence two fish are shown bearing up the entire allegory.

The fourth high-relief represents a crowned, two-headed eagle opposite a bare heraldic shield. This signifies the union and "volatilisation" (or evaporation) of the male and female principles, now immersed in eternity. The presence of a bare oval shield under the two heads recalls that the eagle dominates Earth and Heaven by virtue of its Temporal and Spiritual Powers. This is why the two-headed eagle was often chosen as the symbol of imperial rule.

Finally, just above the entrance to the palazzo, the crowned female head is the traditional human symbol of alchemy.

Palazzo Lezze takes its name from Giovanni De Lezze, an important military and political figure who died around 1624. The De Lezze family had engaged in trade and ship-building and came to Venice around 973 from Lecce (Puglia), hence their name. Giovanni De Lezze was close to Emperor Charles V, and was undoubtedly influenced by the numerous exponents of hermetism who frequented his court.

ALCHEMY

Most religious orders of the Middle Ages and the Renaissance considered *alchemy* (from the Coptic term *Allah-Chemia*, or divine chemistry) as the *Art of the Holy Spirit* or *Royal Art* of the divine creation of the world and man. It was connected to Orthodox Catholic doctrine.

The followers of this art divided it into two principal forms. *Spiritual alchemy* exclusively concerns the inspiration of the soul, transforming the impure elements of the body in the refined states of spiritual consciousness, which is also called the *Way of the Repentants*. *Laboratory alchemy*, called the *Way of the Philosophers*, reproduces the alchemical universe of the transmutation of nature's impure elements into noble metals, such as silver and gold, in the laboratory. These two alchemical practices are generally followed in combination, thus becoming the *Way of the Humble*, where the humility is that of man faced with the grandeur of the universe reproduced in the laboratory (in Latin *labor + oratorium*); the alchemy of the (interior) soul is expressed exteriorly in the laboratory. Those who practise *Laboratory alchemy* with the sole purpose of finding silver and gold, and thus neglect the essential aspects of the betterment of the soul, will fail and become *charlatans*, who might have a wide-ranging culture but certainly not the required moral qualities. To avoid becoming a *charlatan* (it was this heretic form that was condemned by the Church), followers must balance the heart and soul, culture and moral qualities, penitence and humility, to become a true philosopher.

ALCHEMY IN VENICE

Throughout the 16th and into the 17th century, the European centre of alchemy was Prague. In the 15th century, the city's archbishop had already been condemned by the Council of Konstanz for his interest in such practices. However, at that time, Venice also had its share of alchemists and charlatans, the latter posing a true threat to the city because of the trickery and fraud they employed in the pursuit of money, fame and power. It was not uncommon, for example, for such cheats to build false-bottomed boxes in which they would hide gold in order to then produce it after a miraculous "transformation" of base metals. Another trick was to bleach gold using mercury, and then restoring the glow of the metal by subsequent heating.

A flagrant example of such crooks was Italian priest Giuseppe Marini. His interest in alchemy was purely financial, not spiritual, and thus he entirely failed in his aims. His *Alchemical Treasury*, written in Venice in 1664, describes how he lost family and friends, power and illusions, all through a perverted use of alchemy. Because of such tricksters, Venice passed a law in 1530 condemning alchemists to death. It was this persecution – and the need to keep their discoveries secret – that led real alchemists to develop a language rich in symbols and metaphors that could only be understood by the initiated. Text, painting, drawing and sculpture could all take the form of alchemical "treatises", often under the name of *Philosophical Rose Gardens* or *Marian Rose Gardens*. (The Virgin Mary was the patron saint of their art because she had produced the living "Philosopher's Stone", Christ.)

Created in 1470, the secret society *Voarchadumia* attracted such members as the alchemists John Dee and George Ripley. Involved in the practice of alchemy and in communication with celestial beings via a magical language known as Enochian (after Enoch, the son of Noah), it was this society that was mainly responsible for the publication of alchemical works in 16th-century Venice. These included the *Chrisopoiae libri tres* (1515) by Giovanni Aurelio Augurello (1441-1524), an Italian alchemist and poet who dedicated this work to Pope Leo X (to whom he also handed over an empty purse, saying that a man who knew how to make gold had no need for a bag in which to keep it). Other alchemical works published in Venice were: *Continens Liber* (1529), a monumental medicinal treatise based on the concepts of the Persian Abu al-Razi (c. 865-925), whose works on alchemy and medicine were very influential in medieval Europe; *Pretiosa Margarita Novella de Thesauro, ac Pretiosissimo Philosophorum Lapide* (1564), by Petrus Bonus, who probably lived in the 14th century and was a philosopher and alchemist from Ferrara; and *I Libri Segreti* (1561 and 1580) by Leonardo Fioravventi, a doctor and alchemist from Bologna who had also published his 1564 medical treatise *De Capricci medicinali* in Venice.

Alchemy in Venice was principally linked with philosophical concerns and the exercise of charity, with chemical compounds and other concoctions being freely used in medicinal treatments. Evidence of this interest can still be seen in the esoteric symbols present on a number of ancient buildings and monuments within the city.

THE MIRACULOUS STATUE OF THE BLESSED VIRGIN OF THE GRACES ㉕

Church of San Marziale
Lauds 7:15am; Rosary 6pm; Mass 6:30pm
• Stations of the Cross on Friday at 3pm

> **A rare work of acheiropoesis**

Ignored by tourists and by numerous Venetians themselves, the church of San Marziale contains a miraculous image of the Virgin, located on the left side of the building. Legend has it that, in 1286, the work – carved by a shepherd called Rustico from the trunk of a single tree – was defaced one night by the Devil but was then completed by two angels, who sculpted the Virgin's face (for a definition of *acheiropoesis*, see p. 255). The vessel on which the statue was loaded at Rimini was then driven by angels towards Venice, coming to dock near the church of San Marziale. With the arrival of the statue another miracle took place: a blind man and his son (mute since birth) were immediately healed. In the sacristy are five paintings recounting this legend (by an unknown 16th-century Venetian artist).

The altar beneath the statue also has fine bas-reliefs recounting the same story. Simply hold back the cloth draped in front to get a good view. The nave ceiling has a painting by Sebastiano Ricci, *The Angels Sculpting the Face of the Virgin*, which again is related to the legend.

At Covignano (near Rimini), the miracle was commemorated in 1290 by a chapel located on the site where the statue was carved. It was replaced by a Franciscan church in 1396, which is still a place of pilgrimage.

SIGHTS NEARBY

A SATANIC LION ㉖
Calle Diedo 2386/A

Running alongside Palazzo Diedo, the narrow Calle Diedo contains a doorway surmounted by a curious carving: a small but menacing lion's head framed by what look like bat's wings. It is undoubtedly because of its very discreet location that the work has survived the passage of time so well. Now occupied by courthouse offices, the palazzo once belonged

to the illustrious Diedo family. Originally from Altino (*Altinum*, a Roman city that had stood on the shore of the lagoon), this family provided the Venetian Republic with architects, bishops, soldiers and men-of-letters.

THE ARZANÀ COLLECTION

Calle delle Pignatte 1936/D
Visits by appointment: 347 2625999 – 340 3097191 – 334 3318621
info@venetianboat.com

> **The world's only _gondolin da fresco_**

The old Venetian saying *Barca xe casa* (Your boat is your home) is perfectly true at the premises of Arzanà, the association which promotes the study and preservation of traditional types of Venetian boat. It is located in the old Squero Casal (*squero* = boatyard) in Rio dei Servi, which was already in use in the 15th century.

The eclectic and rather atmospheric jumble within the boatyard comprises a private collection of numerous maritime treasures: vintage sails, boat floats in cork and glass, boat-building tools and old fishing equipment, small stoves for *burci* and *trabacoli* (the vessels that brought wine from Sicily and timber from Istria), an original *felze* (the covered structure for passengers that used to be located in the centre of a gondola), boat lamps and 19th-century lights, *forcole* (the upright into which the gondola oar fits), hemp ropes and cotton nets, models of boats used in the lagoon, and lots of other materials either donated by private individuals or recovered from abandoned workshops.

The association also has a small fleet of about forty working vessels – all in wood and all vintage! – that includes the last *peata* to be found in Venice. But the real "jewel in the crown" is an authentic *gondolin da fresco*. It is the only one in the world and is in a fine state of preservation. Also known as a *gondola filante*, this vessel was narrower across the beam so that it could go faster. This particular *gondolin* was built in 1870-80, in this very *squero,* and would have been used for summer outings into the lagoon to enjoy the fresh breeze off the water.

The interest that the association members have in the history of Venetian boats has fortunately meant that a number of vessels have been saved from destruction. In the past, old boats were used for firewood, with only their iron fittings being recycled.

Various films shot in the lagoon (including *The Merchant of Venice* and *Casanova*) have used the old boats from the Arzanà collection, rowed by the association members themselves.

A BOAT TRIP AROUND THE *SQUERI*

In collaboration with authorised tour guides, Arzanà offers fine boat trips that take in the various *squeri* within the city. Starting from the Squero di San Trovaso, one ends at the Squero Casal, having completed a route that illustrates the various activities linked with this precious part of the lagoon heritage (for information: Paola Brolati. Tel: 348 2932772).

WHAT IS THE ORIGIN OF THE NAME FONDAMENTA DEGLI ORMESINI?

Following on from Fondamenta della Misericórdia, Fondamenta degli Ormesini took its name from the numerous shops here that once sold *ormesin*, a sort of light silk used in clothing. Originally, the fabric had come from the city of Hormuz (in present-day Iran), hence the name *ormesin*.

THE CHAPEL OF THE *VOLTO SANTO*

Centro Pastorale Universitaria Santa Fosca
Fondamenta Daniele Canal 2372

- Visit by appointment, and sometimes by direct request
- Tel: 041 7155775 (opening hours: 8am to 12pm, 5pm to 8pm)
- Mass on Tuesday at 9pm, in theory only for students
- cpu@santafosca.it

By prior appointment – or perhaps by direct request at reception – it is possible to visit the chapel of the Holy Visage (*Volto Santo*) near Santa Fosca. Built against the church of I Servi (see below) in 1360 to serve the community of people from Lucca (Tuscany), the chapel was consecrated in 1376. It was also known as the *Oratorio del Genturone*, because the Christ on the Crucifix was girt in a leather loincloth known as a *Genturone*.

Despite the damage it suffered in the 19th century, the chapel still has its fine ceiling, with images of the Fathers of the Church and symbols of the Four Evangelists. A crucifix that hangs from the ceiling recalls the one venerated at Lucca, where the Basilica of San Martino houses the miraculous acheiropoetic Cross (see p. 246).

> Other areas in Venice record the presence of a community from Lucca in the city. See the Corte del Volto Santo (p. 247) and Rialto (p. 19).

REMAINS OF THE CHURCH OF I SERVI

Centro Pastorale Universitaria Santa Fosca
Fondamenta Daniele Canal 2372

- Open admission or by appointment (same e-mail and telephone as for the Cappella del Volto Santo).

All that remains of the magnificent 14th-century complex of Santa Maria dei Servi are two majestic doorways that lie off the beaten track, and thus tend to be ignored by tourists. The superb dichromatic Porta del Pellegrino (Pilgrim's Doorway) on Rio dei Servi is reminiscent of the Tuscan style associated with the early Servites,* who came to Venice from Tuscany at the beginning of the 14th century. Nowadays, the site houses student accommodation and a youth hostel.

Begun in 1318 and completed in 1491, the church occupied a sizeable surface area. It was one of the three biggest in the city, along with I Frari and Santi Giovanni e Paolo. You get some idea of the size when looking at the relative position of the two existing doorways; the second is to the left as you enter (often open on weekdays). However, this massive structure was so badly damaged by fire in 1813 that it was demolished. The tombs of the doges Andrea Vendramin and Francesco Donà – now in Santi Giovanni e Paolo – originally stood here. It was for the refectory of this monastery that Paolo Veronese painted his *Cena in casa del Fariseo* in 1570-76. This important work was later given to the French king Louis XIV and is now at Versailles. The Servite monk Paolo Sarpi lived and died here.

---

* Established by a group of seven people in Tuscany in 1223, the Servite Order of the Blessed Virgin Mary is a mendicant Order of the Roman Catholic Church that combines a life of contemplation with apostolic work.

FOOTPRINTS ON THE PONTE SANTA FOSCA ㉚

> ***Traces of the street violence of yesteryear***

Walking over the Ponte Santa Fosca, it would be easy to miss the four footprints in Istrian stone set into the pavement at each corner of the top of the bridge. Less well-known than the San Barnaba bridge that leads out of Campo Santa Margherita, this bridge was also a *Ponte de la Guera* (War Bridge), a fact recorded by these footprints, which are known as *sampe*.

It was here that, from September to Christmas, *Nicolotti* and *Castellani* gangs fought each other in fights held according to special rules. For example, each side chose a "godfather" to act as referee, and, before the general free-for-all, there were individual and group combats. Just as in a game of rugby, the groups advanced in combat formation to occupy the area at the top of the bridge, fighting with fists and feet (with no prohibition on hitting "below the belt"). In those days, the bridges had no parapets, so combatants could often end up in the canal beneath, perhaps after receiving a sound thrashing. Those who managed to raise their "standard" at the top of the bridge – red for the *Castellani*, black for the *Nicolotti* – were declared the winners.

THE RIVALRY BETWEEN THE *CASTELLANI* AND *NICOLOTTI*

The *Castellani* lived in the eastern area of the city, in the *sestiere* known as Castello. They were predominantly workers at the Arsenale and identified themselves by their red berets and scarves.

The *Nicolotti* – who wore black berets and scarves – were predominately fishermen and lived in the western area of the city, the extreme point of which was formerly identified by the church of San Nicolò dei Mendicoli.

No one knows how the combats between these two groups started, though perhaps it was because of the murder of a Castello bishop by one of the *Nicolotti*. We do know, however, that sticks and clubs were used in the first fights, but that combatants later had to make do with their fists alone.

DIVIDI ET IMPERA

These street punch-ups not only guaranteed the Venetian State a ready supply of men used to hand-to-hand fighting, but also meant that no form of general coalition was formed amongst the populace as a whole. Indeed, the government's tolerance of this intra-class rivalry was inspired by the ancient Roman notion of *dividi et impera* (divide and rule). Furthermore, these fights allowed the more aggressive members of society to let off steam on specific occasions in specific locations, without posing a threat to general law and order.

Other locations for such factional fighting were the famous Ponte dei Pugni at San Barnaba (also with still-existing *sampe*), the Ponte dei Carmini near Santa Margherita, and the Ponte de la Guera at Zan Zulian (not far from San Lio).

1705: THE LAST FIGHT ON PONTE DEI PUGNI

There were cases when pushing rivals into the canal was not enough. In 1705, Ponte dei Pugni at San Barnaba was the site of a clash between the two rival factions that was so violent it led the Grand Council (*Maggior Consigilio*) to ban this popular tradition forever. Indeed, things had

got so out of hand that day that the combatants had first started slinging stones and then drew knives. The fighting was so intense that no one took any notice of the violent fire that had broken out at San Gerolamo. In the end, the parish priest of San Barnaba had to be brought in to separate the combatants, brandishing a crucifix as he courageously waded into the mêlée with little regard for his own safety.

THE ERCOLE D'ORO PHARMACY

• Tel. 041 720600
• Visits during the Santa Fosca pharmacy's opening hours: Monday to Friday from 9am to 12:20pm and from 3pm to 7:30pm. Saturday from 9am to 12:45pm

Santa Fosca's miracle-working tablets

Alongside the modern chemist's shop of Santa Fosca is the old *spezieria* "All'Ercole d'Oro", where a magnificent old room still contains its original furnishings and the ancient jars for drugs and medicines. The recent restoration has entirely stripped away the dark 19th-century patina that used to cover the woodwork, leaving it agleam with the warm shades of colour that are typical of walnut. The room has maintained all its Baroque charm. Note the doors, the counter and the large cabinets of carved solid wood, along the top of which the jars – all made in Bassano – are carefully aligned. The entire furnishings seem to have been carved so as to be in keeping with the richly decorated doors, which could have come from a church or a religious confraternity. The wooden sculptures have been attributed to the sons of Francesco Pianta, who was himself a pupil of Brustolon.

The *Spezieria All'Ercole d'Oro* was frequented by learned patricians, clergymen and scholars, who treated the pharmacy as a sort of coffee-shop, a place for erudite conversation and intellectual discussion. Specialising in the preparation of more unusual drugs, the pharmacy has its own *Sala dei Veleni* [Poisons Room] where rare herbs, medicinal potions and spices, often from far-distant countries, were stored. The pharmacy was renowned for a laxative preparation known as "Santa Fosca purgative pills", or the *pillule del piovan*. Tradition had it that the remedy was first concocted by a parish priest (*piovan*) who lived in the area. Much appreciated for their effectiveness, these pills were used far beyond the confines of the city itself and were still being manufactured in 1975.

SCORPION OIL: ONE HUNDRED SCORPIONS DROWNED IN TWO LITRES OF OLIVE OIL

The old druggists of Venice (*spezier da medicine*) had everything they needed at their disposal. The glass instruments and vessels used in concocting medications were actually produced in the lagoon and imports from the East brought a vast variety of herbs, medicines, spices and compounds. They could thus produce such curious specialities as *Olio di Scorpioni* (Scorpion Oil), which was used to treat wounds and was produced by drowning some 100 live scorpions in two litres of olive oil. However, they were most famous for their *Mitridato*,* a concoction of herbs and *castoreum* (an oily extract from the sexual glands of the beaver), and for *Teriaca* (see p. 44).

---

* King Mithridates VI (132-63 BC) was famous for his immunity to poisons.

CINERES
THOMÆ TEMANZ...
MDCCLXXXII.

WHY IS THIS CHURCH NAMED AFTER MARY MAGDALENE?
Besides the long-standing veneration of Mary Magdalene, the church owes its name to the end of hostilities between Venice and Genoa in 1355. Though the peace treaty between them was agreed on 1 July of that year, it was not announced and made official until 22 July, the feast day of St. Mary Magdalene.

MASONIC SYMBOLS IN THE CHURCH OF LA MADDALENA

32

Campo della Maddalena
• Open for exhibitions and during the Venice Biennale

> *The last religious building built by the Venetian Republic*

Designed by Tommaso Temanza, the church of La Maddalena was begun in 1763 and completed in 1790. This makes it the last religious building undertaken under an independent Venetian Republic. All subsequent buildings date from the time of Napoleonic, French or Italian rule.

Open only when hosting exhibitions (some of them during the Venice Biennale), the church is noteworthy for its round form (the only other round churches in Venice are La Salute and San Simeon Piccolo) and for the presence over the main doorway of an eye enclosed within a triangle (see following double page). On the pediment, there is the inscription *Sapientia aedificavit sibi domum*, which might be translated to read "Wisdom built this House Herself" – a motto that some take as being too secular for a church, as it denies the role of God.

Round churches have existed since Classical Antiquity (see the Pantheon and the church of Santo Stefano Rotondo in Rome). Similarly, the eye within the triangle is a Christian symbol. However, there is also the probable influence here of Freemasonry. It was the Age of Enlightenment, and the rationalism associated with the Masons was in vogue. Hence, Temanza was probably influenced by their ideas. We know, for example, that he frequented the circle of Andrea Memmo, a *procuratore di San Marco* who, together with his brothers Bernardo and Lorenzo, was among the first well-known Freemasons in Venice. They were initiated into the order by Casanova himself (see p. 142-143).

Further evidence for this supposition is to be found inside the church. Whilst two additional altars were subsequently created, perhaps to "erase" this Masonic influence, the church initially had only a single altar "for a single Supreme Being", as the Masonic creed urged. There was no altar to the Virgin, to Mary Magdalene or to any other saint, contrary to the custom in other Venetian churches. There had been such altars in the old church (probably dating from the 11th or 12th centuries) on the site of which La Maddalena was built.

And there is one final piece of evidence. Inside, in front of a secondary doorway, is the tomb of the architect Temanza, bearing his date of death (1789) and a compass, ruler and set-square. Whilst these tools are clearly associated with his profession as an architect, they are also well-known Masonic symbols.

THE EYE OF THE TRIANGLE

The eye of the triangle tradition, which can be seen in most Christian temples, has its origin in the first apostolic preachers of Christianity. It was inherited from pharaonic Egypt as preserved in Persian writings that Christians collected in Alexandria, in Egypt. The central, radiant Sun god (*Ra*) was replaced by the Eye of Divine Providence enveloped in a luminous aura of glory covering the Triangle (Luminous Delta).

Whereas for the ancient Egyptians the equilateral triangle represented the *Osirian Triad* of Osiris – Horus – Isis, for the Christians it became the Holy Trinity of the Father – Son – Holy Spirit. Viewed as one indivisible Being incarnated by the Eye or Sun of Egypt, it is often replaced by the name of God, *Jehovah*, and generally broken down into four Hebraic letters, *Iod-He-Vau-Heth*.

It is through its equal sides and angles that the equilateral Triangle symbolises the Most Holy Trinity, or rather, three Hypostases emanating from the unique Logos expressed by the Sun of Egypt or "All-Seeing Eye", a way of saying that the Absolute rules over the entire Universe.

The presence of the Trinity and the Triangle is practically universal, as it is found in most traditional religions – in the Hindu *Trimurti* (Trinity) manifested by Brahma – Vishnu – Shiva, but especially in ancient Egypt where this symbol appeared over several eras of its history. Beside the *Osirian Triad*, there was the *Memphite Triad* of Ptah – Nefertem – Sekhmet (Father – Son – Mother) and the *Theban Triad* of Amon – Khonsu – Mut, the primordial gods of this civilisation's pantheon. In Persia, there was Ahura Mazda – Vohu Mano – Asha Vahista, that is the Master Sage, Good Thought and Best Rectitude. It was this Trinity that served as the inspiration for the one conceived by the Christians.

In the 18th century, with the appearance of speculative Freemasonry, the Masons immediately adopted this symbol, calling it the Luminous Delta. Their symbol depicted a Sun, an Eye or simply a G in the centre, representing the Grand Architect of the Universe, the Divinity that created everything and everyone, the supreme Surveyor.

Sometimes Freemasons replace the Triangle by three dots (one at each point of the triangle) that signify the Past, Present and Future, while the full triangle represents Eternity or the Eternal God. The three angles thus represent the three phases of the perpetual evolution of existence: Birth – Life – Death, an evolution that God governs without being governed.

In short, the radiant Eye of the Triangle is the emblem of the Divinity that is Una (unique) in its essence and Trina (threefold) in its manifestation. For this reason it is considered to be the expression of the Perfect Spirit and of the True Initiate united in a Triune God.

THE WAGNER ROOMS AT CA' VENDRAMIN CALERGI

Ca' Vendramin Calergi 2040. Guided tours organised by the Associazione Richard Wagner di Venezia (ARWV)
• Access solely by booking by name; Tuesday and Saturday morning and Thursday afternoon.
• Contact the ARWV by 12pm on the day before the visit
• Tel 041 2760407 • 338 4164174 • ARWV@libero.it
• Bring valid ID. Admission is via the entrance to the Venice Casino

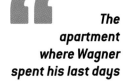

The apartment where Wagner spent his last days

The mezzanine floor of the Palazzo Vendramin Calergi houses the Museo Richard Wagner. It is the largest private collection of material relating to the composer after that of Bayreuth, the Bavarian city that hosts the *Bayreuther Festspiele* every year, a festival founded by Wagner himself in 1876 and still dedicated exclusively to his ten operas. The key part of the tour comprises three of the 25-28 rooms that were actually occupied by Wagner and his family. The others have been given over to the offices of the Venice Casino, which is housed within the palazzo. Wagner always felt an artistic and sentimental attachment to Venice, his favourite Italian city. He visited the city six times between 1858 and 1883. During his last visit, he rented the entire mezzanine of Palazzo Vendramin Calergi, including the "White Wing" with its great views onto the Grand Canal and a very efficient heating system (very important for a composer who was susceptible to the cold). Wagner spent his last winter (1882-1883) here, along with his wife and four children. He died in his private studio on 13 February 1883. The museum has various objects and documents relating to the great composer. In 2003, it also acquired the Joseph Lienhart Collection comprising precious musical scores, programmes, facsimile manuscripts, autograph letters, books, records, paintings and lithographs. The entire collection is available for consultation by scholars and researchers upon request.

WAGNER CONCERTS IN THE SALONE DELLE FESTE AT CA' VENDRAMIN CALERGI

The programme and invitations (available on a "first come, first served" basis) can be obtained from the Secretary, ARWV, Venice. Tel 041 2760407 – 3384164174 – ARWV@libero.it

The Venice Richard Wagner Association also has a number of activities intended to promote the study and knowledge of the great composer's literary and musical work. The rich calendar of events includes conferences, symposia, round tables, exhibitions and film screenings.

Held in collaboration with the Fondazione La Fenice and the Venice Casino, the "Concert of Homage to Richard Wagner: A Musical Encounter with the Young Musicians of Bayreuth" is an annual event. During the "Wagner Days" cycle of concerts, young musicians also play music by Wagner himself and those composers who influenced – or were influenced by – him.

THE INSCRIPTION *NON NOBIS DOMINE, NON NOBIS*

34

Façade of Palazzo Vendramin Calergi

> *"It is deliberate sin that is true death"*

On the left of the main façade of Palazzo Vendramin Calergi, giving onto the Grand Canal, the inscription *NON NOBIS DOMINE, NON NOBIS* has long intrigued scholars.

Drawn from the Old Testament (Psalms 114:1 in the Latin Bible, but 115:1 in the Jerusalem Bible), this phrase is in fact the opening part of the famous phrase associated with the Knights Templar: *NON NOBIS DOMINE, NON NOBIS, SED NOMINI TUO DA GLORIAM*, which translates as "Not for us, Lord, not for us but for the glory of Your name". It is interesting to note that the deep meaning of this psalm as a whole may be summarised as: Glory to the one God; Christian humility; protection of the weak, the old and the young; physical death is but a departure on a journey, while it is deliberate sin that is true death.

Completed in 1509 and designed by Mauro Codussi, the palazzo was originally built for Andrea Loredan, who is thought to have maintained the ideas and heritage of the Templars. The phrase would subsequently become the Loredan family motto.

The oak leaves around the inscription were, in the Latin tradition, associated with the wreath that crowned a *defensor urbi*, the defender of the city and the public well-being. They would later come to symbolise the humble veneration of the Loredan and other Venetian patricians of the day towards God and the glory of the Venetian Republic itself.

THE TEMPLARS IN VENICE

The Templars arrived in the lagoon in the mid-12th century, and legend had it that they had brought with them a treasure which they then buried on the island of San Giórgio in Alga. The historical facts of the matter are rather different, for that island was the site of a Benedictine – and later Cistercian – monastery (founded around the year 1000) where the Templars had first found refuge. It should not be forgotten that the very Rule of the Order of the Knights Templar was written by St. Bernard of Clairvaux, who – as a Cistercian – followed the Benedictine Rule. The treasure referred to in the legend, therefore, was not a material one but the spiritual wealth which the Templars and their monastic scriptural teachers enjoyed by virtue of their closeness to esoteric Christian mysteries. In 1397, the island saw the foundation of the Benedictine Order of the *Canonicos Regulares de San Giórgio in Alga*, which later produced the popes Eugenius IV and Gregory XII, as well as St. Lorenzo Giustiniani. Clearly, this Order drew upon the initiation into Christian mysteries of which the monks and Templars had knowledge. The relation between the Templars and Venice was a close one. Trade with the East was an important mainstay of Venetian wealth, and the city at the time was suffering from attacks on its mercantile fleets by Mediterranean pirates and from the shortage of forces to impose its overall supremacy on the area. This is where the Templars played such a part: their ships and their territorial possessions in the Holy Land were of great importance in guaranteeing a flow of trade between Venice and the East. Furthermore, the Order had a trading depot in Venice (see page 144), and the Templars served as personal guards to Pope Alexander III during his visit to the city in 1177.

At the beginning of the 14th century, however, the French king, Philippe IV, became the enemy of an Order whose wealth he hoped to seize for himself, ultimately forcing the pope to suppress the Templars. Upon fleeing from Rome, a number of the knights initially found refuge in Venice, which had long championed religious freedom in the face of opposition from Rome. However, taking advantage of the Templars' various defeats in the Holy Land and their loss of important territorial possessions there, Philippe IV formed an alliance with Venetian and Genoese merchants against the Order in 1307. Accused of heresy, sodomy and sorcery, the Templars were thus ultimately persecuted by an alliance that included Venice's merchant oligarchy.

A short time later, most of the Templars in Europe would take refuge in Portugal, where they were warmly welcomed – as long as they undertook to change the name of the Order. Thus, the Knights Templar became the Knights of the Order of Christ and another chapter in their history would begin (see our guide *Secret Lisbon*).

THE KNIGHTS TEMPLAR: LEGEND AND FACT

The Order of the Poor Knights of Christ and of the Temple of Solomon (*Pauperes Commilitiones Christi Temlpoque Salomonici*) — more commonly known as the Order of the Templars or the Order of the Temple — was the most famous religious-military Order of the Middle Ages. Founded upon return from the First Crusade (1096) with the declared purpose of protecting Christian pilgrims to the Holy Land, it would exist for more than two centuries.

Officially recognised by Pope Honorius II in January 1128, the Order of the Temple quickly became the most highly regarded charitable order in Christendom, growing rapidly in both numbers and power. Distinguished by a white robe (revealing that they followed the Cistercian Rule of Cluny) bearing a red cross *pattée*, they formed the elite fighting force of the Crusades. The non-combatant members of the Order ran a vast financial empire that extended throughout Christendom (even inventing the letter of credit, which was the first step towards our modern banking system). Ultimately, the Knights Templar had forts and churches throughout Europe and the Holy Land. This magnificent organisational structure had a double goal: the formation of what would today be called a United States of Europe, and the provision of free and obligatory education (in keeping with the principles of the Templars themselves). Thus, the Order became established at two levels: one was outwardly visible to the whole world, the other was a more inward, esoteric existence. The "secular" arm, as it were, comprised dynamic men of action and soldiers, whilst the esoteric arm was made up of the Order's true elite, the wise men and priests who formed the "rearguard" to a body of knights and warriors.

The two groups answered solely to the Grand Master of the Order and not to any king or pope. This is what led them to be suspected of heresy, even if all they were doing was observing a rule of obedience. Similarly, the secrecy surrounding the Templars' ceremonies caused people to imagine that they engaged in heretic worship, something that was never proved because "civilians never enter into the houses of the military". The Order undoubtedly adhered rigorously to Apostolic Catholicism, even if some of its members had an intellectual interest in other cultures and theologies, and Gnosticism in particular. Gnostic symbols are sometimes to be found in the churches and castles the Templars built.

The spiritual mentor of the Order, St. Bernard of Clairvaux, had initially selected nine members of its elite to go to Jerusalem, where King Baldwin III allowed them to establish their premises in the underground stables beneath the ruins of the Temple of Solomon. Certain traditions have it that they there discovered the Cup of Solomon, which had been hidden or lost since the time of Jesus Christ (the famous Holy Grail). The Templars are supposed to have brought this Grail to the West, which from that point onwards extended its dominion over the whole world, just as the Order itself grew to dazzling heights.

With the loss of the Holy Land, the support the Templars enjoyed from Europe's monarchs began to wane. The French king, Philippe IV, who had no way of paying off a substantial debt to the Order, began to put pressure on Pope Clement V to take measures against the Templars. Evidence was forged and rumours spread, both with regard to their sexual practices and religious orthodoxy. It was said, for example, that the Templars worshipped a bizarre demonic figure called *Baphomet*, of which little is known exactly, except that it was a figure of pure invention. Finally, in 1307, a large number of Templars in France were arrested and tortured until they made false confessions. They were then burnt at the stake or sentenced to service on the galleys. Philippe IV thereafter kept up the pressure on the pope, and Clement V finally dissolved the Order on 22 March 1322.

In Portugal, however, King Dom Dinis considered the Templars to be innocent, affording immediate protection to the sizeable number who had fled there from France. After the dissolution of the Order, the king immediately founded another that incorporated the former Templars: the Military Order of Our Lord Jesus Christ, also known as The Order of Christ.

The abrupt disappearance of most of the "infrastructure" created in Europe by the Order of the Temple gave rise to a number of more or less extravagant legends and suppositions.

THE MIRACLE OF THE *VOLTO SANTO*

Legend has it that the *Volto Santo* (Holy Visage) bears a physical resemblance to Christ himself. Joseph of Arimathea and Nicodemus were the two disciples who took Christ down from the Cross. Nicodemus later set about making a faithful reproduction of the scene, but soon realised he had little talent as a sculptor. Then, overnight, he found the crucifix miraculously completed by an unknown hand. Hidden in a safe place after Nicodemus' death, the crucifix was said to have been sent to Christian Europe some 600 years later by Bishop Gualfredus, acting upon orders from an angel. Carried by ship, the crucifix arrived at the town of Luni in Liguria, whose inhabitants wished to keep it for themselves. However, the final destination was decided when the two oxen drawing the cart headed in the direction of Lucca. The *Volto Santo* is now housed in a small chapel within the city's cathedral, San Martino, and is a particular object of veneration on 13 September, when a special procession – *La Luminara* – is held.

THE FACES IN CORTE DEL VOLTO SANTO

Corte del Volto Santo
• Vaporetto stop: San Marcuola

> **The remains of the old Scuola dei Lucchesi**

A keen-eyed stroller along Rio Terà di Maddalena (near the San Marcuola canal) will spot a high-relief of a head wearing a crown. When you go into the courtyard itself, you find the same face on the wellhead and on the wall to your right.

This is non other than a reproduction of the famous *Volto Santo* (Holy Visage) of Lucca (see our guide *Secret Tuscany*), and served to mark the area where merchants from that city resided.

Around thirty patrician families and more than 300 artisans fled Lucca in

1309 (1317 according to some sources), when Castrucccio Castracani became lord of the city. Having settled in Venice, they set about developing the silk trade that had already made Lucca's fortune. In 1360, they formed their own guild or corporation (the *Scuola del Volto Santo*, also known as the *Scuola dei Lucchesi*) and bought the present site on 6 September 1398. The *scuola* itself was destroyed in the immense fire that swept through the entire neighbourhood in 1789.

A painting by Francesco Guardi depicts the fire of 20 November 1789. It is now in the Accademia. The fire is said to have started accidentally in an oil warehouse near the Campiello del Tagliapietra, not far from here. It destroyed around 60 houses that were home to a total of 140 families, a good 50 of them paupers.

COMUNITÀ EBRAICA DI VENEZIA
JEWISH COMMUNITY OF VENICE
ק"ק ויניציאה יצ"ו

—— Confini dell'Eruv
Borders of the Eruv
גבולות העירוב

Aree non comprese nell'Eruv

THE CORTE SCONTA DETTA ARCANA DOES NOT EXIST

Numerous visitors to the Ghetto try to find the Corte Sconta detta Arcana, which Hugo Pratt mentions in his book on Venice. This courtyard does not exist in the Ghetto; the author based it on the Corte Botera near the church of San Giovanni e Paolo (see p. 250).

THE MAP OF THE *ERUV* OF VENICE

Spanish School
• Open during services (Friday at sunset; Saturday morning at 9am) or
during organised tours

> *An unusual adaptation of an ancestral Hebrew custom*

On the ground floor of the Spanish School, just before the staircase on the right leading up to the synagogue proper on the first floor, there is a curious map of Venice which shows the limits of the *eruv*.

The traditional interpretation of two passages in the Book of Exodus (16:29 and 36:6) means that, on the Sabbath and during the feast of Yom Kippur, Jews are forbidden to transport anything more than 2 metres from a public to a private space (or vice versa). Taken literally, the ban imposes a severe restriction, for it covers the transport of all things of all weights. For example, you are not allowed to carry spectacles in your pocket (though you can wear them), nor can you carry a book or any other heavier object.

In order to circumvent these difficulties, the Jewish community in Venice reached an agreement with the City Council. Via payment of a modest rent, various public areas alongside private properties were to be considered as belonging to the Jewish community as a whole. Known as *eruv*, these areas were thus exempt from the ban on transport because they too were private property.

SIGHTS NEARBY

THE HINGES OF THE OLD GHETTO GATES

Ponte Farnese and Ponte Vecchia

Nowadays, three bridges lead into the Ghetto, but in the past there were only two; the one over the Rio de la Misericórdia did not exist. At the threshold of the houses that mark the two access points to the historic Ghetto, you can still see the holes in the walls for the hinges to the gates that closed off the entire area at nightfall.

When you look at a map of the city, it is clear just how easy it was at the time to completely isolate this area from the rest of Venice.

CORTO MALTESE: AN IDEALISED SELF-PORTRAIT OF HUGO PRATT?

Corto Maltese made his first appearance in 1967, in *The Ballad of the Salt Sea*, and last appeared in *Mû* in 1988, just a few years before his author's death in 1995. It took less than twenty years for this cosmopolitan sailor to become a legendary figure, always ready to defend freedom as he travelled in pursuit of adventure. Ironic, anarchic and libertarian, Corto Maltese is in many ways an idealised self-portrait of Pratt himself. He is the incarnation of the romantic heroes whose travels, regardless of their ostensible purpose, are episodes in a quest for one's own identity.

SOME PLACES IN VENICE MENTIONED IN *CORTO MALTESE*

For those who wish to follow the famous sailor in his movements around Venice, the following is a list of some of the imaginary poetic place names that figure in the *Favola di Venezia*.

Ponte della Nostalgia: Ponte Widmann, near Campo dei Miracoli, Cannaregio.

Sotoportego dei Cattivi Pensieri ("sotoportego of Bad Thoughts"): Sotoportego dell'Anzolo, which leads into Calle Magno alongside the Arsenale, Castello.

Campiello de l'Arabo d'Oro ("campiello of the Golden Arab"): Corte Riotta at San Martino, near Campo do Pozzi, Castello.

Corte del Maltese o de Bocca Dorada ("Courtyard of the Maltese or of the Golden Mouth"): Corte Buello, near Corte Nova, behind the grating at number 2862 Castello.

Calle dei Marrani: Salizada Santa Giustina, near Campo San Francesco della Vigna, Castello.

Corte Sconta detta Arcana ("The Secret Courtyard of the Arcana"): Corte Botera, near the church of San Giovanni e Paolo, and not in the Ghetto, as at the beginning of the tale *Corte Sconta* (1979).

The hotel that figures in the Corto strip cartoon is the ***Trattoria da Scarso*** on the small square at Malamocco, where Hugo Pratt liked to meet up with his friends.

Pratt chose the house of the painter Titian as the home for Corto Maltese. It is in **Corte del Tiziano** (Cannaregio), alongside Campo de la Carità (not far from Calle del Fumo).

The success of the books was such that they actually had an effect upon the place names of the real city. An actual *Corte Sconta* was created within a restaurant in Calle del Pestrin in the Bragora district near the Arsenal; and within the Hotel Sofitel (Santa Croce 245, near the Papadopoli Gardens), a **Campiello Corto Maltese** was created. The hotel was a favourite of the writer's, who was a friend of the owner.

THE REAL-LIFE INSPIRATION FOR THE FEMALE CHARACTERS IN *CORTO MALTESE*

Women play a considerable role in the Corto Maltese stories. They are almost always beautiful, bewitching women, but there are also episodes in which the female characters actually existed at the time of Corto's adventures (the early 20th century). One need only mention as examples the young and unscrupulous Art Deco painter **Tamara de Lempicka** (a veritable symbol of the wild years of the 20s-30s) and **Louise Brookszowyc**, whose character evokes memories of the refined actress Louise Brooks. Then, of course, there is *Valentina* (who appears in an act of homage to her original creator, Guido Crepax). However, the most striking and powerful female personalities are the following:

Esmeralda, Corto's gypsy friend. Nini Rosa, a great friend of Pratt's and an expert tango dancer, inspired the character of the entrancing and dusky Argentine gypsy who figures in many of Corto's adventures.

Golden Mouth, the magician-helper. Golden Mouth is a Creole fortune-teller from Bahia. An expert in Caribbean voodoo, she is a sort of South American *pasionaria* who brings together esoteric ritual and the business affairs of the Atlantic Marine Transport Finance Society. Corto's faithful confidante, she often provides him with good advice while puffing on her *cigarillo* between one hand of Tarot cards and the next. It seems she was inspired by an early love of Pratt's.

Venexiana Stevenson, the legendary enemy. The model for Venexiana Stevenson was Mariolina, the wife of Guido Fuga (who, together with Lele Vianello, was the artist's assistant and travelling companion). However, Venexiana's character and apperance are very different. She is an adventurer with whom Corto clashes more than once as they pursue the same treasure or the same dreams.

WHY CORTO *MALTESE*?

Corto may be a British subject – born in Valletta (Malta) on 10 July 1887 to a mother who was a Seville gypsy and a father who was a Cornish sailor in the Royal Navy – but his clearly Mediterranean looks and name pay tribute to the island's independence. They are a sort of response to the constraints which American strip cartoons imposed on the genre at the time when Pratt produced his first works.

For the real Pratt *aficionado*, who may be keen to see where the first *Corto Maltese* stories were drawn, the most interesting address of all is the apartment occupied by Pratt and his family in the 1960s. It is on the upper floor of the building at 21 Via Doge Galla at Malamocco (on the Lido) and can be reached by the bus which goes from the Piazzale Santa Maria Elisabetta to Alberoni.

THE ORSONI LIBRARY OF ENAMELS

Calle dei Vedei 1045
- For information and to organise a visit: call 041 2440002-3
- info@orsoni.com

> **The only
> glass kiln
> in the city centre**

The Orsoni glassmakers have the only glass kiln still active within the city centre. The family firm was founded in 1888 to revive the Byzantine art of mosaics and exploit the techniques for making pure glass enamels that had been developed on Murano in the Renaissance period. Set in the midst of a rich garden, the company now produces mosaic *tesserae* in glass of polychrome enamels and gold leaf. The workshops are open to the public.

The various phases of work carried out here still follow an age-old pattern. First, the raw materials are blended together in a mortar to form an opaque white paste, to which are added the different metal oxides that produce the different colours. Then the mix is rolled to obtain "slabs" of glass paste which are fired in the kiln. After gradual cooling to room temperature, these slabs are then cut up into *tesserae* using what look like marble scissors (an invention of the company's founder, Angelo Orsoni).

The whole factory hinges around the "Library of Enamels". The fruit of long and painstaking research, this library is an archive of more than 3,000 different shades that can be used to form an infinite variety of colour combinations. Everyday, in fact, the factory ships off hundredweights of *tesserae* in glass enamel and gold leaf to destinations all over the world. As a result, the company name has been associated with various mosaic masterpieces: in St. Paul's (London), the Sagrada Familia (Barcelona) and the Trocadero and Sacred Heart Basilica (Paris).

MOSAIC WORKSHOP

The company also organises one- or two-week full-time courses for amateurs who wish to learn the art of mosaics, or for artists, architects and designers who wish to develop knowledge of certain specific mosaic techniques (for information: www.orsoni.com).

The Calle and Sotoportego dei Vedei owe their name to the nearby abattoir where calves (*vedei*) were once slaughtered to supply the city with veal.

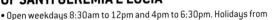

THE CHRIST OF THE CHURCH OF SANTI GEREMIA E LUCIA

39

• Open weekdays 8:30am to 12pm and 4pm to 6:30pm. Holidays from 9:30am to 12:15pm and from 5:30pm to 6:30pm
• Mass at 6pm on weekdays and 10am on holy days

A miracle-working acheiropoieton of Christ

To the right of the chapel of Santa Lucia, the church of Santi Geremia e Lucia houses an *acheiropoietic* sculpture of Christ. The Greek term means "not made by the hand of man" (see opposite) and, in this case, the Capuchin father who had begun the work found himself unable to complete the face of the statue in the way that he wished. Before his death, he entrusted the unfinished work to Father Colombano, who shortly after the death of his friend realised the statue was perfectly finished. After passing Lent 1602 in the church of San Geremia, Father Colombano presented the sculpture to the parish, urging that it should be the object of particular devotion, given the numerous examples of miraculous grace it had already granted.

During the Jubilee year of 1700, the Christ was taken to Rome, where again it worked numerous miracles.

WHEN ARTICULATED LIMBS MADE IT EASY TO TRANSPORT MIRACLE-WORKING RELIQUARIES...

During Jubilee years (once ordained every 100 years, now every 25), there was a tradition for all miracle-working images throughout Italy to be taken to Rome. Certain miracle-working images of Christ were thus designed to be more easily transportable, their articulated arms making it easier for them to be fitted in place on the Cross.

ACHEIROPOIETIC WORKS OF ART

In the Christian tradition, the term *acheiropoieton* refers to works of art "not made by the hand of man". Thus it relates to images created either by transposition from direct contact (as with the Shroud of Turin and the Veil of Veronica) or by divine intervention.

This term was apparently coined by St. Paul himself in a particular context: during a stay at Ephesus, he rose up against pagan idolatry and especially against the numerous many-breasted statues of Artemis, mother of the gods. He declared that the "gods made by the hand of man are not gods". With the use of this term *acheiropoieton* he showed respect for the Judaic prohibition of images, attacked pagan idols by setting the actual body of Christ against them, and limited eventual abuse by also claiming that this body of Christ was exclusively in the form it took after the Transfiguration (see p. 21), in other words after an event that followed the Resurrection.

Besides the celebrated Shroud of Turin and the Veil of Veronica (see *Secret Rome* in this series of guides), tradition holds that a few other rare *acheiropoietic* images still exist today. One example is to be found at Mount Athos in Greece: this theocratic monarchy, isolated on a peninsula in northeastern Greece since the 11th century and out of bounds to women, children and female animals, is home to two *acheiropoietic* icons. One is in the monastery of the Great Lavra and the other in the monastery of Iviron.

In France, there is also an *acheiropoieton* in the church of Notre-Dame-des-Miracles at Saint-Maur near Paris (see our guide *Banlieue de Paris Insolite et Secrète*, not yet available in English).

Similarly, the Holy Visage of Edessa, now in the Bartholomite Church of Genoa, is said to have been painted by Christ himself.

The painting of Christ in the Sancta Santorum of the Lateran in Rome is said to have been drawn by St. Luke and then completed by angels, and the famous sculpture of the Holy Visage in Lucca (Tuscany) is said to have been started by Nicodemus (who, together with Joseph of Arimathea, was present at Christ's crucifixion), but then completed by angels (see our guide *Secret Tuscany*).

THE SHOP IN THE CHAPEL OF SANTA REPARATA ⓵

Church of Santi Geremia e Lucia

• Open from the end of May to the end of December, from 10am to 2pm and from 4pm to 7pm

Since 2005, the chapel of Santa Reparata in the church of Santi Geremia e Lucia has – from May to Christmas time – housed an extraordinary temporary shop of Murano glass. The grandiose decor of the chapel remains unaltered and serves as a most unusual setting for these true works of Murano glass (not the Chinese and Taiwanese fakes to be found in a number of such shops in the city). The entrance is discreetly located, which protects the shop against floods of tourists and exaggeratedly high prices. An open door to the right of the main entrance to the church leads to an external corridor (the old main façade of the church itself, but now a place for tombstones moved here from elsewhere). At the end of the corridor, on the left, is a second door leading into the shop. In winter (from January to May), the chapel, which is easier to heat than the main church, is sometimes used for 10 o'clock morning mass.

THE ALTAR IN THE CRYPT OF THE CHURCH OF SANTI GEREMIA E LUCIA ⓶

Church of Santi Geremia e Lucia

• Open weekdays 8:30am to 12pm and 4pm to 6:30pm. Holidays from 9:30am to 12:15pm and from 5:30pm to 6:30pm
• Mass at 6pm on weekdays and 10am on holy days

First built in the 13th century, the church of San Geremia was in a parlous state by the middle of the 18th century. In 1753, thanks to the numerous donations received because of the presence of the miracle-working image of Christ (see previous double page), it was decided to demolish the old church and build a new one. The superb altar that housed the *acheiropoeton* was moved to the crypt, where it still stands. A polite request may gain you access to see it. Recently restored, the altar is decorated with depictions of a number of the instruments of Christ's Passion: Judas's hand and the purse of silver; the soldiers' lantern; the cock whose crowing reminded St. Peter of his denial of Christ; the jug of water that Pilate used to wash his hands; the nails, hammer and tongs; and the dice the soldiers threw when dividing Christ's garments.

A PLAQUE MARKING THE FORMER SITE OF THE CHURCH OF SANTA LUCIA ⓷

Just in front of the steps leading up to the Venice railway station, a discreet plaque trodden underfoot every year by millions of people recalls that the construction of this station required the destruction of the church of Santa Lucia. The veneration of the saint and her relics was moved to a new chapel added to the nearby church of San Geremia, which thenceforward became the church of Santi Geremia e Lucia (see p. 254).

CASTELLO

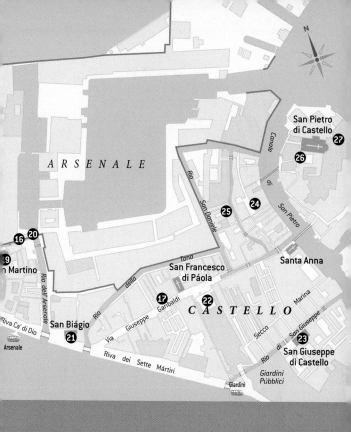

GIUSEPPE LUCARINI

L'INTERO SUO PATRIMONIO
AL PATRIO SPEDALE CIVICO
LEGAVA

LA PREPOSITURA
DEI PII ISTITUTI RIUNITI
POSE
MDCCCLXVIII

M IN VENEZIA NEL DI XVI GENNAJO MDCCCLXVII

SALA SAN MARCO
BIBLIOTECA

THE LIBRARY OF SAN MARCO

❶

Campo San Giovanni e Paolo
• Free entry for individual visitors, Monday to Friday 8:30am to 2pm (except holidays, the week of 15 August and from 24 December to 1 January)
• Note: Given the chilling nature of some of the surgical instruments, children under 14 are not admitted unless accompanied by their parents or by teachers, who assume full responsibility

A forgotten gem

Housed in the old Chapter Room of the Scuola Grande di San Marco, the rich Biblioteca San Marco is one of the best-kept secrets in Venice. It is reached by passing through the old entrance hall of the Scuola – the reception area of the present-day Hospital of San Giovanni e Paolo – and then turning right up the stairs to the first floor. There, one finds a magnificent carved and gilded ceiling that is a fitting expression of the power of the old Scuola (Confraternity) that occupied these premises. At the centre is the Lion of St. Mark with its open book, surrounded by symbols of the other great confraternities in the city: the eagle (*San Giovanni Evangelista*), the cross with concentric circles (*Carità*) and the seals "SR" and "SMV" (*San Rocco* and *Santa Maria di Valverde*; the latter was also known as *La Misericórdia*). Since 1985, this room has housed a medical-scientific library and a permanent exhibition entitled *The Memory of Health Care – Venice and its hospital from the sixteenth to the twentieth century*. The exhibits comprise important ancient texts (treatises, anatomical atlases, engravings and drawings), the designs for the refurbishment of the hospital complex and a vast range of surgical instruments, including a kit of everything needed for trepanning (complete with bone saws). The Scuola di San Marco itself was both devotional and practical, providing assistance for the poor and sick. Destroyed by a fire in 1485, its premises were immediately rebuilt with help from the city's Senate. The Chapter Room is decorated with paintings involving St. Mark, of which those by Palma il Giovane (*Christ in Glory with Saints Mark, Peter and Paul*) and Domenico Tintoretto, son of Jacopo (*The Transport of the Body of St. Mark, The Arrival in the Lagoon of the Ship Bearing his Body, St. Mark Blessing the Islands of Venice*) can still be seen. Before being stripped of

its treasures by Napoleon's army, the Scuola was also home to four works by Jacopo Tintoretto himself, three of which are now in the city's Accademia (*The Miracle of the Slave, St. Mark Saving a Saracen from Shipwreck, The Body of St. Mark Rescued from the Pyre after his Martyrdom*). The fourth work is in the Brera in Milan (*The Discovery of the Body of St. Mark*). In 1806, the Scuola was converted into a barracks, then into a military hospital. In 1819, it became the city's hospital, with beds for just over 120 patients. The complex was substantially restored and expanded in 1948.

A GRAFFITI IMAGE OF A HUMAN HEART

Façade of the Venice Ospedale Civile

Memento of a brutal matricide

On the receding expanse of wall between the main entrance of the Venice City Hospital (the former Scuola Grande di San Marco) and the right-hand side of the façade, about 30 centimetres from ground level, a curious work of graffiti can still be seen: a man holding a human heart in his hand. This is the only existing trace of a very strange story.

A woman resident of the neighbourhood had a child by a Jew who was a Turkish citizen. The son then lived with his father on the Giudecca, often visiting his adoring mother. Half Venetian, half Levantine, the young man dressed in the Turkish fashion and found it difficult to establish a personal identity, being something of an outcast in both communities. The result was a certain violence of temper, which led him frequently to beat his mother, who however always forgave him out of maternal love.

One evening, in a particularly violent fit of temper, the young man lost total control of himself, stabbing his mother and then tearing her heart from her chest. Seized by horror at what he had done, he then ran off through the streets, still gripping the bleeding heart in his fist. When he got to the bridge just in front of what is now the hospital, he tripped on the first step and dropped the heart, which, legend has it, then uttered the words, "Have you hurt yourself, my son?" The murderer then ran off towards the lagoon behind the hospital and drowned himself.

The whole dramatic scene was witnessed by Cesco, an old stonecutter, who slept in the portal of the Scuola di San Marco every night. It made such an awful impression upon him that he immediately scratched an image of the young man holding his mother's heart into the stone. Seen in profile and wearing a turban, the figure grasps the heart in his left hand.

Directly opposite are other graffiti carvings, also apparently by Cesco. They show boats loading and unloading merchandise in the Campo. The stonecutter, who had lost his young wife to disease in 1501, was in fact one of those who had worked on the creation of the Scuola's magnificent façade. Inconsolable after his wife's death, he ended up a beggar, sleeping rough at his previous place of employment, where every now and again he carved depictions of the things he saw.

THE FRESCO OF MARCANTONIO BRAGADIN, ❸
SKINNED ALIVE

Church of Santi Giovanni e Paolo
• Open daily from 7:30am to 6:30pm (Sundays from 12pm to 7:30pm)

*Skinned
alive!*

Located to your right, just inside the entrance to the church, the altar dedicated to Marcantonio Bragadin has an urn bearing his portrait bust. Above is a fresco depicting the horrible way in which this Venetian hero met his death. The urn actually contains the man's skin, but it is not visible to the public. It was last opened by specialists in 1961, and for obvious reasons is not likely to be opened again any time soon.

Appointed governor of Cyprus in 1569, Marcantonio Bragadin set sail for Famagusta, the seat of civilian government on the island. However, the modern fortifications that he had built did not prevent the fleet of Turkish sultan Selim II from landing troops there on 3 July 1570. Having taken Nicosia, the Turks beheaded the commander of that garrison – Niccolò Dandolo – and sent the head to Bragadin as a warning, before invading the city of Famagusta itself in September 1570. Despite overwhelming odds (6,000 Venetians to 200,000 Turks), the city held out heroically for almost a year. Finally, in July 1571, the Turks breached the walls and captured Bragadin, punishing him for his resistance by skinning him alive. His limbs were then divided between the various parts of the Turkish army, whilst his skin was stuffed with straw and sewn back together. This macabre trophy – together with the heads of Alvise Martinego and Gianantonio Querini – was then mounted on the ship of Turkish commander Lala Mustapha Pasha and taken to Istanbul.

Bragadin's skin would eventually be stolen from the Istanbul military magazine in 1580 by a Venetian slave, Gerolamo Polidori, and brought back to Venice. Initially, it was kept in the church of San Gregorio, but is now at Santi Giovanni e Paolo.

SIGHTS NEARBY

THE MISSING ARM OF THE STATUE OF POMPEO GIUSTINIANI ❹
To the other side of the nave, as you make your way to the choir, you will find the statue of Pompeo Giustiniani. Before entering the service of Venice and becoming governor of *Candia* (the old name for Crete), Giustiniani fought with the Spanish forces at the siege of Ostend, during which his right arm was taken off by a cannonball. After his death in 1616 – when fighting for the German forces – a statue was raised to his memory. It shows Giustiniani on horseback, from the left side, thus his missing arm is not visible.

PLACES ASSOCIATED WITH CASANOVA

A man of wit and culture, Giacomo Casanova (Venice 1725 – Dux, Bohemia, 1798) has gone down in history for adventurous amours that crossed all social divides. However, he was also a spy for the Inquisition, a Freemason, a devotee of occult sciences and a great traveller. Various periods of his life were spent in Venice, before his final banishment to Dux in 1783. The following are some of the places associated with this colourful character.

Priest for the space of a single sermon in the church of San Samuele – Campo San Samuele (San Marco)

Now used for art exhibitions, the small church of San Samuele (near Santo Stefano) was where Casanova preached his first sermon. He had quickly embraced an ecclesiastical career at the behest of his mother Zanetta, an actress who thought this was one way of guaranteeing the two of them some financial security. The sermon preached by the fifteen-year-old cleric was a great success, especially with the female part of the congregation, who showered the youth with money and *billets doux*. His second sermon – delivered after a heavy drinking bout – was such a fiasco that Casanova immediately abandoned all thought of a clerical career.

Violinist at Palazzo Soranzo, to make ends meet – Campo San Polo 2169-2171 (San Polo)

In Casanova's day, the façade of Palazzo Soranzo, which can now be seen from Campo San Polo, was still decorated with frescoes by Giorgione. It was here, in 1746, that the young seducer would – for three nights in a row – play as a violinist at the magnificent celebrations held for the wedding of Canziana Soranzo and Girolamo Corsaro. At the end of the party, Casanova noticed that the Consul Matteo Bragadin had dropped a letter as he was getting into his gondola. He immediately picked it up and returned it, for which Bragadin was so grateful that he offered to take the young man on his next official journey. During the trip, the consul fell dangerously ill and later credited his survival to the fact that Casanova had promptly had him bled. Thus came about Casanova's solid friendship with the man who would be his most generous protector and patron.

An adopted son and Kabbalist at Palazzo Bragadin Barabba – Ramo Bragadin 6050 (Castello)

For ten years, Giacomo lived in this palazzo as Consul Bragadin's adopted son, receiving the monthly allowance of 10 sequins (a far from negligible sum at the time). It appears that the twenty-year-old Casanova was in the habit of amusing the consul by organising séances (according to a ritual that was largely invented by his cronies). These events also involved his patrician friends Marco Dandolo and Marco Barabo, who were both passionately interested in the occult.

Seducer at the *Hostaria del Salvadego* – Bocca di Piazza 1238 (San Marco)

Located in a building behind St. Mark's Square that is now occupied by a hotel, the Hostaria del Salvadego was a famous and respected inn for almost five centuries; it finally closed in 1870. Casanova used to come here for dinner with his latest conquest, ready to continue the evening later in the rooms on the floors above. It would seem that the building – in the Venetian-Byzantine style – had originally been used as a sort of prison, which would explain the presence of bars at the windows and the rather grim façade (better suited to a gaol than to a hotel).

Gambler at the *Ridotto* – Palazzo Dandolo – Calle Vallaresso 1332 (San Marco)

Like many other Venetians of the time, Casanova adored gambling. His favourite gambling-den was the *ridotto* (see p. 53), where – hidden behind a mask – he often tried his luck at cards or in love.

Santa Maria degli Angeli, the convent of "M.M.", Casanova's nun-mistress – Fondamenta Venier (Murano)

Just to the left of the "Murano Venier" vaporetto stop is a Gothic archway leading through to the former convent of Santa Maria degli Angeli, which has long been abandoned. It is here that, again hidden behind a mask, Casanova came to spend the night with the beautiful M.M., a nun with whom he was having an affair. Many of the nuns in this Augustinian convent came from some of the best families in Venice and had been obliged to take religious vows at a very young age. This was one of the ways such families protected themselves against a division of their wealth.

Palazzo Morosini del Pestrin: M.M.'s family home – Ramo Pestruin 6140 (Castello)

Now private property, M.M.'s family home has an internal courtyard decorated with two neo-classical statues (visible through the railings). The term *pestrin* comes from the fact that the palazzo – not far from Santa Maria Formosa – stood alongside a dairy (*pestrin* in Venetian); such places were generally also flanked by a barn for the cattle. There have been numerous theories as to the identity of the mysterious "M.M.". It is highly likely that the initials are those of the beautiful aristocrat Marina Morosini, who was born in this palazzo in 1731 and who entered a convent at the age of 8.

A surprising meeting at the horse – Campo San Giovanni e Paolo (Castello)

In his *Memoirs of My Life*, Casanova describes an assignation with M.M. at the foot of the equestrian monument to Bartolomeo Colleoni in Campo SS Giovanni e Paolo. As night fell, Casanova saw a gondola approach down Rio dei Mendicanti, coming from the direction of Murano. When the boat docked, a figure got out, but Casanova was frozen to the spot when he saw it was a masked man. He was about to leave when he recognised "disguised as a man, my angel", who had prudently chosen this way of protecting her identity.

OTHER TRACES OF THE RISORGIMENTO IN VENICE

- **The cannonball lodged in the façade of the church of San Salvador** (at the end of the Mercerie). It was fired during the Austrian siege of Venice (1849), which put an end to the short-lived Republic declared in 1848.
- **The column in Campo San Salvador commemorating the glorious Venetian resistance of 1848-1849**. Raised in 1898, it bears a bronze band with the date 22 March MDCCCXLVIII, the day when – temporarily – the city threw off the yoke of more than fifty years of foreign rule.
- **The Austrian shell in the façade of the church of San Nicolò ai Tolentini**, near Piazzale Roma. Again, fired during the 1849 siege.
- **Hotel San Fantin** (San Marco, 1930, near the Fenice Opera House). Built in 1869, it is decorated with shells and cannonballs that the Austrians fired against Venice during the siege.
- **The sculpted portraits of Risorgimento figures** in Calle Larga dell'Ascension (near the entrance to St. Mark's Square, between the Museo Correr and the Post Office).

THE HIDDEN INITIALS
OF KING VICTOR EMANUEL II

Ponte de Borgoloco

⑤

L eading into Campo Santa Maria Formosa by the side of Palazzo Ruzzini, the Borgoloco bridge has elegant volutes of cast iron which bear a concealed political message. At first sight, the graffiti beneath the parapet look like hearts, but closer inspection

> *A bridge with a hidden political message*

reveals that they are three letters, "V V E" – the initials of the expression *Viva Vittorio Emanuele* (King of Italy).

Given that during Austrian rule the open discussion of various subjects – and especially political matters – was banned, the Italian patriots of the Risorgimento often addressed the populace using these encoded messages.

ANOTHER EXAMPLE OF A CONCEALED SLOGAN: *VIVA VERDI* IN THE FILM *SENSO*

Apparently addressed to the opera composer, the slogan *Viva Verdi* was in fact a Risorgimento acrostic of *Viva V[ittorio]E[manuele]R[e] D'I[talia]* (Victor Emanuel, King of Italy).

In Luchino Visconti's *Senso* (1954), a sequence shot in the Fenice Opera House plays upon the link between what is happening on stage and the feelings in the theatre beyond it. When the choir sings *All'armi all'armi! Eccone presti/ a pugnar teco, teco a morir* ("To arms! To arms! Here we are ready/to fight alongside you, to die with you"), it becomes a cry of defiance aimed at the rows of Austrian officers in the stalls watching Verdi's *Il Trovatore*. At this point, cries of *Viva Verdi!* and *Viva L'Italia!* erupt whilst Risorgimento patriots scatter leaflets from the gallery, singing a hymn exalting a unified Italy. The film is, in fact, set in 1866, the last year of Austrian rule in Italy.

WHAT DOES *BORGOLOCO* MEAN?

The term is thought to derive from the Venetian expression *tegnir uno a loco e foco* (literally "to offer someone a fire and a bed"). This area around Santa Maria Formosa was full of hotels and places offering rooms to let.

THE HOLE AND THE ANGEL
AT PALAZZO SORANZO

6

Façade of Palazzo Sopranzo
San Marco

> **Did the Devil pass through this hole in 1552?**

Walking along the south wall of St. Mark's Basilica, continue along Calle Canonica then take the first street on your left. Follow it for 50 metres and you will come to the so-called Ponte dell'Angelo, from where you get the best view of the angel sculpted on the façade of Palazzo Soranzo. In his hand, the figure holds a globe decorated with a cross. Above it, there is not only a very badly damaged fresco of the Virgin and Child between two Angels, but also a hole. It is associated with a very strange story that dates back to 1552.

At the time, this building was home to a lawyer in the ducal Chancellery. Though he had acquired his wealth dishonestly, the man affected a devout public persona and one day he invited the Capuchin monk Matteo da Bascio to dinner. Having been told that all the household duties in the palazzo were performed by a trained monkey, the cleric asked to see the animal. But when it was produced, he immediately recognised it as the Devil in disguise and set to asking it questions. The Devil told him that he was there to carry off the lawyer's soul to hell – a fate he deserved for a vast number of reasons but which he had so far avoided because every evening he said a prayer to the Virgin before going to bed. The very moment he would forget that prayer, the Devil said, his soul would be carried off to eternal damnation.

Father Matteo ordered the satanic animal out of the house, but the monkey would only agree to leave if he was allowed to do some damage. The priest accepted, on condition that it was he himself who chose what damage should be done. Hence, the only act of destruction he allowed the Devil was this large hole he made when leaving the palazzo – a mark that would serve evermore to show he had been there.

Father Matteo then sat down to eat with the lawyer, reproaching him for the errors of his past life. To illustrate his point, he took a napkin and twisted it, causing blood to flow from the fabric. That, he told the lawyer, was the blood of all the poor people he had exploited. Seized by remorse, the lawyer wept bitterly and thanked the monk for the grace he had obtained. However, he said he was worried that the Devil might return through the hole he had made in the palazzo wall. Don Matteo reassured him, suggesting that he raise a statue of an angel near the hole – that would be more than sufficient to drive off any evil spirit trying to enter the building.

THE LIBRARY OF THE SCIENTIFIC ASSOCIATION OF PALAZZO CAPPELLO

Calle Cappello 6391
Open to the public
• Tel: 041 5221307

More than 10,000 books on stucco-work and its restoration

The very attractive Palazzo Cappello actually appears in the background of Giovanni Bellini's painting *The Miracle of the True Cross near the Bridge of San Lorenzo*. Today, it houses a number of organisations whose premises, contrary to what you might expect, are all open to the public: the Scientific Association of Palazzo Cappello, the International Centre for Interior Decoration and Restoration, and a Library and Study Cabinet concerned with the planning of architectural restoration.

Specialising in the restoration of Baroque and neoclassical stucco-work, the library occupies some fine rooms with decorated ceiling beams (16th-century fresco work) and magnificent Venetian-style floor-paving encrusted with fragments of malachite. The valuable collection – more than 10,000 books occupying most of the wall space – can be consulted by teachers, university researchers and students preparing their degrees and doctorates. It is also available for use by all those who are interested in the history of stucco-work and its restoration.

The place is also home to a curious private collection put together by the director of the association, professor and architect Francesco Amendolagine. It comprises a series of old calculating and measuring instruments dating from the end of the 17th century right up to the beginning of the 20th. One fine exhibit is an 18th-century English ruler.

In the 1930s, the palazzo was a centre of Venetian social life, being home to the *salon* of Signora Ivancich, the aristocratic widow of Elti di Rodeano, a descendant of a Trieste family of ship-owners who had moved to Venice. In the 1970s, the *piano nobile* on the first floor was used by the Benedetti High School.

Nowadays, the association holds conferences and exhibitions here concerned with themes relating to Baroque and neoclassical decoration and its restoration. Working under its director, the coordinated team of professionals at the Centre for Architectural Planning has also been active in such ambitious projects as the restoration/replacement of the decor and accessories at the Fenice Opera House and the redevelopment of the Molino Stucky.

CHAPEL OF THE VISION OF ST. MARK ❽

Courtyard of the Patronato della Chiesa di San Francesco della Vigna
• Opened upon request during church opening hours

> **A key place in the history of the foundation of Venice**

Completely forgotten nowadays, the chapel of the Vision of St. Mark at the far end of the monastery of San Francesco della Vigna is however one of the key places in the legend surrounding the foundation of Venice. It is said to stand on the spot where St. Mark came ashore after being caught in a storm during his return from (or, according to other sources, departure for) a mission to preach the Gospel in Aquileia. An angel is said to have appeared to him, saying, "Peace be with you, Mark. Here your body will find its rest" – words that would become part of the official seal of Venice (*Pax tibi Marce Evanglista meum*).

Upon hearing the words, the apostle thought his last moments had come, but then the angel continued, "Fear not, Evangelist of God, you have long to endure yet. After your death, a city will be raised here to which your body will be borne and you will be its protector."

Having returned to Rome, Mark told this to Peter, his master, and also asked him to appoint Ermagoras, who had witnessed the vision, as Bishop of Aquileia.

Initially built in wood in 774, the chapel of "San Marco in Gemini" was rebuilt several times, the last time probably in the 18th century, as can be seen from the style of the present chapel.

Now used as a storeroom, the chapel is of no particular aesthetic or artistic interest.

WAS THE SEIZURE OF ST. MARK'S BODY ORGANISED TO THWART AQUILEIA?

Certain historians argue that the whole story of the vision of St. Mark was invented by the Venetians to assert their political and religious hegemony over a region that also included the cities of Aquileia and Grado. The latter, for example, enjoyed a certain status because, in 628, the emperor Heraclitus had given it the so-called "Throne of St. Mark", which was later taken by Venice.

The Mantua Synod of 827 had resulted in a serious reversal for Venice and its attempts to impose its authority over Grado. The patriarch of Aquileia, Maxentius, had managed to link his diocese with Grado, stressing the fact that St. Mark had preached the gospel in Aquileia itself. Venice's reaction was swift and effective. Just one year later (828) it managed to seize the body of St. Mark from Alexandria. Some argue that the entire story of St. Mark's vision was invented at the same time in order to claim (without any solid proof) that the apostle had stopped on the island of Venice itself and not on any of the other islands in the lagoon. Furthermore, the key version was that he had stopped on his way to – not back from – Grado and Aquileia, which thus justified the primacy of Venice over its rivals.

Another interesting consequence of the possession of the saint's body was that it allowed Venice to throw off the tutelage of the Western and Eastern Roman empires, symbolically affirming the independence of the Church of Venice.

THE GARDENS AND VINEYARDS OF SAN FRANCESCO DELLA VIGNA

Church of San Francesco della Vigna
• Open daily 8am to 12:30pm and 3pm to 7pm
• Visits sometimes possible (especially in September) upon request

A taste of Heaven

An on-the-spot request can sometimes get you admission to the extraordinary vineyards of the monastery of San Francesco della Vigna.

A visit in September is particularly charming. The monk who acts as your guide along the pathways through the garden will probably allow you to taste the grapes plucked directly form the vine. Various types of grapes are grown here, including the famous *fragola*, which has the unmistakable taste of strawberries (*fragole*) and is used to make the famous Fragolino dessert wine.

These vines are most likely the descendants of those that originally gave the monastery its name. The initial vineyards were donated to the Franciscan Friars Minor in 1253 by Marco Ziani, son of Doge Pietro Ziani.

THE KABBALAH-INSPIRED MEASUREMENTS ⑩ OF THE CHURCH OF SAN FRANCESCO DELLA VIGNA

Church of San Francesco della Vigna

A Pythagorean musical Kabbalah

First built in the 13th century by Marino di Pisa, the church of San Francesco della Vigna was in such a precarious state by the 16th century that the doge, Andrea Gritti, who owned a nearby palazzo, ordered it to be rebuilt. It was the doge himself who laid the foundation stone on 15 August 1534, according to the initial plans drawn up by Sansovino. The plans were later substantially modified by the Franciscan monk Francesco Zorzi, who was in charge of the work.

Applying the principles of Kabbalistic music (see p. 282), Zorzi (see p. 280) tried to make the building's proportions reflect Pythagorean musical consonances. The aim was for the church to "entirely reflect the harmony of the universe" as described by hermetic writers (see p. 174). To this end, Zorzi made extensive use of the number 3, which he saw as a divine number and the symbol of the Holy Trinity of the Father, Son and Holy Spirit. Hence, the church's length was to be three times its width: 27 (3^3) feet as opposed to 9 (3^2) feet. Similarly, the side chapels were to be 3 feet wide, whilst the chapel behind the altar was to measure 6 feet wide and 9 feet long (see the floor plan alongside).

The number 3 also refers to the three vibrations of the notes that are the basis of Pythagorean musical tradition: C, G and E, each in harmony with the musical requirements of rhythm, melody and harmony. In the musical Kabbalah, these notes represent the Holy Spirit (C – Body; the length of the nave), the Son (G – Soul; the width of the side chapels) and the Father (E – Spirit; the height of the chapel behind the choir).

In addition to proportions based on the number three, another element that was very important for Zorzi was the relation between the various dimensions of the church, which were to correspond to musical intervals (see the text on Kabbalistic music, p. 282). For example, relations in the ratio 4:3 correspond to musical fourths, in the ratio 3:6 to an octave and 6:9 to a musical fifth.

The unit of measure used in building the church was the Venetian foot, of which there is still a standard measure at the entrance to the military shipyard of the Arsenale. You can see it by asking at the reception desk there.

THREE: A DIVINE NUMBER

The number 3 is said to have been Moses' inspiration in his construction of the Ark of the Covenant. Similarly, as St. Paul points out in his Letter to the Corinthians, it is also implicit in the proportions of the human body. Furthermore, it was said to have inspired the proportions of Solomon's Temple in Jerusalem.

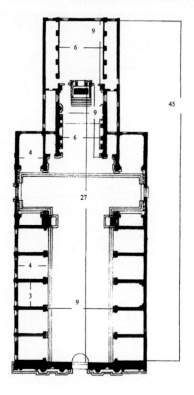

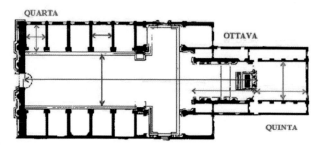

FRANCESCO ZORZI (1453 - 1540): A STUDENT OF THE KABBALAH

Born in Venice in 1453 to a noble family, Dardi Francesco Giorgio became a member of the city's Grand Council (a sort of parliament) at the age of 18, thanks to his father. However, following his religious vocation, he later became a Franciscan monk under the name of Francesco; his mother disinherited him for having given up the family name of Dardi. Having been ordained at San Francesco della Vigna – where he would live almost all his life – he rapidly became an expert on Platonism and the Kabbalah. In order to be able to measure his ideas against those of Jewish scholars, he travelled to Palestine between 1490 and 1500, visiting all the holy sites and learning Hebrew. Having returned to Venice, he became the spiritual director of two nuns at the Venice convent of the Holy Sepulchre, Chiara Bugni and Orsola Ausnaga, in 1504. These two women quickly achieved a saintly reputation and Zorzi (the Venetian equivalent of the Italian name "Giorgio") became an eye-witness to a number of their miracles, including those in which they made a piece of metal sprout flowers and in which they received an ampoule of Christ's blood from the Saviour himself. In 1510, the monk was appointed to oversee work on the sanctuary of the Madonna of Miracles at Motta di Livenza, where the Virgin had appeared to Ludovico Cigana on 8 August that year. Pope Clement VII even consulted him with regard to the issue of the divorce requested by Henry VIII of England. Already a respected figure consulted on a number of matters, Zorzi published his *De Harmonia Mundi* in 1526. Dedicated to Clement VII, this *magnum opus* is very close to the theories propounded by Pico della Mirandola and Marsilio Ficino in particular. In this work, Zorzo develops his own ideas for the construction of San Francesco della Vigna in line with the principles of both the Jewish Kabbalah (see p. 173) and Kabbalistic music (see following double page).

Condemning the decadence of contemporary morals, he himself experienced the division that occurred in the early 16th century between the Observantist Franciscan Friars Minor, to whom he himself belonged, and the so-called Conventuals. The former group was anxious to return to the original austerity and poverty preached by St. Francis, while the latter favoured the development of the Order in keeping with the times. Later, within the Observantists themselves, Zorzi saw the emergence of the reform movement that led to the foundation of the Capuchin Franciscans. Nevertheless, as the Provincial of the Franciscans, he was always firmly opposed to any form of schism. At the end of his life, Zorzi retired to the monastery of St. Jerome in Asolo, a town of the Venetian mainland, where he died on 1 April 1540. Zorzi's interpretations of the Holy Scripture, in line with the principles of the Kabbalah, naturally earned him a number of opponents, and his works were placed on the *Index* in various European countries.

THE OBSERVANTIST FRANCISCANS OF SAN FRANCESCO DELLA VIGNA AGAINST THE CONVENTUAL FRANCISCANS OF THE FRARI

The rebuilding of the church of San Francesco della Vigna took place at a time when a veritable schism within the Franciscan Order was occurring between the so-called Friars Minor or Observantists (who advocated a return to the austerity and poverty of St. Francis of Assisi) and the so-called Conventuals (who claimed the Order should develop). The Observantist Franciscans of San Francesco della Vigna were thus the rivals of the Conventuals of the Frari at San Polo. The prestige of their respective churches became an important element in this dispute.

F R A N C I S C I

GEORGII VENETI,
MINORITANÆ FAMILIÆ,
de harmonia Mundi totius Cantica) tria. Cum
indice eorum, quæ inter legendum ad-
notatu digna visa fuere, nunc
recens addito.

➤ *Talia probarint, spiritus quibus spirat.*

Cum priuilegio.

PARISIIS
Apud Andream Berthelin, via ad diuum Iacobum, in domo
Gulielmi Rolandi sub insigni aureæ coronę: & in vico Lon-
gobardorum in domo eiusdem G. Rolandi.

1 5 4 5.

PRINCIPLES OF KABBALISTIC MUSIC

Kabbalistic music is inspired by the Pythagoreans' claim, which is disputed by Aristotle, that in their revolution around the Earth the planets emit a sound that is inaudible to the human ear but can be heard by God (the concept of "the music of the spheres"). Similarly, the very distance between the planets was of musical significance. Pliny the Elder, for example, argued that the distance between the Earth and the Moon corresponded to a musical key. The same also applied to the planets' speeds, Cicero claiming in his *Dream of Scipio* that the Moon, which turns very slowly, emits the lowest of all tones.

Given that the created Universe above the sublunary level was, by definition, considered to be perfect, if it were possible to understand and reproduce its sounds, then it would become possible to recreate universal harmony here on Earth. The initial step towards this goal was taken by Pythagoras, who was the first to offer a conceptual analysis of musical intervals, with Plato subsequently seeing a link between these intervals and the "music of the spheres". The result was a view of music as a means towards propagating celestial harmony. Later, musical intervals would also be reflected in architecture, with structural proportions being inspired by the proportions that generated harmonies in music. Hence it was possible for buildings themselves to recreate the harmony of the heavens.

The legend goes that it was after noting the differences resulting from variations in the length of an ironsmith's hammer that Pythagoras (Samos, c.571 BC – Metapontum, c.497 BC) was led by the gods to his discovery of the mathematical relations behind sounds. Taking a piece of rope of the same length, he depressed the cord some three-quarters of the way from one end and then plucked it, noting that the tone was one-fourth above the tone emitted when the entire cord was plucked. Holding the rope at a point two-thirds of the way along the length, he heard a note that was one-fifth above, whilst nipping the chord in the middle he obtained a tone one octave above the one obtained when plucking the whole string. It was this experiment that resulted in these musical intervals becoming known as "Pythagorean consonances". For example, if the original cord is taken to be 12 units in length, reducing it to 9 units results in a fourth, to 8 units results in a fifth and to 6 units results in an octave. Applying these ratios to the lengths of strings in an instrument called a "canon" or "monochord", the Pythagoreans were thus able to determine the tonality of an entire musical system mathematically. As a result, music became a natural extension of mathematics, and when Plato took up what Pythagoras said about music, it also became a philosophical theme.

The ancient Pythagoreans, from whom Ptolemy drew his notions regarding astronomy, considered that each of the seven planets of the known solar system corresponded to both a note and a colour: the Sun corresponded with the note D and the colour orange, the Moon with the note B and violet, Mars with the note C and red, Saturn with the note F and green, Venus with the note A and blue, Mercury with the note E and yellow, and Jupiter with the note G and purple. The fusion of these notes and colours was visualised on Earth as a sort of symphonic rainbow, which Pythagoras himself referred to as "the music of the spheres".

Pythagoras' musical and mathematical discoveries would have a crucial effect upon the development of music and, during the Middle Ages and Renaissance, upon the transposition of numerical principles to architecture. It is St. Augustine and Boethius (c. 4th century AD) who are to be credited with preserving the Pythagorean symbolism of music which figures in the great religious architecture of Europe during the Middle Ages and beyond – a tradition exemplified, for example, in the Venetian church

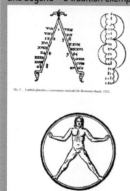

Dis. 2 - Lambda platonico e consonanze musicali (De Harmonia Mundi, 1525).

of San Francesco della Vigna (see p. 278).

Experts also recognise that the musical Kabbalah is also to be found in the works of various great composers – primarily Bach, but also Beethoven, Mozart and Wagner.

However, the Copernican Revolution of the 16th century, which established that it was the Earth which revolved around the Sun rather than vice versa, would undermine the very foundations of Kabbalistic music.

In the same way, a study of the proportions of the human body, itself a divine creation, meant that these proportions could be applied to architecture and make it possible to create buildings that were perfectly "in tune" with the harmony of the universe. This is the inspiration, for example, behind Leonardo da Vinci's famous illustration of the Vitruvian Man, which can now be seen in the Venice Accademia. In more modern times, Le Corbusier's work on the "modulor", a sort of update of the proportions of the Vitruvian Man, was inspired by exactly the same concept.

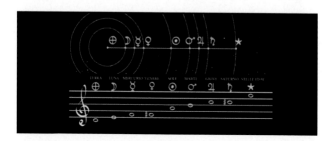

THE PROPHECIES OF ST. MALACHY: REVELATIONS IN VENICE REGARDING THE END OF THE ROMAN CHURCH?

Born in Armagh (Ireland) in 1094, St. Malachy was a Benedictine who was still an adolescent when he became abbot of his monastery. His visions began in 1139 at the time of his first visit to Rome, during which he met Pope Innocent II (pontiff from 14 February 1130 to 24 September 1143). After this visit, Malachy O'Morgair would write down his prophecies, made up of 111 Latin phrases associated with 111 pontiffs, from Celestine II (1143-1144) to the last pope, *Petrus Romanus* (Peter the Roman), the penultimate at this point being the present pope, Benedict XVI.

According to St. Malachy, under *Petrus Romanus* – whom some suggest will be Portuguese – the Roman Catholic Church will complete its cycle of existence. "*Petrus Romanus* will arise during the last persecution suffered by the Roman Catholic Church and will have to guide his flock during a period of travail. Once this travail has been passed, the city of the seven hills will be destroyed and the Incorruptible Judge will judge his people." This apocalyptic text is written in Latin, however, and thus its actual interpretation continues to be a matter of dispute.

St. Malachy died at Clairvaux on the exact date he had predicted – 2 November 1148 – comforted by his great friend St. Bernard of Clairvaux.

He was canonised by Pope Clement III on 6 July 1199 and the Prophecies of St. Malachy were placed in the Vatican Archives. They were left forgotten there until a figure known as "the Monk of Padua" published some of them in Venice in 1527, under the title "Prophecies of the Monk of Padua". An incomplete selection, they covered the names of only twenty or so popes.

In 1595 Arnold de Wyon completed the list, publishing the *Prophecies of St. Malachy* in Venice as part of his own book *Lignum Vitae*. Though this work added De Wyon's own annotations, it did include all the prophecies.

The choice of Venice as the place for the publication of the *Prophecies of the Monk of Padua* and the entire collection of Malachy's prophecies was probably due to the fact that this city had produced – and would continue to produce – various popes. Gregory VII, Eugenius IV, Paul II, Alexander VIII and Clement VIII were all born in the city (see opposite).

THE VENETIAN POPES IN THE PROPHECIES OF ST. MALACHY

Gregory XII (Angelo Correr). Pope from 30 November 1406 to 4 July 1415 Malachy's reference: *Nauta de ponte nigro*. The term *nauta* (the root of the word "nautical") recalls the man's origin in Venice, whilst *ponte nigro* refers to the fact that Gregory XII had been bishop of the island of Negroponte (or Euboea), a Greek island in the Aegean (close to the Black Sea), which, in the 15th century, was under Venetian rule. **Eugenius IV** (Gabriele Condulmer). Pope from 3 March 1431 to 23 February 1447. Malachy's reference: *Lupa coelestina*. The *lupa* (female wolf) figures in the arms of the city of Siena, where Eugenius had been bishop. The *coelestina* refers to the Order of the Celestines, which had been absorbed by the Augustinian Order within which Eugenius had taught. **Paul II** (Pietro Barbo). Pope from 30 August 1464 to 26 July 1471. Malachy's reference: *De cervo et leone*. The lion (*leone*) is clearly a reference to that of St. Mark in Venice, where Paul was born. However, he had also been the bishop of Cervia (which takes its name from the word for "stag": *cervo*), a small city on the Adriatic coast near Ravenna. **Alexander VIII** (Pietro Vito Ottoboni). Pope from 6 October 1689 to 1 February 1691. Malachy's reference: *Poenitentia gloriosa*. The "glorious penitence" is an allusion to the life of penitence lived by St. Bruno, Alexander VIII being elected to the papacy on his feast day. **Clement XIII** (Carlo della Torre Rezzonico). Pope from 6 July 1758 to 2 February 1769. Malachy's reference: *Rosa Umbraie*. The "Rose of Umbria" is a direct reference to Clement XIII, who had been governor of Rieti in Umbria, the region that contains Assisi, the birthplace of the "Rose of Christianity": St. Francis. **Pius X** (Giuseppe Melchiorre Sarto). Pope from 9 August 1903 to 20 August 1914. Malachy's reference: *Ignis ardens*. Born in Riese (in the Veneto), he became Patriarch of Venice in 1896. The "ardent fire" is an allusion to the Great War, because, when hostilities broke out, Pius X wanted to go to the battlefront at all costs to put an end to the fighting.

Twentieth-century Venice has produced two other popes who were not born in the city but were patriarch of the diocese. **John XXIII**. Cardinal-Patriarch of the city from 1953 to 1958, his own gifts of prophecy are displayed in a little-known work entitled *The Prophecies of John XXIII*. They are similar to Malachy's apocalyptic prophecies, though they stress the redeeming role of the Mother of God, referred to as "the White Rose" or "the Blue Sea". In the *Prophecies of St. Malachy*, John XXIII (Angelo Giuseppe Roncalli; pope from 4 November 1958 to 3 July 1963) is referred to as *pastor et natua* (shepherd and pilot), a reference to the pastoral work of the Church emphasised by the Second Vatican Council, which began and ended during his papacy and would give a new direction to the Church. **John Paul I** (Albino Luciani; pope from 26 August 1978 to 28 September 1978). Born in 1912 in the Veneto, he was Cardinal-Patriarch of Venice when he was elected pope. Malachy refers to him using the expression *De medietate lunae* (of the half-moon), a reference to his birth at Canale d'Agordo in the diocese of Bel*luna* (*luna*= moon).

Palazzo Altieri near Viterbo (Italy) has a collection of papal portraits that, from Celestine II onwards, bear the Latin phrase identifying each pope in the *Prophecies of St. Malachy*.

THE RED STONE IN THE *SOTOPORTEGO* DE LA CORTE NOVA

**A miracle
in the time
of the plague**

The inscription in the lunette above the *sotoportego* de la Corte Nova recounts the wonders worked here through the intercession of the Virgin Mary. The story concerns a number of inhabitants who, through the power of faith, were spared during the terrible epidemic. A further reminder of the whole incident is one of the paving stones.

It was during the terrible plaque of 1630, which killed more than 50,000 people in Venice alone, that a young girl named Giovanna, a resident of Corte Nova, urged her neighbours not to give up hope. She made a picture of the Holy Virgin together with St. Roch (the patron saint of those afflicted with the plague), St. Sebastian and St. Lawrence (protectors against epidemics), and then placed it in the *sotoportego*, where the residents used to gather every day for prayer. The ravages of the plague continued, but did not extend beyond the painting, thus the inhabitants of the courtyard were spared.

To commemorate this wonder, it was decided to install a slab of red Verona marble within the paving of the courtyard. It is still there today, and some – particularly students – believe it brings good luck to walk across it. However, there are also those who say it can have the opposite effect.

During the First World War (1914-1918), residents in the same courtyard followed the example of their predecessors and implored the Madonna for safety during enemy shelling. It would seem that, once again, faith bore fruit and acted as a "shield" for the residents of the area, as not one of them was injured during the bombing.

Every year on 1 May and 21 November, Our Lady of the Rosary is venerated in the *sotoportego* of Corte Nova. The place becomes a veritable shrine, complete with flowers and candles (for information, telephone 041 5206102).

THE GRAND PRIORATE OF THE ORDER OF THE KNIGHTS OF MALTA IN VENICE

⑫

Palazzo Malta
Castello 3253
• Tel: 041 5222452
• www.ordinedimaltaitalia.org
• Visits by appointment. Tel: 041 2410027

See the palazzo and church of the Order of the Knights of Malta

Prior appointment will now gain you access to the Grand Priorate of the Order of the Knights of Malta in Venice.

For centuries, the Lombardy and Venice Grand Priorate of the Sovereign Order of St. John of Jerusalem, also known as the Order of Rhodes and the Order of the Knights of Malta (see following page), served as a monastery, hospital and military barracks. The complex, complete with church and palazzo, is laid out around a central cloister and opens onto one of the largest gardens in Venice (which served both as an open-air space for the monastery and hospital and also as a garden of simples).

Founded in Jerusalem in the second half of the 11th century, the Order quickly spread throughout Europe. In 1187, Monsignor Gerardo, bishop of Ravenna, provided the knights of the Order, who were already present in the lagoon, with a site where they might establish their headquarters.

Dedicated to St. John the Baptist, the patron saint of the Order, the church was soon joined by a small hospital. Then, during the course of the 14th century, the larger hospital of Santa Caterina was added. In 1451, part of the establishment was ceded to the Order of the Confraternity of Saints George and Tryphon, also known as the Order of the Slavs (the name for the Dalmatian community in Venice). A smaller part of the same hospital also went to the Confraternity of St. John the Baptist, which, unlike the premises of the Dalmatian confraternity, no longer exists, even if an inscription to the right of the façade bears witness to its past existence: *Schola de S. Zuane del Tempio* (Confraternity of St. John of the Temple).

Numerous walls must have had frescoes , as illustrated by the cycle dedicated to the *Life of St. Catherine of Alexandria*, which dates from the 14th century. The large painting over the main altar, depicting *The Baptism of Christ*, is attributed to Giovanni Bellini's studio (early 16th century). It shows the donor, Prior Sebastiano Michiel, who commissioned the work, kneeling in prayer.

Extensively reworked in the 16th, 17th and 18th centuries, the palazzo (and church) were confiscated by the State when the Venetian Republic fell to Napoleon in 1797. It was only in 1841 that Austrian Emperor Ferdinand I restored a monumental part of the complex to the Order. In the meantime, numerous other parts of the buildings had been sold off to private individuals.

It was then that the Venice Priorate was linked with that of Lombardy to form the Grand Priorate of Lombardy and Venice.

The church, which had been stripped of all its artwork, was refurbished by the Priorate, which managed to obtain the restitution of the original altarpiece by the Bellini studio and installed the high altar that had once stood in the church of San Geminiano (see page 88).

During the 19th century, the Priorate also reassumed its medical role with the reopening of its dispensary. The Grand Priorate of Lombardy and Venice still exercises its authority over the Order of Malta in North Italy and Sardinia.

Contrary to popular belief (which has been misled by the "*Schola de S. Zuane del Tempio*" inscription), this site was never the Venetian headquarters of the Knights Templar. In the Middle Ages, the future Order of Malta was also called the Order of St. John of Jerusalem and the Order of Saint John of the Temple. Furthermore, whereas the future Order of Malta always had St. John as its patron saint, the Templars were particularly devoted to the Virgin, not St. John.

THE ORDER OF MALTA: THE ONLY PRIVATE ORGANISATION IN THE WORLD WITH THE ATTRIBUTES OF A SOVEREIGN STATE – EXTRATERRITORIALITY, EMBASSIES ...

The Sovereign Military Hospitaller Order of St. John of Jerusalem of Rhodes and of Malta, variously known down the ages as Knights Hospitaller, Order of the Knights of Rhodes, or Order of Malta, is one of the most ancient Roman Catholic religious orders whose current mission is to defend the faith and assist deprived and sick people.

Founded in Jerusalem in the latter half of the 11th century by merchants of the ancient Marine Republic of Amalfi to care for pilgrims in the Holy Land, this monastic community dedicated to John the Baptist was recognised as a religious order by Pope Paschal II in 1113.

The Hospitallers rapidly became militarised after the taking of Jerusalem during the First Crusade of 1099, a few years before the arrival of the Templars in the Holy Land. After the fall of Jerusalem and Saint Jean d'Acre in 1291, the Order retreated to Cyprus from 1291 to 1309. As the knights' rivalry with the King of Cyprus was creating difficulties, they conquered the island of Rhodes, then under Byzantine rule, and made it their new headquarters in 1310, ruling there until 1523. The island situation led them to acquire a fleet that became the scourge of Muslim shipping. Eventually vanquished by the Turks, the knights sailed to Civitavecchia and then Viterbe, in Italy, before travelling to Nice and in 1530 finally settling in Malta, given to them by the Holy Roman Emperor Charles V who had understood how useful they could be against any Ottoman advances. But Napoleon drove them out when he occupied the island in 1798, and they were finally welcomed in Rome by the pope in 1834.

Before the loss of Malta, most members of the order were monks who had taken the three vows of poverty, chastity and obedience. Even today some members are monks, but most of the knights and dames that now make up the Order are lay members (there are 12,500 of them). The military function has not been exercised since 1798.

Although, in the past, the knights of the Order had to come from chivalrous and noble Christian families, current members need only distinguish themselves by their faith, morality and the virtues sought within the Church and the Order itself. Although volunteers are always welcome, you can only become a member by invitation.

The Order maintains diplomatic relations with 104 countries through its embassies. It has a very special status, making it the only private institution that is treated almost like a country in itself. Activities are financed by donations from members themselves and other private parties, as well as income from the Order's properties.

Its headquarters are at two sites in Rome, which have been granted extraterritoriality. These are the Magistral Palace at 68 Via dei Condotti, where the Grand Master resides and meets with government bodies, and Villa Malta on the Aventine Hill, which houses the Grand Priory of Rome, the Embassy of the Order to the Holy See and the Embassy of the Order to the Italian Republic.

CROSS OF THE ORDER OF MALTA OR CROSS OF THE GRAND MASTER?

The famous cross of the Order of Malta is in fact that of the Grand Master of the Order of Malta, not of the Order itself.

The Order uses a simple white cross on a red background, similar to the arms of the House of Savoy.

Over time, because of the analogy between them, the cross of the Grand Master became confused with that of the Order.

THE MALTESE CROSS

Founded in 11th century Jerusalem by merchants from Amalfi (near Naples), the Sovereign Order of the Knights Hospitaller of St. John of Jerusalem (the future Knights of Malta) had originally taken as their symbol that of the port of Amalfi, merely dropping the blue background. Then, in 1130, Raymond de Puy transformed the charitable brotherhood into a military Order and obtained from Pope Innocent II the right to a white cruciform emblem; the colour was chosen to avoid confusion with the red cross of the Templars. Shortly after being driven off the island of Rhodes by the Turks in 1523, the Order would settle on Malta. At that point, the red flag of the island – inherited from the period when it had been occupied by the Normans – became the background to the white cross. And thus the Maltese Cross came into being.

THE MEANING OF THE EIGHT POINTS IN THE MALTESE CROSS

The eight points in the Maltese Cross signify various things:

- the eight sides of the Dome of the Rock at Jerusalem.

- the eight nationalities of the original knights of the Order of St. John of Jerusalem (the future Order of Malta) or the eight principles they undertook to live by: spirituality, simplicity, humility, compassion, justice, pity, sincerity and patience.

- the eight virtues which a knight of the Order of Malta was expected to possess: loyalty, pity, frankness, courage, honour, contempt of death, solidarity with the sick and poor, respect for the Catholic Church.

- the Eight Beatitudes which Christ listed in his Sermon on the Mount (St. Matthew's Gospel, Chapter 5):

Blessed are the poor in spirit: for theirs is the kingdom of heaven. (Verse 3)

Blessed are the meek: for they shall possess the land. (Verse 4)

Blessed are they who mourn: for they shall be comforted. (Verse 5)

Blessed are they that hunger and thirst after justice: for they shall have their fill. (Verse 6)

Blessed are the merciful: for they shall obtain mercy. (Verse 7)

Blessed are the clean of heart: for they shall see God. (Verse 8)

Blessed are the peacemakers: for they shall be called the children of God. (Verse 9)

Blessed are they that suffer persecution for justice' sake, for theirs is the kingdom of heaven. (Verse 10)

REMAINS OF THE FOUNDLINGS' WHEEL AT LA PIETÀ CONVENT

⑬

Calle de la Pietà

> *Abandon your child with an easy mind*

The only visible remains of the foundlings' wheel that used to be set in the wall of La Pietà convent is, contrary to what is sometimes said, the outside of the round wooden door placed at the entrance to the right of Calle de la Pietà. This now forms part of the Hotel Metropole, as the former convent and church of La Pietà formerly stood on that site (see following double spread).

The hotel lobby retains two columns from the church, on the far right as you go in.

To the right of the round door, below the high relief of the Virgin with Child, the inscription "*oferta agli esposti*" can still be read around the edge of a slot into which visitors could drop a donation to help the convent in its work of taking in abandoned babies and bringing them up.

THE FOUNDLINGS' WHEEL

It is said that in 787, Dateus, a priest in Milan, began placing a large basket outside his church so that abandoned infants could be left there. More organised initiatives for the reception of abandoned children were begun by the Hospice des Chanoines in Marseilles from 1188 onwards, with Pope Innocent III (1198-1216) later giving the practice the Church's benediction; he had been horrified by the terrible sight of the bodies of abandoned infants floating in the Tiber and was determined to do something to save them.

So the doors of convents were equipped with a sort of rotating cradle which made it possible for parents to leave their children anonymously and without exposing them to the elements. The infant was left in the outside section of the cradle, and then the parent rang a bell so that the nuns could activate the mechanism and bring the child inside. Access to the "turntable" was, however, protected by a grille so narrow that only newborn infants would fit through ...

Pope Gregory VII, Genghis Khan and Jean-Jacques Rousseau are some of the famous personalities who were abandoned as babies.

Abandoned during the 19th century, the system had to be readopted after some twenty years at various places in Europe due to the sharp upturn in the number of infants abandoned.

Foundlings' wheels of historical significance can be seen at the Vatican and in Pisa and Florence (see *Secret Tuscany* and *Secret Rome* in this series of guides), Bayonne (France) and Barcelona (see *Secret Barcelona*).

THE PLAQUE FORBIDDING CHILD ABANDONMENT

Calle de la Pietà

14

> *Under the threat of being "cursed and excommunicated"!*

On the side of the church of La Pietà is an astonishing plaque. Reminding passers-by of a papal bull issued by Paul III on 12 November 1548, it reiterates that those with sufficient means to support their children are strictly forbidden to abandon them to the care of the convent of La Pietà. Offenders are threatened with being "cursed and excommunicated".

Originally, this plaque stood on the opposite side of the street, alongside the "wheel" or revolving compartment into which abandoned infants were placed (see previous double page). In fact, the original convent of La Pietà was founded in 1348, whereas the existing church dates from 1760. It replaced a small church that had stood at the heart of the convent complex (see the period drawing opposite).

LA PIETÀ: A CHURCH DESIGNED AS A CONCERT HALL

The amazing thing about La Pietà is that from the very start the architect, Massari, envisaged it as a concert hall. In fact, this was where the gifted orphans raised by the convent used to give highly regarded classical music concerts. You can still see the grilles of wrought iron that run down either side of the church and above the main doorway. This is where the child musicians were placed.

The amazing oval form of the church was designed specifically with acoustics in mind. Similarly, the atrium that precedes the doorway into the body of the church was intended to insulate the "concert hall" from the sounds of the street outside.

NO, VIVALDI NEVER PLAYED IN THE PRESENT CHURCH OF LA PIETÀ

Contrary to a persistent legend, Vivaldi never played in the present-day church, for the simple reason that he died in 1743 before it was built (in 1760). He did, however, perform frequently in the old church of La Pietà, two columns of which can now be seen in the Hotel Metropole (on the right, at the end of the reception hall).

Hospitale della Pietá

THE COMTE DE SAINT GERMAIN: A MAGUS IN VENICE

Though not extensive, the evidence for the presence of the famous Comte de Saint Germain in Venice is fairly solid. It is supplied above all by the *Memoirs* of his enemy, the famous Giacomo Casanova (Venice, 2 April 1725 – Dux, Bohemia, 4 June 1798). Whilst Casanova may be considered the embodiment of vice, with a clear inclination towards the black arts – as exemplified in his fictional treatise *Isocameron* (begun in Venice and completed in Bohemia) – the Comte de Saint Germain can be said to have

MARQUIS SAINT GERMAIN DER WUNDERMANN.

Original Gemälde im Besitze der Marquise von Urfé
1783 in Kupfer gestochen von N. Thomas in Paris.
Folio seltenes Blatt

been motivated by virtue. A "Perfect Master" of white magic, he left an illustrated treatise on the subject: *La Très Sainte Trinosophie*, probably begun in Venice and completed in Troyes (the French city's library still has the original manuscript). The dates of the man's birth and death are not certain. What is known is that he appears in connection with the Prince of Transylvania, Francis II Radowsky, around 28 May 1696. However, it is not clear if this is the date of his birth, nor is it certain that the prince in question was his father. As for his death, it is supposed to have occurred at Eckernförd (Germany) on 27 February 1784. However, apart from the church registers there is no real proof, and we do not know if the person named therein is the actual Comte de Saint Germain. Nor is there any evidence as to where he was buried. The Comte de Saint Germain obtained distinction in various European courts as a veritable alchemist, magus and politician. For example, he was involved in the negotiation of various peace agreements, such as that between Prussia and Austria in 1761. A benefactor of the poor, he produced medicinal remedies that he put at their service. Amongst adepts of the esoteric arts, he is considered to have been the "Perfect Master", the "Unknown Master" of the Rosicrucians and the Freemasons. According to Casanova's *Memoirs*, the composer Rameau and the Comtesse de Gergy (widow of the French ambassador to Venice) swore that they had met the Comte de Saint Germain in the city in 1710. He was going under the name of Lorenzo Paolo Domiciani, Marquis de Montferrat, and was accompanied by his wife, Lorenza Annunziata Feliciani. Both of them were remarkably handsome. In challenging the official date of Saint Germain's death, the Comte de Chalons, upon his return from his time as ambassador to Venice, assured Comtesse d'Adhemar (as she mentions in her own *Memoirs*) that he had spoken with the Comte de Saint Germain in St. Mark's Square the day before he himself left Venice as part of an embassy to Portugal. In Venice, Saint Germain was friendly with the British ambassador, Lord Holderness, just as he had been with the French ambassador, Comte de Gergy. In 1764, Saint Germain took up residence in Venice (a city that had been home to numerous chemists and alchemists since the Middle Ages), working to develop a technique for dyeing silk in order to obtain specific colours – purple, in particular. At that time, Venice was also home to Count Maximilian de Lamberg, a brilliant diplomat and witty man of letters, who wrote in his *Memoirs* that, "A character worth knowing is the Marquis de Aymar, or Belmar, who is better known under the title Saint Germain. He has been living in Venice for some time, where – surrounded by nearly a hundred women workers (obtained for him by an abbess) – he is carrying out experiments with linen, which he bleaches to make it identical to Italian raw silk." The women mentioned were probably from the Ospedale della Pietà, a convent and orphanage for young girls which, during the course of the 18th century, would become famous for its music school for gifted orphans. It was here that composer Antonio Vivaldi worked for most of his career (see page 297).

RENAISSANCE VENICE: A REFUGE FOR HERETICS AND PRACTITIONERS OF THE OCCULT AND HERMETIC ARTS

In the 16th century, Rome and Venice were often in conflict. Sometimes caused by immediate political interests, sometimes by religious doctrine, these clashes were primarily inspired by Venice's determination to maintain its independence against a papacy it had quickly come to see as interfering in its affairs. The pope of the day, Clement VIII (24 February 1536 – 3 March 1605), was anything but clement by nature, viewing Venice as an immense refuge for "heretics", Lutherans, Calvinists and the various practitioners of occult arts who promoted religious reform. The city was an intellectual centre for hermetic philosophy, something that was bound to displease the champions of the Counter-Reformation.

Books whose unorthodox ideas had led them to be included in the *Index Librorum Prohibitorum*, a list of forbidden works that Clement VIII had updated in 1596, were freely available in Venice, particularly within the Jewish quarter. Indeed, the Venetian Patriarchate had continually defied the repressive totalitarianism of the Roman Curia, going so far as to set up its own rules for the Inquisition (which included a ban on the use of torture) in 1521.

Clement VIII was noted for his opposition to any form of "progress". Even coffee, first introduced in Venice around 1570, was seen as a Muslim drink and Christians had been forbidden to drink it. However, during his visit to Venice, the pope himself would try some, enjoy it, and lift the ban.

While most of Europe was firmly in the grip of the Roman Inquisition, Venice enjoyed great intellectual freedom, which explains why the city attracted so many of the intellectuals and thinkers who had rebelled against papal intransigence. One of the most famous was Giordano Bruno (1548-1600), a neo-Platonist who settled in Venice in 1590 upon the invitation of Venetian nobleman Giovanni Mocenigo, to whom he was supposed to teach "mnemotechnics", the art of developing one's memory. However, Mocenigo would betray Bruno, handing him over to papal troops who then took him to Rome, where he was burnt at the stake in Campo dei Fiori on 17 February 1600.

Venetian independence from the papacy reached such a level of animosity that, after the assassination of Henri III of France (1521-1589), a figure well known for his interest in magic and the hermetic arts (he had, for example, been the protector of the famous soothsayer Nostradamus), the city immediately offered asylum to the king's cousin and successor, Henri IV (1553-1610).

In 1587, the hermetic philosopher Fabio Paolini founded his *Accademia degli Uranici* in the Venetian monastery of San Francesco della Vigna. This attracted famous exponents of the occult and hermetic arts from all over Renaissance Europe. In 1589, Paolini published a treatise of hermetic neo-Platonism entitled *Hebdomades* (more precisely, *Hebdomades siue Septem de septenário Libri*), which was quickly considered as the most important occultist work published in Venice. The meetings of the Academy of Uranians – often held at members' homes, away from prying eyes – attracted not only freethinkers and exponents of occultism, but also a number of printers and publishers interested in such arts. One of them was Giovanni Battista, known as *Ciotto*, who was a follower of Giordano Bruno's ideas regarding parallel worlds and the owner of the *Minerva* bookshop in the Mercerie.

After a number of years, the Academy had to disband because of pressure from the clergy. The Inquisition even arrested some of the members, who however revealed nothing about the meetings and even went so far as to deny all interest in the hermetic and magical arts.

In 1788, the famous Freemason and "Unknown Superior" of the Rosicrucians, Alessandro Cagliostro, Count of San Leo and Fénix, stayed in Venice for six weeks, introducing the Coptic or Egyptian Rite. A group of Socinians (a Protestant sect that rejected the doctrine of the Trinity) applied to Cagliostro for authorisation to found a Masonic lodge, as they did not want to participate in his magical-Kabbalistic rituals. The Count thus founded the Rite of Memphis here, appointing the Socinians to the lower ranks of the Great Lodge of England and the higher ranks of Freemasonry of the German Templars.

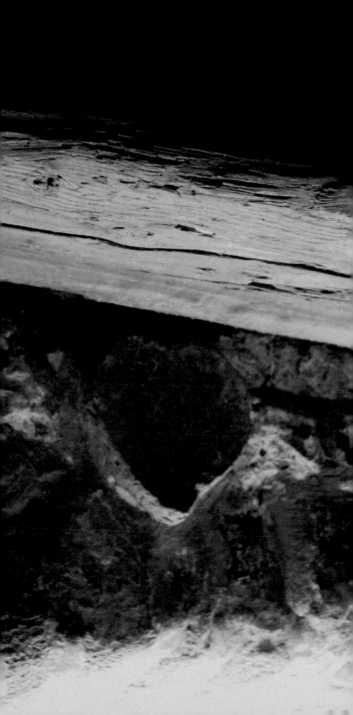

A BRICK HEART IN SOTOPORTEGO DEI PRETI

⓯

Sotoportego dei Preti
Salizada del Pignater

> **Memento of the love of a fisherman for a mermaid...**

Located near the church of San Giovanni in Bragora, the Sotoportego dei Preti links Salizada del Pignater with Calle del Pestrin. Just above the arch opening onto the Salizada there is a curious little heart in red brick.

An amazing legend has it that this house was home to Orio, a young fisherman who used to cast his nets in the area near Malamocco. One night he heard a voice lamenting, "Please, free me. I beg you!" and then he saw the face of a beautiful young girl emerge from the water. "Don't be scared," she said. "I am not a witch; my name is Melusina." And as they both smiled, he saw that her body ended in an enormous fishtail. Nevertheless he fell in love with her, the two talking together until dawn and then promising they would meet up there every night.

One day Orio decided that he wanted to marry Melusina. She agreed, but for the ceremony to take place she obviously needed legs rather than a fishtail and she made the rather odd condition that, until the marriage, they must never see each other on Saturdays. Everything went well for two weeks, but on the third Saturday Orio could not resist and went to their usual meeting-place. Melusina wasn't there, but soon a small whirlpool formed in the water from which emerged a huge serpent that said to him, "I told you not to come! An evil spell condemns me to turn into a serpent every Saturday. But if you marry me I will always be as beautiful as you have seen me."

They did marry and had three children. Then, one day, Melusina fell ill and died, her body being returned to the sea as she had asked.

Left alone with his three children, Orio thought he would not be able to both work and keep up his home. Curiously, however, every time he came back from fishing, the house was perfectly neat and tidy. He thought that it was a kind neighbour who was doing the work without telling him, but then one day he came home earlier than usual and found a serpent in the kitchen, which he killed. From that moment on, the house was no longer miraculously set in order and he realised that the serpent he had killed had been none other than Melusina, now dead forever at his own hand.

It was in remembrance of these events that the brick heart was set in place on their house.

Nowadays, the heart is considered to bring good luck. Touch it and the wish you make will come true before the end of the year, so they say.

THE STANDARD MEASURE OF A *PASSO VENEZIANO*

• Land entrance to the Arsenale • Open during office hours

Just inside the land entrance to the Arsenale, on the left wall opposite the porter's office, are two bars of metal of different length: these are the standard measures of a metre and a *passo veneziano* – the latter having been the common unit of measure used in the city right up to 1875.

The metre was installed in the Arsenale towards the end of the 19th century so that Venetians could familiarise themselves with the new metric system of measurement.

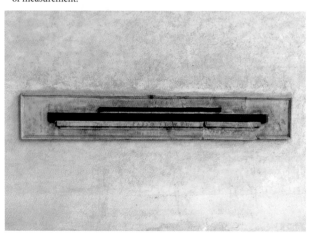

HOW LONG WAS A *PASSO VENEZIANO?*

Adopted throughout Venetian territories, this unit of length was the equivalent of 5 feet (1.738674 m). It was derived from units of measure used by the Romans: the *gradus* (a simple "step" of 2.5 feet, equivalent to around 73.5 cm) and the *passus* (a double "step" of 5 feet).

Before the introduction of the metric system in 1875, different types of *passo* were used, changing name and length from city to city. In Rome, the *passo* was equal to 1.49 m; in Genova, it was the same length but was referred to as the *passo geometrico*; in Bologna, the *passo* was 1.80 m, and in Naples, there was a *passo itinerario* (1.85 m) and *passo di terra* (1.93 m). To complicate things even further, the *passo quadrato* and *passo cubico* (square or cubic measure) changed in value from region to region.

On 20 May 1875, 17 countries (including Italy) signed a convention regarding the introduction of the metre, undertaking to promote the use of the metric system within their respective countries.

HOW IS A METRE DEFINED?

A child of the Enlightenment and the French Revolution, the metre was defined for the first time by the French Académie des Sciences in 1791 and was intended to replace all those units of measures that made reference to the human body (*pouce* / inch, *pied* / foot, etc.). Given that individual bodies tend, by definition, to vary, it had been frequent practice to take the body of the sovereign as the standard of reference, something that was clearly unacceptable to those opposed to the very notion of monarchy.

The Academy thus defined the metre (*metron* in Greek meaning "measure") as being one ten-millionth part of one quarter of a terrestrial meridian. According to this definition, the Earth has a circumference (equal to an entire meridian) of 40,000 km. As at the time it was impossible to measure the quarter of a meridian, the solution adopted was to measure a part thereof and then deduce the total value. The arc of meridian chosen was that between Dunkirk and Barcelona, and it was the French scientists Delambre (between Dunkirk and Rodez) and Méchain (from Rodez to Barcelona and then from Barcelona to Ibiza) who carried out the measurements.

France was the first country to adopt the metre as its official unit of measurement (in 1795). From 1796 to 1797, the Convention installed sixteen standard metres in marble throughout Paris, so that the populace could familiarise themselves with the new unit of measure. Nowadays, two of these marble standards remain: to the right of the porch to number 36 Rue de la Vaugirard and at 13 Place Vendôme, to the left of the entrance to the Ministry of Justice (see our guide *Secret Paris*).

It was 1875 before seventeen other nations signed the "Convention du Mètre". In 1899, the Bureau of Weights and Measures had a standard metre cast in platinum-iridium alloy, which was held to be subject to only infinitesimal variations; that original bar can still be seen at the Pavillon de Breteuil in Sèvres (Hauts-de-Seine).

With the advent of laser technology, the Conférence Générale des Poids et Mesures (CGPM) would in 1960 give a definition of the metre that is rather less comprehensible to the layman: 1,650,763.73 wavelengths of orange-coloured radiation emitted by the krypton 86 atom. In 1983 came an even more esoteric definition: the metre is the length of the path travelled by light in vacuum during a time interval of 1/299,792,458 of a second. Given that, according to the theory of relativity, the speed of light in vacuum is the same at all points, this definition is considered to be more accurate.

SIGHTS NEARBY

MUTUAL HELP ASSOCIATION OF SHIP'S CARPENTERS AND CAULKERS
Via Garibaldi 1791

• Visits only by appointment. Tel: 041 5266813 or smscc@smscc.it

The window at number 1791 Via Garibaldi has a rotating display of old shipbuilding tools and models of vintage Venetian vessels. Inside are other tools that were used by the workers at the Arsenale. These include a *marmotta*, a sort of stool used when caulking the vessels, with sections for all the necessary tools. The association also has its own *mariegola*, a document that combines guild statutes and a registry of apprentices. Amongst the honorary members listed are such illustrious figures as Giuseppe Garibaldi and Umberto di Savoia. There is also a reproduction of the autograph that Garibaldi, the "Hero of Two Worlds", gave the association in 1870 (the original is kept in a bank vault) .

Founded in 1867, this society brought together the *marangoni da nave* (ship's carpenters) and *calafati* (caulkers) in a sort of cooperative. The members, who worked in the city's various private and public shipyards, subscribed to a contribution system that generated a fund for social assistance. Today, the association – which also has a *squero da sotil* (a boatyard for smaller craft) on Fondamenta Sant'Iseppo at San Pietro – is open to all Venetian citizens. The public assistance is provided by sharing out the resources created by the annual contributions of the members. Amongst the members are the very few remaining caulkers left in the city; such trades as the *calafati* and the *squeraroli* (boatyard workers) are fast disappearing.

SURVIVING TRACES OF THE HOMES FOR WORKERS AT THE ARSENALE
Known as *Arsenalotti*, the Arsenale workers were a sort of elite corps among the city's craftsmen. Carpenters, caulkers, joiners, labourers and apprentices worked in a team, proud to serve the naval might of the Venetian Republic. At the election of a new doge, it was they who formed the guard of honour, and it was also they who rowed the *Bucintoro* during official ceremonies. They were also responsible for serving as a fire-fighting force anywhere in the city. One of their perks was free (or very low rent) housing provided close to the walls of the Arsenale.

On Rio delle Forne in San Martino (giving onto Fondamenta dei Penini, which takes its name from the shop that used to sell boiled lamb's feet, known as *penini*), numbers 2446 and 2445 bear old inscriptions. They not only give the old numbering of the houses, but also indicate that they were home to a foreman (*capomastro*) of the Arsenal sawmills and to a caulker (*calafato*): *N° 47 CAPPO MRO ALLE SEGHE* and *N° 46 APPUNTADOR DE CALAFAI*.

SIGHTS NEARBY

TOOLS FROM THE ARSENALE ON THE FLOOR OF THE CHURCH OF SAN MARTINO

Church of San Martino

On the floor of the church, enclosed between two rows of pews just before the choir, are engraved depictions of the tools that the workmen used at the nearby Arsenale. This engraving, like the rest of the church, was restored in 1972.

The workmen also had their own altar (second on the right). The altar has a painting that depicts the bishop St. Phocas, their patron saint, with a rudder at his feet.

The *calafati* (caulkers) also had an altar at Santo Stefano, where their guild (founded in the 13th century) met from 1454 onwards. The altar actually bears the inscription *Altare Artis Calaphactorum* (Altar of the Guild of Caulkers).

St. Martin is the first Christian saint not to have died a martyr.

PEGOLOTI OR *CALAFATI*

These were the Arsenale workers responsible for caulking the hulls of vessels in order to make them watertight. The *calafati da figger* fixed the structure of the hull in place using nails, and then the *calafati da maggio* added the hemp soaked in pitch which sealed all the joints between the planks of the hull and the deck of the vessel. These craftsmen were exempt from military service, and were also allowed to work outside the Arsenale on the building of commercial vessels.

THE RUNIC INSCRIPTIONS ON THE LIONS OF THE ARSENALE

Campo Arsenale

Traces of the Vikings in Venice

Various lions stand guard at the main doorway to the military shipyard of the Arsenale. The one on the left bears some curious inscriptions on its left and right sides.

Brought from Athens in 1687 by Doge Francesco Morosini (the man who has gone down in history as being responsible for the explosion of the Parthenon, used at the time as a powder magazine by the Turks), the lion once stood guard at the entrance to the Greek port of Piraeus, near Athens (which was actually known as "the Lion port").

As booty of war, the lion was sent to Venice, where its inscriptions – which were neither Greek nor Arabic – began to intrigue the Venetians. However, the mystery was not solved until the 19th century, when Danish scholar C. C. Rafn recognised that they were runes, inscribed on the statue in the 11th century by order of the future king of Norway, Harald III Sigurdsson (1015-1066).

After the death of his half-brother, Olaf II, Harald was exiled, ending up in Constantinople as the head of the Varangian Guard, an elite troop of the Byzantine army that was used to put down an uprising in the city of Athens. The inscriptions are said to read as follows: "Haakon, thanks to the aid of Ulf, Asmud and Orn, has conquered this port. These men, together with Harald the Great, suffered heavy losses due to the revolt of the Greeks. Dalk was held in captivity in distant lands. Egil made war, in the company of Ragnar, in Romania and Armenia." The inscription continues: "Asmund carved these runes, aided by Asgeir, Thorleif, Thord and Ivar, by order of Harald the Great, even if the Greeks were opposed."

Harald the Great would later return to his homeland and become King of Norway in 1047. He was killed at the Battle of Stamford Bridge (Yorkshire) in 1066, defeated by the very Harold Godwinson who a few days later would be defeated himself at the famous Battle of Hastings.

BLESSING OF THE THROATS ㉑

Church of San Biagio
Candle Ceremony: 3 February 10am and 6pm
• Blessing of the Candles: 2 February at the 6pm mass
Church is open Sunday morning from 10.30am to 12.30pm; mass at
11.30am; Saturday open from 4pm to 5.30pm

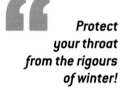

*Protect
your throat
from the rigours
of winter!*

Once a year in the depths of winter – on 3 February, the feast day of St. Blaise – an amazing ceremony of benediction takes place here. After the day's two masses, holy bread is blessed and distributed; the priest also performs a special benediction, holding two candles crossways over each person's throat and reciting the words: "Through the intercession of St. Blaise, bishop and martyr, may God deliver you from ailments of the throat and from every other evil, in the name of the Father, the Son and the Holy Ghost." The source of this tradition is the life of the saint himself (see below).

Given that St. Blaise was Armenian, the 6pm mass on 3 February is celebrated in the presence of the Abbot General of the city's community of Armenian Mechitarist Fathers.

WHY IS ST. BLAISE INVOKED TO PROTECT THE THROAT?

Born in the 3rd century AD in Armenia, Blaise was elected bishop of Sebaste. When the Christians began to be persecuted under Diocletian, he retreated to a cave surrounded by wild beasts, where he carried out several miracles including saving a child who was choking on a fishbone stuck in his throat. Blaise laid his hands on the child and prayed that he and all those who asked in his name should be healed, thus saving the child's life.
Shortly afterwards, at his command, a wolf gave back a pig that it had seized from a poor woman. She later killed the pig and brought him its head and feet, with a candle and some bread. He ate the meat and told her that whoever lit a candle in a church dedicated to him would reap the benefit. These two incidents were the source of the tradition of blessing the throat with wax candles.
Tortured with an iron comb or rake, Blaise was finally beheaded in 287 or 316, according to different sources.

INNUMERABLE RELICS OF ST. BLAISE

Blaise is probably the Roman Catholic saint with the greatest number of "official" relics. If all those who claim possession are to be believed, Saint Blaise would have had over a hundred arms. Although his body is said to be buried at Maratea, in southern Italy, another body lies at San Marcello in Rome. The church of Santi Biagio e Carlo ai Catinari (Biagio is Italian for Blaise) allegedly retains the saint's "throat bone".

Traditional saying: "If on Candlemas day it be shower and rain, winter's gone and will not come again."

STATUE OF GIUSEPPE ZOLLI

Viale Garibaldi

The statue of a ghost

I n 1921, a certain Vinicio Salvi was walking in the gardens near the site of the present-day Biennale when, upon approaching the statue of Garibaldi, he felt a heavy blow on his arm which made him fall to the ground. As he stood up, he saw a "red shadow" disappearing into the distance.

When he told his friends what had happened, they inevitably made fun of him, replying that shadows like that came out of the nearest bar. (In Venetian dialect, the word for shadow, *ombra*, is also used for a "glass of red wine").

A week later, however, the red shadow would make itself visible again, once more near the statue of Garibaldi. This time it was seen first by a courting couple and then by a fisherman, who actually came home with a bump on his head. These incidents caused a certain anxiety and the local police were called in. When they got near the statue, they were suddenly thrown backwards and the red shadow materialised before them, at which point they clearly saw one

of Garibaldi's red-shirted followers. A local resident even recognised the figure as Giuseppe Zolli, who had just recently died. Born in 1838, he had promised Garibaldi during the famous "Expedition of the 1,000" that he would watch over his chief even after death. Out of a feeling of sympathy for the apparition, the local residents then erected a bronze statue of Giuseppe Zolli to watch over and protect his general.

The apparitions of the red shadow immediately came to an end.

RIO AND FONDAMENTA DELLA TANA.
WHERE DOES THE NAME "TANA" COME FROM?

Just behind Via Garibaldi, Rio and Fondamenta della Tana run alongside the south wall of the Arsenale. The name comes from the city of Tana, which stands at the mouth of the river Tanai (now the river Don) in Russia. This was the site of a Venetian-Genoese trading colony and supplied the Venetians with the hemp used in the Arsenale to make ship's cordage.

THE GOLDEN ROSE AND THE *DOGARESSA* MOROSINA MOROSINI ㉓

Church of San Giuseppe di Castello
• Open on Saturday from 5:30pm to 6:45pm and on Sunday from 9am to 12pm

> *A reminder of an extraordinary custom that has long been forgotten*

The very pretty yet little-known church of San Giuseppe di Castello houses the monumental tomb of Doge Marino Grimani (1532-1605), just to the left of the entrance. At the foot of the two columns on the right of the tomb, a bas-relief commemorates the *dogaressa* (doge's wife), Morosina Morosini, receiving the Golden Rose, a sacred adornment that the pope presented yearly to a figure he wished to honour, from the hands of the papal nuncio. It is a tradition that has now been almost completely forgotten (see opposite).

Crowned *dogaressa* on 4 May 1597, Morosina Morosini supposedly set up a lace workshop at Santa Fosca, where a total of 130 people worked. It would appear to be the first organisation of lace production on an (almost) industrial scale, with the industry then spreading to Burano. She was presented with the Golden Rose by Pope Clement VIII, probably as an elegant and original way of entering into the good graces of her husband, Doge Marino Grimani. In fact, during his period as doge (1595-1605), Grimani was an active opponent of the papacy, not only seizing Ferrara (at the time part of the Papal States), but also making it clear that the pope was not to attempt to interfere in the religious affairs of the Venetian State (an interference that made itself felt almost everywhere else in Italy).

THE SEVEN GOLDEN ROSES IN VENICE

All in all, popes would send a total of seven golden roses to Venice, presented in 1177 by Pope Alexander III to Doge Sebastiano Ziani, in 1474 by Sixtus IV to Doge Nicolò Marcello, in 1496 by Alexander IV to Doge Agostino Barbarigo, in 1577 by Gregory XIII to Doge Sebastiano Venier, in 1597 by Clement VIII to Morosina Morosini (wife of Doge Marino Grimani), in 1759 by Clement XIII to Doge Francesco Loredan, and in 1833 by Gregory XVI to the Basilica of St. Mark's itself. The latter is still in the Treasury of the Basilica. All trace of the other six has been lost.

WHAT IS A GOLDEN ROSE?

The Golden Rose is a sacred adornment that usual depicts a single rose (sometimes a spray of roses) in solid gold. Every year, the pope presented one either to a sovereign, a place of worship, a place of pilgrimage or even an entire community, as a special mark of honour.

Since many of these objects were subsequently melted down for their gold, only a few roses still exist: one in the Treasury of the Basilica of St. Mark's (see above), one in the Paris Musée de Cluny (see photo below), one in

the Palazzo Comunale of Siena (Tuscany), two in the Treasury of the Hofburg in Vienna (Austria), one in the Treasury of the Cathedral of Benevento and one in the Museum of Sacred Art in the Vatican Library. Recently, popes (including John Paul II) have presented golden roses to Lourdes, to the Brazilian Basilica of Our Lady of Aparecida (1967 and 2007) and to the Sanctuary of Guadalupe (Mexico).

The first mention of such a golden rose was in 1049, in a papal bull issued by Pope Leo IX, whilst the earliest mention of one being presented by a pope dates from the end of the 11th century. In 1098-1099, Urban II gave one to Count Foulques d'Anjou for preaching the First Crusade.

As the message that always accompanies it makes clear, the Golden Rose is a secular honour with a spiritual significance. Just as the rose is considered the most beautiful and finely scented of all flowers, its presentation as a gift expresses the pontiff's wish that the heart and spirit of the recipient will be bathed in an equally divine perfume.

SOTOPORTEGO ZURLIN

**The lowest
sotoportego
in the city**

L ocated in Campo Ruga, Sotoportego
Zurlin is the lowest one in the entire
city. The place is a delight for holiday
photographers and for children, the only ones
who can pass through it without ducking their
head. The Corte Zurlin, to which it leads, is
associated with a ghost story. A doctor was called to visit a sick woman who
lived in the courtyard. However, he later discovered that the young girl who
had brought him here – the woman's daughter – had been dead for a month.

SIGHTS NEARBY

THE LAYET *CASE-RINGHIERE*
Campazzo de L'Erba 394

Just a short distance from Campo Ruga, right at the end of the *sestiere* of
Castello, there is a building that stands out amongst the traditional urban
fabric of Venice; a plaque on the wall gives the year of construction (1890).
This low-cost housing was modelled on a form of development that had
become typical of North Italy: *case-ringhiera*, a block of apartments linked
by an external corridor or balcony (*ringhiera*) that runs the length of the
building and overlooks a central inner courtyard. Initially designed to meet
the housing needs created by the industrial expansion of the 19th century,
this type of working-class accommodation had the advantage of bringing
together housing, workplace and areas of social interaction.

It was a Frenchman, Frédéric Layet, who had this housing block built for the
workers at his metal foundry located on the ground floor. The businessman
had come to Venice to take advantage of the growing demand, both within
the city and across the mainland, for iron-produced urban fixtures such as
streetlamps, railings, and more.

CASE-RINGHIERA IN CANNAREGIO

Another complex of *case-ringhiera* is located in the Vecchia Fornace
area near Sant'Alvise in Cannaregio. Here, too, the need for shift work
led entrepreneurs to create housing that was very unusual within the
surrounding context of traditional Venetian architecture.

THE WHITE STONE IN CAMPO SAN PIETRO

Campo San Pietro

> *The ancient meeting-place of the doge and the patriarch*

On the route that leads up to the church of San Pietro di Castello, an attentive eye will note a white stone amongst the other paving stones. Its position is far from accidental, for it marks the exact spot where, on his way to San Pietro, the doge used to be met by the Patriarch of Venice. Up until 1807, the church of San Pietro was, in fact, the city's cathedral, with St. Mark's being the doge's private chapel. The placing of this stone created a meeting-place which meant that the doge did not have to walk unreceived right up to the threshold of the church, nor did the patriarch have to go to meet him as he disembarked from his boat. The honour of both temporal and secular power was thus maintained.

Napoleon's decision to make St. Mark's the city's cathedral was largely a symbolic one. It meant that, before being received in the basilica himself, a substantial part of the symbolism of the ancient Republic and its doges was removed.

SIGHTS NEARBY

THE ELIO DE PELLEGRINI BOATYARDS
• Open Monday to Friday from 8am to 12pm and 1pm to 5pm

Having passed to the right upon entry, continue around the cloister in the former Patriarch's Palace and you will, at the end wall, come to a narrow corridor that is easy to overlook. This leads to an iron grille, but during the week just ring the bell and you will be admitted to a small boatyard. The main interest of this place is that it affords a view of the rear of both the church of San Pietro and of the former Patriarch's Palace, seen here from a tiny garden-terrrace that gives right onto the lagoon.

ANCIENT EMBLEM OF THE HOSPITAL OF ST. JOHN AND ST. PAUL

In the neighbourhood of San Pietro di Castello, a mysterious-looking symbol can often be spotted. It is, in fact, that of the former hospital of St. John and St. Paul.

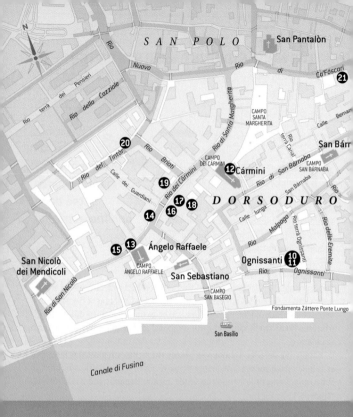

DORSODURO

THE LIBRARY OF THE VENICE SEMINARY

Dorsoduro, 1
30123 Venice
• Tel: 041 2411018
• E-mail : segreteria@seminariovenezia.it or biblioteca@marcianum.it
• www.seminariovenezia.it

*A hidden
gem*

I t is possible, by appointment, to visit the extraordinarily imposing library of the Venice Seminary. Located on the first floor of the building, it is one of the city's best-kept secrets.

The splendid library was originally created for the congregation of Somaschi Fathers,* which was dissolved at the time of Napoleonic rule. Today, it contains a number of precious texts. Primarily concerned with religion, a substantial part of these texts come from the legacy left by the patriarch Federigo

Giovanelli in 1799. There are also two mappemondes by Vincenzo Coronelli and three ceiling paintings: A. Zanchi's *The Burning of Heretical Books* (1705), Sebastiano Ricci's *The Glorification of Learning* (1720), and N. Bambini's *Minerva Crowning Titus Livy*.

The seminary itself was built for the Somaschi Fathers in 1699, to designs by Baldassare Longhena. The Somaschi congregation was dissolved in 1810, by Napoleon, and the building was given to the Venice Seminary in 1815. Previously, the seminary had been located at San Cipriano on Murano.

THE STARRED DODECAHEDRON IN THE LIBRARY

A surprising exhibit in one of the display cases is a starred dodecahedron. It was probably used in mathematical studies of Plato's five solids (see p. 70), and is a further reminder of the link between Venice and the goddess Venus, who was often associated with the dodecahedron (see p. 86).

---

* Founded by Saint Jerome Emilien (1486-153?), the Somaschi Fathers take their name from the city of Somasca (northwest of Bergamo), where their founder died. In 1531, Emilien had decided to abandon all worldly goods and share the life of paupers and orphans; he himself had been orphaned at 10 years of age.

THE PICTURE GALLERY
IN THE VENICE SEMINARY

Dorsoduro,1
30123 Venice
• Tel: 041 2411018
• E-mail : segreteria@seminariovenezia.it or biblioteca@marcianum.it
• www.seminariovenezia.it

By prior appointment – but sometimes during the visit to the library (see previous double page) – you can visit the Pinacoteca Manfrediana.

A neglected collection

The collection comprises paintings bequeathed by Frederico Manfredini (1743-1829) and the most important works of sculpture that came into the seminary's possession thanks to the work of Father Antonio Moschini, who recovered the pieces primarily from various Venetian churches and monasteries that had either been suppressed or stripped by the Napoleonic forces in the city.

Amongst the works of sculpture, note the superb *Adoration of the Magi* by a master of the School of Benedetto Antelami. It once stood over the doorway into the church of Santi Filippo e Giacomo.

Amongst the paintings, there is a fragment of fresco by Veronese (*Fame*, 1551) from the Villa Soranzo in Castelfranco Veneto, and an *Apollo and Daphne* that was once attributed to Giorgione but now to Titian. There is also a *Portrait of St. Lorenzo Giustiniani* attributed to the Circle of Gentile Bellini.

Unfortunately, a large number of the paintings are of little interest and tend to dilute the quality of the collection as a whole. However, the terms of Manfredini's legacy require that the seminary put all the works on public display.

Note the magnificent main staircase with its fresco decoration by Antonio Zanchi (late 17th century). The cloister walls also have numerous tombstones and inscriptions, some of which were again recovered thanks to the work of Father Antonio Moschini.

It would also seem that the plan of the basilica was inspired by the design of the temple of *Venere Physizoa* described in the verse romance *Hypnerotomachia Poliphili* (see following double page). Thus, the Basilica della Salute is a place where devotion to the Virgin Mary overlaps with the ancient *Veneti*'s worship of the Goddess-Mother, Venus (see p. 86). The building is also meant to remind followers that the health of the world is to be sought solely in the strength of faith in Mary.

KABBALAH AND THE DESIGN OF THE BASILICA DELLA SALUTE

❸

Basilica della Salute
• Vaporetto stop : La Salute

> *A ground plan inspired by The Poliphilo's Dream?*

Built as a votive church to the Virgin Mary in thanks for the end of the 1630 plague, the design of the Basilica della Salute incorporates numerous references to the Mother of God. First of all, there is the octagonal floor plan, the number 8 (symbol of Hope and Health) referring to the *Stella Maris* (Star of the Seas), an eight-pointed star. The name of this star is a reference to the *Marialis Stella* (Star of Mary), a title that the Carmelites gave to the Virgin when they became established in Europe in the 12th century. Furthermore, the basilica's dome symbolises the Virgin's crown, with Mary also depicted in the statue that stands atop the building.

Beyond the main building's eight sides and six side chapels, there is the lower cupola between the choir and the altar. So, together with the eight sides of the building, the lower cupola, altar and choir add up to the number 11, a symbol of Strength – the strength of the Venetians' faith that the Virgin could deliver them from the plague.

Taking the *passo veneziano* as the unit of measure (equal to 35.09 cm), a now out-of-print study by German historian Gerhard Goebel Schilling and the bookseller-publisher Franco Fliippi argues that the entire basilica is a design predicated on the numbers 8 and 11. For example, the length of the basilica is 121 (11^2) *passi* and its width 88 (8x11) *passi*; the sides of the octagon measure 44 (4x11) *passi* and the buttresses stand at a height of 66 (6x11) *passi*. Even the foundations extend to 88 (8x11) *passi* into the ground. Furthermore, the campo in front of the basilica is 44 (4x11) *passi* deep, the building is reached by 16 (8x2) steps, and the campo itself ends in 11 steps that lead down into the water of the Grand Canal.

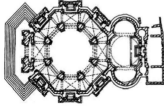

The sum of 8 and 11 is also symbolic. In the Jewish Kabbalah (see p.173), it is the number associated with the Sun of Mary (*Marialis Solis*), which underlies the entire meaning of the church.

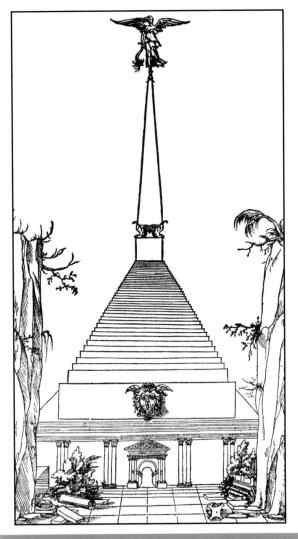

THE UNREQUITED LOVE OF LORENZO DE' MEDICI: AN INSPIRATION FOR POLIPHILO AND SHAKESPEARE?

The doomed love affair of Lorenzo de' Medici and Lucrezia Donati (who was married to Niccolo Ardinghelli against her will) seems to have directly inspired Poliphilo's quest: same name, same events, same timescale (1462-1464)... The love life of Lorenzo the Magnificent is also thought to have provided the material for Francesco Cei, a poet close to Lorenzo, in his poem *Giulia e Romeo* which directly inspired Shakespeare to write the famous *Romeo and Juliet*.

***POLIPHILO'S DREAM OF THE STRIFE OF LOVE*, AN EXTRAORDINARY HUMANIST ROMANCE THAT DIRECTLY INSPIRED THE GARDENS OF VERSAILLES, BOBOLI (FLORENCE) AND BERNINI'S CELEBRATED ELEPHANT-OBELISK IN ROME**

Printed by Aldus Manutius at Venice in 1499, *Hypnerotomachia Poliphili* (Poliphilo's Dream of the Strife of Love) is perhaps the most complex *roman-à-clef* ever published. Illustrated with around 170 exquisite woodcuts, it is also considered one of the finest examples of early printing.

The book, written in a mixture of Italian, Latin, Greek, Hebrew, Arabic, Spanish, Venetian and a few other dialects, was long considered anonymous. Recent research, however, chiefly led by Emanuela Kretzulesco,* have pointed to Francesco Colonna, as the decorative first letters of each of the thirty-eight chapters spell out the following phrase: *Poliam Frater Franciscus Columna peramavit* ("Brother Francesco Colonna dearly loved Polia"). A nephew of Cardinal Prospero Colonna, Francesco Colonna was part of the circle of Enlightenment figures that included Cardinal Bessarion, the future Pope Pius II and Nicholas V, known as the Renaissance Pope, opposed to the succeeding popes and in particular to Alexander VI Borgia. At a time when the Borgias, against the advice of Pius II and Nicholas V, were seeking to grant the pontiff temporal as well as spiritual power, and the papacy was embarking on a dark period of its history, *Poliphilo's Dream* was consequently rendered deliberately obscure in order to escape papal censure. More than a story of Poliphilo's love for Lucrezia, the book is a spiritual quest of a philosopher passionately devoted to divine wisdom (Athena Polias). Developing humanist themes, he transmitted in a cryptic way the spiritual testament of a circle of theologians united around Nicholas V, who had undertaken comparative studies of religious traditions going back to ancient Greece and Egypt with great openness of mind, thus reviving the heritage of Pope Sylvester II (Gerbert of Aurillac). In concurrence with the Florentine Platonic Academy of the Medici and Marsilio Ficino, this group notably included the architect Leon Battista Alberti and Prospero Colonna, as well as being a great inspiration to Pico della Mirandola, Leonardo da Vinci, Nicolaus Copernicus, Giordano Bruno and Galileo.

Poliphilo's Dream reveals that the best way to know God is through Nature, divine creation. With the help of the codes held in the *Hyeroglyphica* of Horus Apollo (Horapollo), it also illuminates the spiritual road that leads there. In an absolutely extraordinary fashion for anyone interested in understanding the background against which *Poliphilo's Dream* evolved, it is clear that it also closely inspired the gardens of Versailles or Boboli in Florence, as well as Bernini's celebrated elephant-obelisk in Rome through the numerous symbols scattered along Poliphilo's route.

WHAT DOES *HYPNEROTOMACHIA* MEAN?

The etymology of the term *Hypnerotomachia* is based on the following Greek words: *hypnos* (sleep) *eros* (love), and *mache* (fight).

Les Jardins du songe. Poliphile et la mystique de la Renaissance. Paris, Magma (only in French and Spanish).

CURIOUS DEATHS AT CA' DARIO ❹

• Vaporetto stop: Salute

A deadly palazzo

With its fine polychrome marble façade, Ca' Dario is one of the most charming *palazzi* in Venice. It is also one of the most mysterious. It seems that purchasing the building can very quickly lead to the ruin or violent death of the owner.

The earliest of such stories associated with the building date back to the very first owner, Giovanni Dario, the Venetian ambassador to Constantinople, who had the place built in the 15th century by architect Pietro Lombardo. Even if he himself did not live there – it served as the home of his daughter, who was married to nobleman Vincenzo Barbaro – Giovanni Dario soon lost his political influence, whilst his son-in-law went bankrupt and his daughter died of a broken heart.

In the 17th century, the palazzo was occupied for a time by a descendant of the Barbaro family, Giacomo Barbaro, who was murdered in Candia (Crete) when he was governor there.

The very next owner, the rich Armenian diamond-merchant Arbit Abdol, lost his entire fortune and died a ruined man.

The story continues in the 19th century. Rawdon Brown, an English scientist who lived in the palazzo from 1832 to 1842, would – like his lover – commit suicide, a ruined man.

And in the 20th century, the American Charles Briggs had to flee the country as the result of a homosexual scandal; his lover committed suicide in Mexico shortly afterwards.

In the 1970s, the palazzo was home to Filippo Giordano delle Lanze, whose lover beat him to death there with a statuette. And in 1981, Christoph Lambert, a manager of "The Who", also died in the palazzo.

The next owner, Fabrizio Ferrari, may not have died, but he did lose a large part of his fortune; his sister Nicoletta, however, was found dead in a field. And again, the famous Italian industrialist Raul Gardini committed suicide soon after buying the palazzo.

There was one last incident. After a serious car accident, tenor Mario del Monaco gave up his plans of buying the palazzo – as did Woody Allen when he learnt of the curse that seems to hang over the place.

Now the building has been bought by a developer who intends to turn it into apartments.

Henri de Régnier, author of *Altana or Venetian Life*, spent a lot of time writing on the *altana* (roof terrace) of Ca' Dario.

THE CHURCH OF THE FORMER OSPEDALE DEGLI INCURABILI ❺

Zattere
Dorsoduro 423
• Open during university faculty hours

> **Outline trace of a church that served as a concert hall**

The present-day Academy of Fine Arts is housed in what was, until 1813, the Ospedale degli Incurabili, which, in addition to being a hospital, provided social assistance to paupers and orphans, some of whom then served as the vocalists and musicians in the concerts given in the church.

The church at Gli Incurabili was the first to adopt a very original oval form. Inspired by the resonance chamber of string instruments, it guaranteed that the sound waves would be propagated in a regular manner. The form is now to be seen in the outline within the present cloister. In fact, the coloured stones that emerge from ground level form a rounded rectangular shape that outlines the exact area occupied by the old church.

Also for acoustic reasons, the building had a wooden roof in the form of an inverted lute, and the side galleries (again in wood) were also designed in the form of the cover of a musical instrument. The same sort of principle can be seen in the extant ceiling in Villa Contarini at Piazzola sul Brenta (there inspired by an inverted guitar).

Built by Antonio da Ponte to designs by Sansovino, the church was razed to the ground by the Austrians in 1832.

SIGHTS NEARBY

THE COLUMN OF CASA VELLUTI ❻
Dorsoduro 46

Looking through the glass door of Casa Velluti, one sees that the entrance to this relatively recent building is adorned with a remarkable column.

However, whilst aesthetically very convincing, it would seem that this column is an early 20th-century copy of one of the columns of the ciborium on the main altar of St. Mark's Basilica. The staircase balustrade (dating from the same period) is a copy of the Gothic balustrade to a staircase at Ca' d'Oro.

THE FOUR HOSPITALS OF THE VENETIAN REPUBLIC: PLACES OF SOCIAL ASSISTANCE AND MUSIC-MAKING

In response to some of the numerous social ills besetting Renaissance Venice, the government founded four hospitals/hospices: Gli Incurabili (see opposite), I Mendicanti (behind the present-day hospital at Santi Giovanni e Paolo), I Derelitti (the present-day Ospedaletto), and La Pietà (see p. 296). These institutions served a double function. As well as caring for the sick, they took in paupers and young orphans who were then taught either to sing or to play a musical instrument. In the 18th century, a good 70% of Venetian noblemen remained unmarried so as to avoid any division of the family's wealth, hence the large number of "courtesans" and of unrecognised offspring classed as "orphans". Just like St. Filippo Neri in Rome (see our guide *Secret Rome*), Girolamo Emiliano* in Venice understood the important role that music (and other crafts) could play in the education of these abandoned youngsters, helping the boys avoid beggary and the girls prostitution. This second role meant that not only could the orphans be kept occupied, but also that, via concerts, the hospitals could raise funds to continue their work. The churches in each of these hospitals became veritable concert halls. Indeed, when the church was constructed or reconstructed specifically to serve the needs of music (as was the case at Gli Incurabili, I Mendicanti and La Pietà), a special narthex was built onto the front of the church/concert hall to insulate it from external sounds. Initially, the church at I Derelitti was simply modified to meet this new use, but then, in 1771-1777, a special concert hall was built (complete with frescoes by Guarana and Mengozzi). Two churches (La Pietà and Gli Incurabili) were designed from scratch to serve as concert halls, and in each case an oval form was adopted in order to have the best possible acoustics (see previous page, Gli Incurabili). Whilst the boys learnt other trades and went to daily mass (the two sexes never attended religious services in the same place), it was the young girls who performed music. Most orphans were admitted to the hospital at around the age of six, but it was only those who demonstrated real musical talent who became part of the *cappella musicale*. The girls/young women would then remain as performers up to the age of 40 or so, when they could decide to become music teachers for the younger orphans, leave to get married or take religious vows. After the fall of the Republic, the four musical *ospedali* were closed and then transformed into civilian or military hospitals at the beginning of the 19th century.

WHY WAS PALAZZO VENIER DEI LEON NEVER FINISHED?

Legend has it that the building was left unfinished because the owner of Palazzo Corner was concerned that the completed building – which promised to be gigantic – would cast his own residence into the shade. A complete model of what Palazzo Venier dei Leon would have looked like can be seen in the Museo Correr.

THE WINDOWS OF PUNTA DELLA DOGANA

Restored by Tadao Ando for François Pinault, the Punta della Dogana has a detail that is the Japanese architect's homage to famous Venetian architect Carlo Scarpa (see p. 354). The grilles across the windows on each side are inspired by those seen in the former Olivetti shop in St. Mark's Square.

---

* also founder of the Somaschi Fathers; see p. 323.

SIGHTS NEARBY

THE HIDDEN CLOISTERS OF THE DON ORIONE ARTIGIANELLI CULTURAL CENTRE

Zattere
Dorsoduro 909/A
• Tel: 041 5224077
• E-mail: info@donorione-venezia.it
• Double rooms: from €135 to €140

As you pass from the Zattere along the east side of the church of I Gesuati, you see a glass door surmounted by the inscription *Don Orione Artigianelli*. This leads through to an old monastery that now houses conference facilities and a hotel. Inside are three cloisters that you can visit upon request.

From the first cloister, to which you gain access immediately, a staircase in the south wall leads into a corridor that continues into a second cloister, of which only half remains. Between the two, note the fine staircase designed by Giorgio Massari. Immediately after the staircase, another passageway leads to the third cloister, a charming little space that gives onto the Zattere.

The site was settled as a monastery in the 14th century by the Gesuati (see below), who also built the church of Santa Maria della Visitazione. The Order was abolished by the pope in 1668 and replaced here a year later by the Dominicans, who built the church of Santa Maria del Rosario (still generally referred to as "I Gesuati"). From 1745 to 1749, Giorgio Massari worked on the extension of the monastery. During the Napoleonic period, the foundation

was suppressed, but the buildings were later occupied by the Somaschi Fathers (see page 323) from 1851 to 1866. After a relatively short period of use by the Congregation of Charity, the charitable foundation of Don Orione Artigianelli took over the buildings, which they still occupy. The term *Artigianelli* ("young craftsmen") comes from the fact that Don Orione, who was beatified for his charity work in 1980, believed that the children supported by his institution should contribute through their own manual labour.

GESUATI AND GESUITI: NOT TO BE CONFUSED

The *Gesuati* (devotees of the name of Jesus) are not to be confused with the *Gesuiti* (Jesuits). The former was an order founded by Siena native Giovanni Colombini, who in 1355 – after reading the life of Saint Mary of Egypt – decided to dedicate his life to the care of the ill and infirm. The church of "I Gesuati" is now a Dominican foundation (see above).

The Jesuits, who at times put the interests of the papacy before those of Venice, have only one magnificent church within the city: the church of I Gesuiti in Cannaregio (see page 196).

THE VAULT OVER THE RIO TERÀ DEI GESUATI ⑧

The best example of a rio terà

Together with the Rio Terà de L'Isola at San Giacomo dell'Orio (see page 117), the Rio Terà dei Gesuati is the best place in Venice to follow the course of a street laid out above a filled-in canal.

Here, you can see the vault over the canal that used to pass under the church of the Gesuati; the vault itself has also been filled in.

REOPEN THE *RIO TERÀ*?

Since the very foundation of Venice, the city's canals have been an essential part of its urban fabric. Around 1500, when the network of such waterways was at its most extensive, the city had more than 37 km of canals, which played a triple role in the life of the city: as a road system, as a way of eliminating rubbish within the city and as channels through which water could flow in and out of the lagoon.

Very few canals disappeared before the fall of the Republic in 1797. Indeed it was the digging of new canals that was then seen as a priority. Before 1600 only five are known to have been filled in, either because of stretches of dead water or for other special reasons; for example, the Rio Batario was filled in 1156, when St. Mark's Square was built. Sometimes, however, in order to limit the impact of the ebbing and flowing of water, a vault was built over the canal, which nevertheless continued to flow under the newly created street.

Things changed dramatically after the fall of the Republic in 1797. Intent upon "modernising" the city, its new rulers filled in about 6 km of canals (20% of the total network). In the short term, this policy had its advantages, for it certainly cost less to fill in a *rio terà* than to maintain a canal. There might even be more specific advantages: the work on Rio Ognissanti was a way of providing employment for those who were protesting in front of the Town Hall.

Contrary to expectations, however, it was not just the French and Austrian forces of occupation that pursued this policy of *rio terà*; both before and after 1866, the Venetian and Italians also applied it.

Nowadays more than 30% of the canals in the San Polo area and 25% of those in Dorsoduro are filled in. Perhaps the time has come to "unfill" some of these waterways. This would not only facilitate the flow of water within the lagoon but also improve the daily life of numerous Venetians by adding to the number of mooring-places (*posti barca*), of which there is now a chronic shortage.

SIGHTS NEARBY

THE HOUND OF ST. DOMINIC

9

On the keystone of the vault over this filled-in canal, a small sculpture indicates the religious order to which the church of the Gesuati belongs. It depicts a dog above a shield with a lily (symbol of St. Dominic's chastity) and a star (a symbol of his wisdom, though certain sources also say it is a reference to the star that is said to have appeared in the sky at his birth).

The story goes that St. Dominic's mother dreamt she gave birth to a dog bearing a torch in its mouth. She interpreted this as meaning that her child would later light up the world with his words. The dog is a reference to the literal translation of the Latin *Domini cani*, "hounds of the Lord" (given the Dominicans' role in pursuing those identified as enemies of the God and his Church). However, the name Dominic (chosen after the pilgrimage that the boy's mother made to the Benedictine St. Dominic of Silos shortly before his birth) comes from *Domenica* (Sunday, the "day of the Lord").

MYSTICAL DECORATION IN THE SACRISTY OF ❿ THE CHURCH OF SANTA TRINITÀ OGNISSANTI

Fondamenta Ognissanti
Dorsoduro
• Open in the morning from 10am to 12am and for mass at 6:30pm
• Tel: 041 5294036

Inlaid symbolism at the back of the monks' choir stalls

Generally ignored by Venetians and tourists alike, the church of Santa Trinità Ognissanti – the former chapel of the Giustinian Hospital – has a quite extraordinary sacristy.

Passing through the doorway of the church, which gives onto the charming Rio Ognissanti, you will find the sacristy directly ahead. Before you go any further, try to find the local parish priest, Father Tarcisio Giuseppe Carolo, who will be only too happy to explain all the detailed symbolism of the place (unfortunately, this treat is reserved for those who can understand Italian).

Designed in 1692 by Don Felice, a monk of the Camaldolese Order, the sacristy originally stood on the island of San Clemente. The story is still told of an exhausted pilgrim who sought shelter at the monastery of San Romulado there. Since it was full, the only place the monastery could accommodate the pilgrim was in the sacristy, whose beauty and spirituality so overwhelmed him that he exclaimed, "This is a place for angels alone to sleep!"

Following the abandonment of the monastery and its subsequent conversion into a luxury hotel, the sacristy was transferred to the church of Santa Trinità Ognissanti at the end of the last century.

The unique appearance of the place is due to the remarkable inlay decoration at the back of each stall. While an untrained eye might well see nothing unusual, Father Carolo will help you decipher a spiritual message that runs the length of all the walls of the sacristy. What initially looks like a mere jigsaw puzzle of shapes gradually forms itself into the outlines of animals, flowers, fruit and monks, and the meaning slowly emerges. The Eagle of St. John, the Lion of St. Mark and the Ox of St. Luke all form part of the essence of Don Felice's work here.

Father Carolo has published a small guide on the subject, *Sacrestia Lignea-Guida alla simbologia e studio ascetico-teologico* (again, only available in Italian). If he offers you a copy, a donation to the church is very welcome, even if he does not ask for any payment.

SIGHTS NEARBY

THE OLD OSSUARY OF THE CHURCH OF SANTA TRINITÀ OGNISSANTI: ⑪
THE VICTORY OF LIFE OVER DEATH

In the central aisle of the choir, a black tomb catches the eye. This was the old ossuary of the church and was in use until Napoleon Bonaparte banned burials within churches and ordered the creation of the cemetery of San Michele. Framed by two groups of eight-pointed stars, the whole ensemble is a magnificent symbol of the victory of life over death, or of the existence of life after death.

THE EIGHT-POINTED STAR: A SYMBOL OF RESURRECTION

In both the sacristy and the choir, you can find numerous eight-pointed stars within the church. These are a Christian symbol of the resurrection. God created the world in six days, rested on the seventh, and the resurrection of Christ is symbolised by the eighth day. Thus, the eight-pointed star became a symbol of this victory of life over death.

THE SYMBOLISM OF THE PATERAS AT THE CHURCH OF I CARMINI

⑫

North door (towards Campo Santa Margherita)

> *Medieval symbols of the struggle between good and evil*

Totalling almost 1,000, the pateras* found on the outside of Venetian buildings date primarily from the 11th to the 13th centuries. The ones on the north door of the church of I Carmini are perhaps the most typical examples of these sculptural works.

Dating from the 12th century, these five pateras in Greek marble depict, from top to bottom and from left to right: an eagle pecking at a rabbit or hare, a gryphon (see p. 49) pecking at the back of a rabbit or hare, another eagle pecking at a rabbit or hare (centre), a wader or pelican with a fish in its beak, and another eagle pecking at a rabbit or hare.

Thanks to its double eyelids, the eagle was the only bird capable of looking straight at the sun and thus was taken as a symbol of spiritual elevation; the sun was frequently associated with Christ. The hare or rabbit are symbols of the lower instincts that humankind has not mastered. By pecking at it, the eagle represents the struggle between good and evil, the ultimate striving to break free of evil through the sacrifice of Christ and the Holy Eucharist. The pelican, too, symbolises Christ's sacrifice, whilst the fish is a symbol of Christ himself (see below).

WHY IS THE PELICAN A SYMBOL OF CHRIST'S SACRIFICE?

For a long time it was believed that the pelican nourished its young with its own blood, pecking its breast to make the blood flow. Hence, in the Middle Ages, the bird became a symbol of Christ's sacrifice. In fact, the bird nourishes its young with regurgitated fish; the young birds peck away in their mother's throat to get at the food.

WHY IS THE FISH A SYMBOL OF CHRIST?

The Greek word for "fish" is *ichthus*, the letters of which are an acronym for *Iesious Christos Theou Uios Soter* (Jesus Christ, Son of God, Saviour). In astrology, Christ's birth was also said to have marked the beginning of the period of the sign of Pisces, the last sign of the zodiac (which, through Christ's advent, thus comes to an end).

* The presence of old pateras does not mean that the building itself is of the same age, as numerous such sculptures have been "recycled". This is the case, for example, with those on Casa Brass, just to the right of the side entrance to the church of San Trovaso, or those on the building of Fondaco dei Turchi. Furthermore, in the 19th and 20th centuries, numerous imitation pateras were produced.

THE *SOCIETÀ BOCCIOFILA* AT SAN SEBASTIANO

Fondamenta San Sebastiano 2371
• Information: 041 2750315 • Open daily, including Sundays, from 10am to 12:30pm and 3:30pm to 7pm

Behind the green door...

N ear Angelo Raffaele, a door on the Fondamenta Briati leads through to a huge bowls ground, whose existence would never have been imagined. There are three regulation-size pitches for the club members, where amateur games alternate with professional tournaments. Time seems to have stopped here, and visitors are very welcome, perhaps to have a glass of wine and a *vovo duro* (a hard-boiled egg) whilst watching the games.

In the 1940s, when bowls were very fashionable, a trattoria near the church of San Sebastiano bought this nearby plot of land to set up a bowls pitch. It was after the Second World War, when television had yet to become available to everyone, that the passion for the sport reached its peak, with bowls runs

(known as *stradoni*) being created alongside numerous bars for use in the summer. When this pastime became a more serious sport, the bowls fans at San Sebastiano joined the Italian Bowls Federation. Today, the Società Bocciofila has around 100 members, most of them pensioners. The club team is considered one of the best in the Veneto.

The game of bowls enjoyed a sort of "golden age" at the time of Italian unification, thanks to Garibaldi. Ultimately, the sport spread throughout the peninsula and then, thanks to emigrants, throughout the world. Since 1991, it has been classed as an Olympic sport.

SIGHTS NEARBY

THE "MARIANO CUCCO" SOCIETÀ BOCCIOFILA

Fondamenta Briati
Dorsoduro 2531
• Open daily from 3pm to 7:30pm
• Tel: 041 524507
• bocc.cucco@libero.it

Located almost opposite Ca' Zenobio, the "Mariano Cucco" *Società Bocciofila* is a place you could pass a hundred times without noticing. The discreet doorway leads into a dark narrow corridor that opens onto the bowls pitch and a small green area that also has a bar. Like the one at San Sebastiano, this club is open to the public.

THE VEGETABLE GARDENS OF PALAZZO MINOTTO

⑮

Ponte del Cristo 2364
• For information, contact the Town Hall at 041 2710012
• To visit the gardens, ask directly on site

Vegetable gardens tucked away between palazzi

At the foot of Ponte del Cristo, near the church of Angelo Raffaele, is a small doorway giving onto the quayside. Identified by a small plaque, it leads into the surprising *Orti degli Anziani* (Pensioners' Gardens) of Palazzo Minotto. The gate is open almost every day as the gardeners go in and out.

With its beds of artichokes, onions, beans and courgettes, you would hardly believe that this place is just a short walk from Piazzale Roma. However, this small area of gardens enclosed by ancient buildings has existed for some twenty years.

Ten garden sheds stand in a plot that has been divided into a total of 40 allotments that are allocated every three years to local residents aged 55 and over who have obtained the requisite number of "points" on a scale established by the Town Hall. In exchange for a small payment, the allotment-holders can indulge their passion for gardening, converse with those who share their interest in nature, and enjoy the very special flavour of salad or soup made with "home-grown" ingredients.

THE ORGANIC VEGETABLE GARDEN AT ANGELO RAFFAELE: LEARNING TO EAT BETTER

Alongside the pensioners' allotments at Angelo Raffaele, an area dedicated to organic gardening has also been created as part of a teaching programme organised by the *Associazione Wigwam Club Giardini Storici Venezia* with the support of the City Council's Environmental Service. The aim of this association is to promote organic gardening amongst not only those pensioners who have allotments, but also the students of Nature Sciences at the nearby Vendramin-Corner Technical High School and all the inhabitants of the city.

The organic garden is inspired by the traditional vegetable gardens of Venice, which comprised herbs, vegetables, flowers and fruit trees and were designed to make the city self-sufficient in the event of siege.

The project involves the organisation of four "celebrations of the seasons". They are open to everyone and illustrate the different phases in the natural cultivation of fruit and vegetables, using methods that cause less pollution and result in healthier produce.

For information: Wigwam Club Giardini Storici Venezia, Tel. 328.8416748 – 320.4678502 giardinistorici.ve@wigwam.it www.wigwam.it.

THE *PUTTI* ROOM

Collegio Armeno Moorat - Raphael
Dorsoduro 2596
• €140 per night
• info@collegioarmeno.it • www.collegioarmeno.com
• Tel: 041 5228770

> *Sleep in a little gem of a room for €140 a night*

While not exactly a hotel, the Collegio Armeno does rent out certain rooms at very reasonable rates (from €30 for a single room to €140 for a room for four people). Of all the rooms, one stands out: the Putti Room.

Overlooking the garden, this room has maintained all its charm; the bed alcove and the profuse stucco-work make it unique in Venice for such a reasonable price. However, do not expect five-star hotel luxury. The palazzo is run as a cultural association, not as a hotel. Next door, in fact, is the room used by a music school (but not at night!). You should book well in advance.

THE ARMENIAN PRESENCE IN VENICE

A place with great spiritual associations for Christianity, Armenia is not only the location of Mount Ararat (where Noah's Ark came to rest after the Flood), but also the source of three of the four rivers that the Bible describes as arising in Paradise itself (the Tigris, the Euphrates and the Pishon; the latter is known in Armenian as the Coroch). Whilst some Armenians were already to be found in Venice, most notably at the monastery of Santa Croce on the Grand Canal (see p. 103), they became a real presence in the lagoon in 1717, the year the Venetian State offered the Armenian monk Father Mechitar the island now known as San Lazzaro degli Armeni. Father Mechitar was, in fact, fleeing from Turkish persecution in Istanbul and would here restore the existing 12th-century church and set up a monastery on the island (which had been abandoned since the 16th century). The foundation even survived the suppression of religious houses in the Napoleonic period, as, in 1805, Napoleon recognised the importance of the scientific and scholarly work carried on there. Signed by the emperor himself, the manuscript decree granting the monastery continued existence as an independent foundation is still kept on the island. Since that period, the monastery has grown to four times its original size, now occupying a full three hectares.

There is also an Armenian church in the heart of Venice, Santa Croca degli Armeni. Open on the last Sunday of the month for mass at 10:30am, it stands a short distance from the church of San Zulian (San Giuliano). See p. 55.

THE *PIANO NOBILE* OF CA' ZENOBIO

Collegio Armeno Moorat-Raphael
Dorsoduro 2596
• Open during the Biennale (free admission) or upon reservation (€3 per person)
• info@collegioarmeno.it • www.collegioarmeno.com
• Tel: 041 5228770

> **The most spectacular ballroom in Venice**

Built around 1690 by Antonio Gaspari for the Zenobio family, rich Venetian patricians of Greek origin, this is one of the finest examples of a late Baroque palazzo in Venice. It stands on the site of the old 14th-century Palazzo Morosini and is now most famous for its remarkable ballroom, with frescoes by French artist Louis Dorigny. The gallery that runs around the main room was intended to house the musicians, who thus were out of sight of the guests.

A mass of mirrors, stucco-work and *trompe-l'oeil* painting, the ballroom can be visited during most of the Contemporary Art Biennales (held in alternate years from June to November). However, outside this period, you can book a visit of the ballroom and oratory for €3 per person (see below).

On the first floor of the palazzo, the small *portego* (central hall) has paintings by Luca Carlevarijs and three frescoes by Gregorio Lazzarini (18th century). There are also two frescoes by Gaspare Diziani in the small room to the left of the ballroom itself. The palazzo also has a pleasant garden, at the end of which stands the old Zenobio family library; it was built by Tommaso Temanza in 1777 and now houses an Armenian Culture Study Centre and Archive.

It was in 1850 that the palazzo was purchased by the Armenian Mechitarist community. A congregation founded by the Venerable Mechitar, it has its Mother House on the island now known as San Lazzaro degli Armeni. Since 1836, the community's premises within the city itself had been at Ca' Pesaro, but – thanks to a generous bequest from an Armenian merchant from Madras (India) – the Mechitarists were able to transfer here in 1851.

The ballroom can also be hired for private events.

SIGHTS NEARBY

THE CA' ZENOBIO ORATORY
Less well-known than the ballroom, the palazzo's oratory (located above the *piano nobile*) is worth the visit, particularly for its stucco ceiling.

The Fondamenta Briati owes its name to the presence of the glass kilns of Giuseppe Briati in the 18th century. It was in 1736 that, owing to the dire state of Venice's economy, the State overruled the Maggior Consiglio's 1291 ban on the presence of such fire risks in the heart of the city and allowed Briati to make his glass objects "in the Bohemian manner" within Venice. The reason he could not set up his works on Murano was that any newcomer (hence new competitor) there was far from welcome.

A COLUMN FROM CAPE SOUNION ⑲

Dorsoduro 2530
Fondamenta Briati, opposite Ca' Zenobio

> **A 2500-year-old column**

The building now houses the premises of the Literature and Philosophy Faculty of the University of Ca' Foscari. The garden is usually open on weekdays during university opening hours. You could walk along Fondamenta Briati any number of times without noticing the column that stands alone in the middle of the garden opposite Ca' Zenobio on the other side of the canal. The piece is, however, of historical interest, being made up of five parts of a column from the Greek temple of Poseidon on Cape Sounion (at the south-east tip of Attica in Greece), which was built in 444-440 BC. These remains were part of a small private collection of antiquities put together during the second half of the 19th century by the Busetto family, which owned this building from 1855 to 1920. The column itself was set up at its present location in 1862, after having first been raised in Palazzo Erizzo (near the Arsenale) when the Busettos had first arrived in Venice in 1826. It was that very year that the Marchese Amilcare Paolucci delle Roncole, the admiral commanding the Mediterranean fleet of

the Austrian emperor, had taken the sections of the column as war booty during his passage around Cape Sounion. Whilst not forming a complete column, these fragments certainly come from the Cape Sounion temple, as evidenced by such characteristic features as the form and size of the capital, the diameter of the various sections, and the fact that the channelled shaft has sixteen grooves rather than the twenty that were usual in columns of the Doric order. The fragments must have been carved out of the same marble as the rest of the temple, which came from the Agrilesa quarry in the Laurion Hills near Sounion. Another peculiarity of the remnants is the presence of inscribed tourist names, such as are found all over the Sounion temple. On the abacus of the Venetian column is the clearly legible name of a French Navy brigantine, along with the year it passed Cape Sounion (LE ZEPHYER BRIC DU ROI 1816). In the grooves around the fourth and fifth section of the column can be read (top to bottom) the inscribed names of what are probably other ships and their date of passage (FLEUR DE [-]C[HE]VALIER VE 1822; AUNE 1814)

The Lion of St. Mark that stands atop the capital of the column dates from the 19th century.

A PLAQUE FORBIDDING BULL-BAITING

Fondamenta dei Cereri

Precursor of the bullfight ?

Opposite Ponte Rosso on Fondamenta dei Cereri, you can still see an engraved plaque reporting the edict of the Council of Ten (16 February 1709) banning bull-baiting. The plaque originally stood in Corte San Rocco (no longer in existence), which was where such bull-baiting took place; it was moved in 1856. The Confraternity of San Rocco owned various areas of land (such as Corte San Rocco) around its Scuola, as well as land within the parish of Angelo Raffaelle, stretching to the old church of Santa Maria Maggiore and including the present-day Fondamenta dei Cereri.

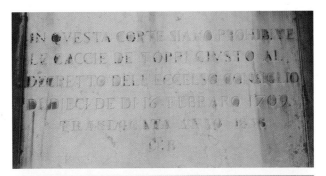

BULL-BAITING

Much appreciated in Venice, the "sport" of bull-baiting took place in the more extensive, open-air areas of the city and involved releasing dogs and bulls into an open space to fight.

On the last Sunday of Carnival, there was even bull-baiting in the courtyard of the Doge's Palace. Such events were also sometimes held in St. Mark's Square as part of the celebrations to honour a visiting prince.

Traditionally, however, the venues were Corte Grande (Giudecca), Campo Santo Stefano, Campo della Bragora, Campo San Geremia, Campo Santa Maria Formosa, Campo Rusolo and Corte San Rocco, though bull-baiting was also known to take place in Ruga degli Orefici (Rialto) and Calle dei Botteri (San Cassiano).

The last recorded bull-baiting took place in Campo Santo Stefano on 22 February 1802. Following the collapse of bleachers overloaded with spectators in front of Palazzo Morosini, this form of "entertainment" was banned once and for all.

OTHER WORKS BY CARLO SCARPA IN VENICE:
The former Olivetti shop, St. Mark's Square;
The entrance to the Architecture University building, at I Tolentini (IUAV);
The Querini Stampalia Foundation;
The wall to the left of the façade of the church of San Sebastiano;
The interior courtyard of the Italian Pavilion at the Biennale Gardens;
Part of the San Michele Cemetery;
The interiors of Ca' d'Oro;
The Monument to the Woman Partisan, near the "Giardini" vaporetto stop.

THE SCARPA ROOM AT THE UNIVERSITY OF CA' FOSCARI

㉑

Dorsoduro 3246
30123 Venice
• Visits by appointment
• Tel: 041 234 83 23
• urp@unive.it

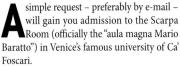

A little- known creation by a great Venetian architect

A simple request – preferably by e-mail – will gain you admission to the Scarpa Room (officially the "aula magna Mario Baratto") in Venice's famous university of Ca' Foscari.

Located on the second *piano nobile* of this palazzo, it has, like the rest of the building, recently been the object of a thorough restoration, completed in 2006.

Accompanied by a member of the university staff, you will have the chance to see one of the least-known achievements of a famous Venetian architect, who remodelled this interior for the first time in the 1930s, then a second time in the 1960s. However, the furnishings, also designed by Scarpa, were not installed until after the architect's death. On the walls are two paintings dating from 1932-33: *The School*, a fine Cubist work by artist Mario de Luigi, and *Venice, Italy and Scholarship* by Mario Sironi, a work in an unadulterated Fascist style. On that subject, the two plinths framing the desk on the lecture platform once held busts of Mussolini.

Another interesting feature of the room is the balcony, which affords superb views of the Grand Canal. The palazzo is located at a wide bend in the canal and thus, more than any other spot, provides full views in either direction. It is no coincidence that during the *Regata Storica*, in September, the floating bleachers for the city authorities are set up here.

Again, upon request, you can visit the rooms housing the "Club Foscari", in the middle of which are the existing remnants of the old floor of the palazzo, which the Doge Foscari had painted in fresco. This would appear to be the sole vestige of this kind of work in the city.

In the Palazzo Giustinian alongside, note the pretty Modernist statue of *Niobe,* weeping for the Italians who have died in the nation's various wars. It is by Napoleon Martinuzzi, a Murano-born sculptor best known for his work in glass (you can see his pieces in the Museo Correr) and for his Monument to The Fallen in the Basilica of Santa Maria e San Donato on Murano.
The palazzo also has rare period chimney pots. Others can be seen on the Palazzo van Axel (open regularly during the various Venice Biennales) and Palazzo Papadopoli on the Grand Canal (not open to the public).

GIUDECCA
& SAN GIORGIO

THE CONCLAVE CHAMBER AT SAN GIORGIO MAGGIORE ❶

Monastery of San Giorgio Maggiore
• Visits possible by asking one of the monks during church opening hours

The only pope elected in Venice

On 29 August 1799, the 83-year-old Pope Pius VI died at Valence in France. A prisoner of the French Directoire, he had been taken there by the retreating army of General MacDonald. Invaded by Napoleon's troops, Rome at that time was in such chaos that the election of a new pope could not be held there, hence the decision to hold the conclave at the monastery of San Giorgio Maggiore in Venice, an Austrian-occupied city where numerous cardinals – including Cardinal Albani, head of the Sacred College – had taken refuge.

It took more than three months of voting, from 13 December 1799 to 14 March 1800, to elect a new pope, Pius VII, who did not leave for Rome until 3 June of that year (when the city was no longer under French occupation). Surprisingly, the man chosen to be pope was Barnaba Chiaramonti, who belonged to the same Benedictine order as the monks of San Giorgio and was the Bishop of Imola at the time. Carefully orchestrated by Napoleon, who had organised a magnificent funeral for the previous pope in January 1800, Chiaramonti's election was something of a slap in the face for Austria, even if the new pope was not particularly hostile to Viennese interests. Indeed, the entire Sacred College of Cardinals had offered the Venetians an abject lesson on how to stand up to the Austrians. Today, you feel a certain emotion when visiting the conclave chamber, which is hidden away on the first floor of the

magnificent monastery complex of San Giorgio Maggiore. The cardinals' chairs, each complete with a name, are still in place, along with a portrait of Pius VII and a neglected work by Carpaccio, *St. George Slaying the Dragon*. You can visit the room by asking one of the monks during church opening hours.

SIGHTS NEARBY

CHAPEL OF THE DEPOSITION ❷

• Sunday mass: 11am

Every Sunday at 11 o'clock, mass is held in the Chapel of the Deposition, which otherwise is closed to the public. The mass gives you the chance to admire Tintoretto's very last painting, *The Deposition*. It is sometimes possible to see the chapel during a visit to the conclave chamber and the sacristy. A space on a stunning scale, the latter is generally closed to the public.

**THE SYMBOLS AND LEGENDS ASSOCIATED WITH THE GONDOLA.
IS THE GONDOLIER A LIVING SYMBOL OF THE BATTLE BETWEEN
ST. GEORGE AND THE DRAGON?**

The first recorded use of the word *gondola* dates from 1094, in a decree by
Doge Vitale Falier that mentions a boat called a *gondulam*. The etymology
of the word is uncertain. Some say it may come from *cymbula* (little boat),
or from the diminutive of *cuncula* (shell). However, it might also come from
such Greek terms for boats as *kundy* or *kuntòhelas*.

Legend has it that in the very depths of the lagoon lived a mysterious
dragon (or large crocodile) which feared no man except the gondolier. Just
as St. George's spear killed the dragon, the gondolier's oar was a permanent
threat to the underwater dragon. The word *gundu* is, in fact, very close
to the word *guntu*, which in the German dialect means "warrior". Whilst
the dragon might sometimes get angry – its breath causing the mists
that enveloped the lagoon – it never rose to the surface because of the
incessant to and fro of the gondoliers.

Note also that the presence of a Benedictine monastery on the island of San
Giorgio Maggiore (St. Giorgio the Great) is no coincidence: the prayers and
canticles of the monks helped to calm the wrath of the legendary monster.

Finally, as it was linked with Venus (which itself was linked with the moon;
see p. 86), it is no coincidence that Venice should have as its characteristic
vessel one that is in the form of a half-moon.

Furthermore, it is also no coincidence that the colour of Venice is red, which
is the colour associated with St. George, whose legend dates back to the
5th century. When he killed the dragon with his spear, some of the blood
was said to have stained his white cloak. And blood/water runs throughout
Venice, with the wounded body of the monster left sunk in the lagoon. So,
perhaps red is also the colour of Venice's victory over the dragon of heresy
and apostasy.

VILLA HERRIOT

Calle Michelangleo 54/P
Vaporetto stop: Zitelle
• Open during the week, notably Tuesday and Thursday from 10am to 1pm

> **The chance of a nice siesta away from the crowds**

Hidden within the narrow streets behind the Zitelle but clearly visible from the other side of the Giudecca, the Villa Herriot is a very interesting neo-Byzantine villa built in 1929.

In effect, made up of two small *palazzi* which the unprepared might mistake for being very ancient indeed, this villa today houses various organisations: the International University of Art (which specialises in restoration), the European Cultural Association, the Venetian Institute for the History of the Resistance and Contemporary Society, and the "Lorenzo Bettini" library of pedagogical material. Discretion or a polite request will gain you admission to the first of the villas; its interior walls are adorned with crossed weapons, making it look rather like a medieval hunting-lodge. The place also has a pleasant garden for a nice, leisurely stroll. Far from the madding crowd of tourists, here you have the chance to rest and enjoy a magnificent view of the southern part of the lagoon.

Standing on the site of a former soap factory, the villa was built in

1929 by the architect and painter Raffaele Mainella as a second home for the Frenchman Herriot. After the death of her husband, Madame Herriot bequeathed the villa to the city of Venice in 1947, on condition that it be used to house a school. Thus, the "Carlo Goldoni" Elementary School came about. Nowadays, the conditions of Madame Herriot's bequest are met by the presence of the International University of Art.

"SOME SAY HOUSES ARE MADE OF WALLS; I SAY THEY ARE MADE OF WINDOWS " (HUNDERTWASSER)

Born in Vienna in 1928, Friedensreich Hundertwasser died in New Zealand in 2000 whilst travelling aboard the *Queen Elizabeth II*.

An artist and architect, his real name was Friedrich Stowasser. Since "sto" means "100" in Czech ("Hundert" in German) and his Christian name, Friedrich, contained the German root word "Frieden", meaning "peace", Stowasser did not hesitate to transform his name so that it quite literally meant "The Kingdom of Peace – One Hundred Waters". In 1990, he proclaimed himself the "physician of architecture" (a title that reflected his own particular approach to his work).

Hundertwasser had a profoundly ecological vision of architecture. Some of his buildings have trees at the windows (see his famous Hundertwasser House in Vienna) and roof terraces, and some are even entirely enclosed in plant life (like the Thermal Spa Hotel in Rogner Bad Blumau). Pure geometrical lines were banished and surfaces were covered in bright colours.

Hundertwasser had no qualms about voicing his ideas and theories loud and clear. His praise of mildew is famous: "Homo, Humus, Humanitas. Humus is the real black gold. The smell of humus is the smell of god, the smell of resurrection, the smell of immortality" (*The Sacred Shit Manifesto*, Pfäffikon, 1979).

In 1960, he organised the *Action Orties* in Paris, inviting the public to try nettle soup. "Did you know it is easy to live without money? All you have to do is eat nettle soup. Nettles grow all over the place, and they don't cost anything. Eat them!"

Hundertwasser also drew up a manifesto proclaiming "the right to windows". In his opinion, "A home-owner should have the right to lean out of his window and change whatever he wants to about the external wall, as far as his hand can reach. From the street one should be able to see that this is where a human being lives, someone different from everyone else."

A fine new edition of *A Garden In Venice* was published in 2003 (Publisher: Frances Lincoln). It includes engravings that are reminiscent of *Poliphilo's Dream of the Strife of Love*, the romance published in Renaissance Venice.

WHAT IS LEFT OF THE GARDEN OF EDEN ?

Located behind the men's prison in Giudecca, the legendary Garden of Eden is one of the best-kept secrets in Venice and probably one of the city's richest sources of urban myths, perhaps partly due to its name, which it owes to its first owner, Frederick Eden, the great-uncle of British Prime Minister Sir Anthony Eden.*

By one of those miraculous strokes of luck sometimes enjoyed in Venice, we had the immense pleasure of visiting this garden recently and so can immediately refute the often-repeated claim that the garden is in a totally wild state, the statues have disappeared and the house is in ruins. True, the grounds may not be wonderfully kept, but they are tended a few times a year by gardeners who tear out the weeds that threaten to overgrow the place. As for the house, it is well-maintained, though there is the one – sizeable – eyesore of a horrible concrete addition on the first-floor terrace. Curiously enough, the façade is adorned with three flags. One has a combination of the Star of David and the green crescent of Islam (a symbol of peace**?), another has three Maori figures from New Zealand, and the third has a spiral (apparently the personal symbol of the architect, Hundertwasser).

And the statues? Well, they are still there, even if – as far as could be seen – they are of little artistic interest.

Nevertheless, with the exception of the house, the property does seem to be in pretty poor shape. The Hundertwasser Foundation, which inherited it from the last owner, fanciful artist and architect Friedensreich Hundertwasser (see opposite page), simply does the bare minimum to maintain the garden. And one last myth to quash: the Garden of Eden is not up for sale. Furthermore, in order to discourage the curious, it is not available for rent or for visits.

It was in 1884 that Sir Frederick Eden bought an old outbuilding of the Convent of Santa Croce.*** Frequented by such artists and writers as Proust, Cocteau, Rilke and Aragon, the garden became the property of Princess Aspasia, the Danish-born wife of Alexander, King of the Hellenes, in the 1920s. The marriage took place in 1919, but Aspasia was left a widow just a few years later when her husband was bitten by his favourite monkey.

Hundertwasser bought the garden in 1972 and, until his death in 2000, showed a very original approach to gardening. In his own words, "one shouldn't trim, but leave everything to nature; nurture spontaneous growth and leave everything to sprout without ever cutting back. There is an urgent need to negotiate with our gardens, to sign a peace treaty." Accused of criminal negligence, he responded, "People who understand nothing go around saying that I am letting the garden go wild. Not at all: I don't like wild plants. I am always re-bedding the nettles and brambles. Look how harmonious these greens are! And those thickets of branches look like embroidery!"

* And a cousin to the Sir William Eden who was involved in an acrimonious court case with Whistler over a portrait of his wife.
** The name Frederick includes the root "Frieden", which means "peace" in German (see opposite).
*** The epic story of the creation of the garden is recounted in the charming book *A Garden in Venice*, published for the first time in London in 1903.

THE CAPUCHIN MONASTERY VEGETABLE GARDEN

Giudecca 195
• Entrance to the left of the Church of Il Redentore
• Telephone Father Cesare, between 1pm and 8pm
• Tel: 041 5224348

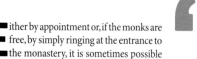

Town and country

E ither by appointment or, if the monks are free, by simply ringing at the entrance to the monastery, it is sometimes possible to visit the vast vegetable garden that occupies more than a hectare of land behind the church

of Il Redentore. Extending to the other side of the Giudecca, it affords superb views of the southern lagoon and the islands of San Clemente and La Grazia. The visit varies substantially depending on the personality of the monk who acts as your guide.

> The Capuchin monastery also has a very fine old pharmacy that may sometimes be visited by appointment.

SIGHTS NEARBY

THE ANATOMICAL BUSTS IN THE SACRISTY OF IL REDENTORE

Church of Il Redentore
• A visit can be arranged by appointment (Monday to Saturday, 10am to 5pm) by telephoning Father Cesare between 1pm and 8pm
• Tel: 041 5224348

Along with its numerous reliquaries, the sacristy of the church of Il Redentore contains an amazing collection of wax busts modelled in the second half of the 19th century, a period when a substantial number of Capuchins were either beatified or canonised. These saints and blessed martyrs are depicted here, including: Felix of Cantalice, Fidelis of Sigmaringen, Joseph of Leonessa, Seraphin of Montegranaro, Bernard of Corleone, Lorenzo of Brindisi, Bernard of Offida, Crispin of Viterbo, Angelo of Acri, Nicolas Molinari and Veronica Giuliani (of the Poor Clares, the female equivalent of the mendicant Order of the Capuchins). The twelfth bust is, therefore, rather anachronistic, as it depicts St. Francis of Assisi (1181-1226), the founder of the Franciscan Order to which the Capuchins belong.

> The Capuchins owe their name to the pointed cowl (*capuche*) they wear. In 1525, an Observant Friar had a vision of St. Francis of Assisi wearing a habit with this type of cowl. This vision would ultimately lead to a split with his original Order, the Capuchins themselves being officially recognised by Pope Paul III in 1536.

CANTINE MENSA INTERAZIENDALE ❻

Giudecca 554
• Tel: 041 2411413
• Open Monday to Friday 11:45am to 2pm
• Fixed menu: € 12

Lunch
in a hidden-away
boatyard

This is not "La Mistra", the restaurant in a large boatyard on the Giudecca featured in some guidebooks. Located in a quiet alleyway behind the Giudecca waterfront, the *Cantine Interaziendale* is housed in the small Giovanni Toffolo boatyard, which overlooks the lagoon to the south of the island. Well off the usual tourist routes, this place offers a welcoming atmosphere and a real-life ambience (the customers are local residents or those who work in the neighbouring boatyards), and the cooking is simple but good.

Well into autumn, you can also lunch "on the terrace" in the sunlight. A couple of tables are set up outside amongst the new or repaired boats so that you can enjoy a very relaxed terrace atmosphere.

The 11-euro menu comprises a hors-d'oeuvre, a plate of pasta, a main meat course, mineral water, wine, coffee and fruit.

A good deal.

THE OLD ROPE FACTORY ON THE GIUDECCA
Giudecca 595

A few steps from the Palanca vaporetto stop, a private alleyway at number 595 was, right up to the 1990s, the location of the last rope factory in Venice. The *Corderia Inio* (named after the owners) moved here from Santa Lucia (Cannaregio) in 1848-1850, when numerous other workshops and industrial factories did the same. The new workshop ran the entire width of the Giudecca, from the Giudecca canal to the side overlooking the southern part of the lagoon. The *corderia* also had a stable and its own cow, which was harnessed to the small cart used in making the ropes. Fed on the grass that was still plentiful on the island, the cow was also a source of milk. In the 1930s, the rope works employed up to 30 people.

THE MARKET OF THE WOMEN'S PRISON ON GIUDECCA

8

Fondamenta delle Convertite
Giudecca 54N
• Vaporettto stop: Palanca
• Market every Thursday morning from 9am to 10am

> *When women prisoners turn greengrocer ...*

If you stroll along the Fondamenta delle Convertite at around 9 to 10 o'clock on a Thursday morning, you will see a surprising sight. Outside the gate of the Giudecca Women's Prison there are a dozen or so people patiently – or almost patiently – waiting in line. On the quayside itself is a display of fruit and vegetables and a pair of scales. What everyone around here calls "the prisoners' market" is about to begin.

The real show is in the queue itself, with these Giudecca grannies jostling for position, lying about who arrived first and sometimes making use of the odd elbow or empty shopping-basket to prove their point. The stakes are high, because, unlike a normal market, this one does not guarantee that there is plenty for everyone, so there is the risk that after having queued for 30 minutes or more you end up getting next to nothing.

And it's difficult to wait patiently. The magnificent aubergines fresh from the prison's biological garden seem to be disappearing all too quickly. Those wonderful courgettes you had planned for lunch are being snapped up by Giudecca grannies who jump the queue with supreme nonchalance. When you arrived, you had a clearly planned lunch menu in mind, and you stand there gradually re-working it as the fruit and vegetables you wanted are snapped up….

Everyone seems good-humoured, the chatter seems friendly – but it's cut-throat out there! Claiming she had already asked if there was anyone else who wanted apples, the woman behind you is suddenly filling her bag with the very last of those great apples you had your eye on. Don't let her get away with it! Insist upon your rights! The apples are delicious and well worth the confrontation. The folklore is fine, but it's the wonderful produce you're there for – entirely organic and much cheaper than elsewhere.

A good plan, if you have the time, is to get there a little before 9 o'clock. You will have to wait a little longer, but you will be the first and will thus avoid the hostilities which generally begin around 9:15. Or you could try getting there around the end of the market – 9:30 to 9:45 – when there are sometimes a few good surprises left.

THE REMAINS OF INDUSTRIAL VENICE

It is difficult to imagine nowadays, but Venice was once home to sizeable industrial facilities, some traces of which still remain.

The *Fabbrica Birra Venezia* (Venezia Brewery) originally stood in the Santa Chiara area near Piazzale Roma. Forgotten for decades, its *Venezia* beer has once again reappeared on the market. In 1902, the factory was transferred to the island of Giudecca (alongside the Mulino Stucky), thus making way for the Dreher Brewery (on a site now developed as housing, see photo). The *Cotonificio Venezianto* (Venice Cotton Works) was one of the most important textile factories in the region. Located in the Santa Marta area, it was active from its foundation in 1883 right up to the 1960s. Today, the premises are occupied by facilities of the University of Ca' Foscari and the Venice Architecture Faculty. The *Macello Comunale* (City Slaughterhouse) in San Giobbe in Cannaregio was opened in 1843, when the Austrians centralised an activity that had previously been carried out at different points in the city. It, too, has been converted into university premises.

Located near Piazzale Roma, the *Manifattura Tabacchi* (Tobacco Works) was opened in 1876 and was one of the largest factories in the city, both in terms of workforce and turnover. It now houses part of the Venetian law courts. The *Saffa* match factory (a leading Italian brand right up to the 1950s) was located in Cannaregio, near the station. Some traces of it are still visible, even after the development of the buildings as housing in 1981-1985.

With Venice's annexation by the Kingdom of Italy in 1866, a number of foreign entrepreneurs began to invest in the city. The Swede **Teodoro Hasselquist**, managing director of the *Società Veneta di Navigazione a Vapore Lagunare*, was responsible for the first steamboat links between the city centre, Chioggia and the various islands of the lagoon. The *De Frigiere-Cottin-Mongolfier* company built the city's first gasworks at San Francesco della Vigna (Castello) in 1841. You can still see the imposing metal structures near the church. The *Compagnie Générale des Eaux pour l'Etranger* was responsible for the city's drinking water (1875). It built the new water plant at Sant'Andrea della Zirada near the shipping port (*Stazione Marittima*).

This was also the period when the Spanish designer **Fortuny** set up his famous textile works at Palazzo Fortuny. Later, at the beginning of the 20th century, the factory was transferred to the Giudecca, where it still stands. Englishman Henry Gilbert Neville, the son of the engineer who had the metal bridges over the Grand Canal built at the Accademia and opposite the church of Gli Scalzi, became the owner of the *Privilegiata e Premiata Fonderia Veneta*, a foundry alongside San Rocco that employed a workforce of around 100 men. After being in operation for fifty years, the factory was dismantled in 1905, and the vast area of around 14,000 m^2 between the apse of the church of San Rocco and Rio della Saccole (San Polo) was divided up and developed as low-cost housing. The sole trace of the industrial past of the area is the name of the alleyway behind the church of San Rocco, *Calle della Fondaria* (Foundry Alley).

During this period, numerous industrial businesses were established on the island of Giudecca, where there was no shortage of space. Here, within the building of the old church of Santi Cosma e Damiano, the German **Herion** set up a factory to produce thread and textiles. The place would generate a number of other relatively hi-tech industries. Another German business, **Junghans**, set up factories to produce precision instruments (watches, timers and detonators for grenades in wartime). The *Junghans* premises have recently been converted into housing, complete with a theatre and university residence hall.

At the western end of the island, Stucky, a Swiss businessman, built

the imposing neo-Gothic mill that still bears his name. Designed by an architect from Hanover, this massive structure in Northern style was initially greeted with little enthusiasm, however Stucky found a way of winning over the locals. When he threatened to sack his entire workforce, the city council immediately withdrew its objections and approved the project. The mill was in operation until 1955 and has now been converted into a luxury hotel complex.

AN ISLAND OF CATTLE AND FILM STARS: *CINECITTÀ* ON THE GIUDECCA

When the Second World War broke out, Venice put itself forward as a possible new *Cinecittà*, providing a unique setting that was also free from the risk of bombing raids.

Directly behind the Mulino Stucky, the Rome production company **Scalera Film** set up its studios in what had previously been cowsheds for more than 150 head of cattle. Scalera would make a total of 13 films there, continuing to be active for a few years after the war. Most notably, it produced such full-length feature films as *Ruy Blas* (1947) by Pierre Billon and Jean Cocteau, which was based on Victor Hugo's novel. It also did post-production work for such famous films as Orson Welles' *Othello* (1952), Luchino Visconti's *Senso* (1954) and David Lean's *Summertime* (1955), which starred Katherine Hepburn. Today, there is almost no trace of these studios, as the area has been redeveloped as housing.

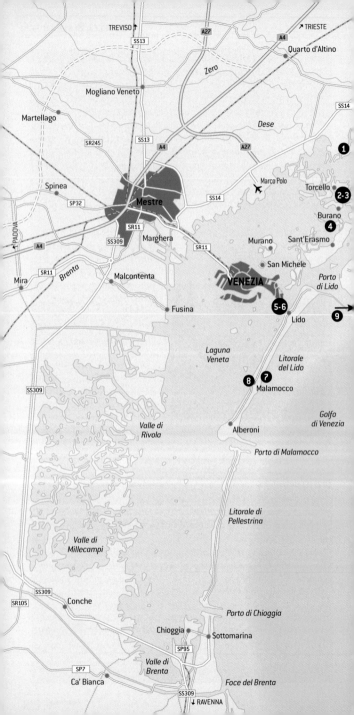

AROUND THE LAGOON

"DA TONI" RESTAURANT

- Open daily without reservations; closed in January
- Tel: 338 8211229
- Toni speaks Italian and English
- € 35 per person, wine included
- How to get there: from the mainland, Toni can pick you up at Porto Grande in his boat (20-minute boat ride); otherwise, you have to own or rent your own boat to get there

A magical journey...

Hidden away in the north of the lagoon behind Torcello, Da Toni's is one of the best-kept secrets in Venice, and a magical place. The very journey to get there takes you through some of the most beautiful parts of the lagoon, to an area that is totally unspoilt, giving some idea of what the lagoon must have been like even before the foundation of Venice itself. Indeed, from the terrace of the restaurant, the only buildings that are visible are the bell-towers of Torcello and Burano.

The restaurant – if that term can be used here – is a simple fisherman's cabin of some 12 m², with a terrace of the same area, all of it resting on wooden piles. It stands on a natural canal that Toni still uses for fishing: several times a day he lowers the *bilancia* that holds his immense net (400 m²) suspended over the canal to capture any passing fish. The fare could not be fresher, because a good part of what he serves is the fish caught in this traditional manner, of which Toni is one of the few remaining practitioners.

Simple but tasty, the cuisine is typically Venetian and uses solely fish and shellfish: fish soup (excellent), mussels, clams, crab, fried fish, and more – all served with red wine and Prosecco* according to taste. Another immense advantage of the place for those who are familiar with the lagoon is that there are no mosquitoes. The almost permanent breeze (a very attractive feature in the summer heat) is strong enough to get rid of them.

A piece of advice: if possible, ask to be seated on the terrace. It is much less interesting inside.

Without needing a boating licence, you can hire your own boat to travel around Venice and the lagoon from www.brussaisboat.it/. The office is at the entrance to the Canareggio canal, near the Ponte delle Guglie.

---

* Prosecco: a sparkling white wine. The Italian equivalent of champagne, only sweeter and less of a luxury.

THE *CASA DI BEPI* ON BURANO

Via Al Gottolo, 339. Burano
For information: info@casabepi.it

> **Bepi Suà's kaleidoscopic house**

I n a small side street off Burano's main thoroughfare (Via Galuppi) stands a very unusual house. The powerfully contrasting colours of its façade create a kaleidoscopic effect that could have been produced straight from a painter's palette.

The building belonged to Giuseppe Toselli, better known on the island as *Bepi Suà* (Sweaty Bepi). Born on Burano in 1920, Bepi sold sweets. A great lover of films, he also worked as a projectionist at the Cinema Falvin in the 1940s. When the cinema closed down, he inherited the large hand-wound projector. On summer evenings, he would use it to project great film classics in the courtyard in front of his technicolour home, the local residents bringing out their chairs to appreciate these free screenings of the adventures and loves of bygone stars.

Bepi's other great passion was painting, to which he gave full – and imaginative – vent in painting his house. Everyone still remembers him sitting there on a stool, working with all the concentration of a monk illuminating a manuscript. Thanks to the changing artistic inspiration of its owner, the house often changed colour. Bepi loved to work on his "creature", coming up with new ideas and continually adding new details and decorations.

After his death (in 2002) the new owner entirely restored the house, using the same technique that Bepi had used in order to give new lustre to the colours of the *maestro*'s most unusual home.

THE COLOURS OF BURANO

Some claim that the origins of the coloured houses of Burano stretch far back in time. During the Middle Ages, it is said, those houses which were infected with the plague were disinfected with white quicklime, whilst the houses that were spared were painted in all the colours of the rainbow (the same ones that the fishermen used to identify their boats). A further advantage of these colours was that, when the lagoon was foggy, the returning fishermen could identify their homes more easily.

THE *CASA DEL PROFESSORE*

❸

Via Terranova, 79
Burano

Located in a less-frequented part of the island, the house at number 79 Via Terranova strikes a note of sober contrast on an island famous for its colour.

> *A house without colour on the most colourful island in the lagoon*

The building was home to artist Remigio Barbaro, known as *Il Professore*, who lived here until his death in 2005. A sculptor of some renown, he was also known as "the hermit of the island", his reserve leading him to shun mondaine social occasions. Another nickname earned by his simple and frugal lifestyle was "the Franciscan sculptor". Indeed, he had a famous line from St. Francis' *Canticle of All Creatures* engraved on his house: LAUDATO SIE MI SIGNORE CUM TUCTE LE TUE CREATURE (Praised be thee, O Lord, with all thy creatures).

It is no accident that the emblematic statue of *Il Poverello di Assisi* stands in the centre of the small garden before Barbaro's house, along with a plaster copy of the bust of composer Baldassare Galuppi and a powerful work of sculpture in terracotta depicting a man hung upside down. The latter is a replica of the Monument to the Dead in the town of Santa Lucia di Piave.

The house, which unfortunately is not open to visitors at the moment, also contains other works by the artist. *Il Professore*, in fact, loved to surround himself with *objets d'art* and precious collections of works, forming a random assembly of drawings, sketches and sculpture in terracotta or bronze. In a career spanning more than 70 years, he created a sort of home-studio, a veritable museum of his work in various media, each one of which is imbued with a powerful sense of spirituality and discernable experience.

When Barbaro died in 2005, the contents of the house were catalogued, the first stage in the creation of a home-museum – a project that was very dear to the artist's heart.

In Burano, the main works by *Il Professore* can be seen in Campo Baldassare Galuppi (where the original bust of the famous 18th-century composer stands) and on the boat-stop quayside (a statue of a young woman entitled *Waiting for Peace*). Other sculptures can be found locally at the Procuratie of St. Mark's, Santa Fosca church, the Torcello Basilica, the monastery of San Francesco del Deserto, Cavallino, the entrance to the Mazzorbo cemetery, Mestre, the Venice Lido and the island of San Michele. Pieces can also be found in numerous private collections in Italy and abroad – in London, for example.

A SPIRITUAL RETREAT ON SAN FRANCESCO DEL DESERTO ❹

Island of San Francesco del Deserto
30142 Burano
• www.isola-sanfrancescodeldeserto.it
• E-mail : info@isola-sanfrancescodeldeserto.it
• Visits possible upon booking: Tuesday to Sunday from 9am to 11am and from 3pm to 5pm
• Reservations for spiritual retreats (in Italian): 041 5286863
Length of stays: from Friday to Sunday or from Tuesday to Thursday
Around 30 monastic cells available for retreats

Away from the crowds... The island of San Francesco del Deserto is a truly exceptional place, probably one of the most beautiful in the whole of the Venetian lagoon.

Guided tours, along with a mass of visitors setting off from nearby Burano, only let you visit a small part of the island and give no idea of the whole magic of the place. If you really want to gain an insight into the island and the life of the monks living here, you should go on a retreat for a few days.

After making the reservation by phone (in Italian), you are picked up by boat on Burano by a monk from the monastery; there is no public transport service to the island. Organised around the seven religious offices of the day, a retreat here is a full immersion in monastic life. However, between those seven offices you are totally free to pass the time as you wish. Given the beauty of the island, most of those on retreat choose to go on walks, or meditate in

the remarkable garden where hundreds of aligned cypress trees provide charming areas of shade. The garden also affords views of a number of nearby islands (Burano with Venice in the background, Sant'Erasmo, and the private island of Crevan), providing panoramas that are another inspiration for reverie. One key moment of the visit is a nocturnal walk around the island bathed in moonlight.

St. Francis of Assisi is said to have lived on this island in 1220 or 1224.

SOME PRACTICAL ADVICE

Avoid the summer months of June-September. Besides the heat, you would have to cope with almost unbearable quantities of mosquitoes.

Contrary to the Rule of Benedictine monasteries, that of Franciscan organisations does not impose silence. You can talk at meals, in the garden and with the monks you meet. Those looking for silence are strongly advised to come either during the week or in winter time (when the fog over the lagoon adds to the mysterious magic of the place).

Women are admitted and you can come as a couple, even if each of you will sleep in a separate room.

Depending upon the numbers present, there is also either a collective commentary of a passage from the Bible or a personal meeting with a monk each day. All of these are held in Italian, the only language the monks speak.

In theory, visitors are expected to attend all the religious offices celebrated by the community (a total of seven a day).

CROSSED ARMS AND THE STIGMATA: A SYMBOL OF THE FRANCISCAN ORDER

In the monastery of San Francesco del Deserto as well as in all the places associated with the Franciscan Order – for example, the church of San Francesco della Vigna in Venice itself – one frequently finds the symbol of two crossed arms.

When you look more closely, you see that the hands bear the stigmata, the traces of the wounds borne both by Christ and St. Francis of Assisi. The arm in a sleeve is that of the saint, whilst the bare arm is that of Christ.

THE STIGMATA OF ST. FRANCIS OF ASSISI

The stigmata are the traces of the wounds inflicted upon Christ during his Passion and Crucifixion.

Though the existence of the phenomenon is still contested, there are numerous famous cases of the inexplicable appearance on a person's body of the marks of these wounds, principally on the hands and feet.

The most famous case of all is that of St. Francis of Assisi, who in 1224 is said to have had a vision of a six-winged seraph hovering in the air before him, his body nailed to a cross. When the vision ended, St. Francis became aware of the apparition of stigmata on his own hands and feet.

Other famous cases of stigmata involve St. Catherine of Siena, St. John of God, Padre Pio, Marthe Robin and St. Gemma Galgani (see *Secret Tuscany*).

In our own time, Father Elia at the Calvi monastery in Umbria (not far from Rome) receives the stigmata of the Passion every year during Lent.

It is to be noted that St. Francis was the only case of someone preserving the marks of the stigmata after burial.

TAU: A FRANCISCAN SYMBOL AND A SIGN OF DIVINE FAVOUR

The various chapels that open to the left of the main church all have discreet glass doors marked with the letter tau.

The tau is, in effect, a symbol of Christ's Cross, which was rediscovered by St. Francis of Assisi.

It originates in the Old Testament Book of Ezekiel, chapter 9, where it is said that those who are marked with the tau will be spared divine retribution. (In the translation of the Jerusalem Bible, this information is given in the commentary.) Another allusion comes in the Apocalypse. Tau is also the last letter of the Hebrew alphabet.

THE TREE OF ST. FRANCIS OF ASSISI

St. Francis is said to have lived on the island in 1220 or 1224, during which time he planted a cypress tree that was then uprooted during a violent storm in the 18th century. The trunk of that tree is in the grotto rebuilt in that same century; it is located in the part of the monastery reserved to the monks and those on retreat. Another part of the tree was placed alongside the chapel of Father Bernardino, to the left of the main church.

THE OLD PHARMACY OF SAN SERVOLO

• Visits by appointment • Tel: 041 5240119

Unjustly neglected, the pharmacy on the island of San Servolo is well worth
a visit for its fine collection of jars decorated with the Lion of St. Mark, and
the recently restored bookcases in solid walnut. In 1716, during war with the
Turks, the monastery on the island was converted into a military hospital
run by the monks of the Fatebenefratelli monastery. The pharmacy was
reorganised, with the addition of a garden of simples, a workshop for the
preparation of medicines and the rich library you can still see today.

WHAT REMAINS OF VENICE'S OLD PHARMACIES?

Known as *spezierie*, the city's pharmacies were refined places adorned with paintings, statues, gilded leather and carved wood furnishings. Only four have remained well preserved, one of which is on **San Servolo** (see opposite). The one known as *Ai do San Marchi* had fine carved fittings in walnut and majolica jars for such substances as *Oleum Vulpin*. It used to stand in San Stin, but in 1935 was bequeathed to Ca' Rezzonico; the restored interiors can now be seen on the third floor of the museum, complete with workshop, back-shop area and the *speziaria* proper (for information, tel: 041 2410100).

The **All'Ercole d'Oro** pharmacy at Santa Fosca is also worth a detour. Its splendid decorations and antique jars and containers make this a place where time seems to have stood still (see page 235). Unfortunately, the 16th-century pharmacy of **I Cappuccini** on the Giudecca is not open to the public.

Other pharmacies have maintained parts of their original fixtures and fittings. The one known as **Alla Gatta** (on Fondamenta degli Ormesini) has old-fashioned scales, a mortar and a curious collection of thermometers and densimeters, as well as 19th-century jars and late 18th-century furnishings created by craftsman Samuel Cohen. The pharmacy **Alla Colonna e mezza** (in Campo San Polo) still has its mosaics and its late 19th-century decor, complete with two statues of Galen and Aesculapius, the fathers of ancient medicine. The original name – "Alle due Colonne" – was changed by law in 1586 because there was already another of the same name that specialised in the production of *Teriaca Fina* (see p. 44). Now, outside the original **Alle due Colonne** (in San Canciano) you can see the hole in the ground used to hold the mortar for pounding the ingredients of that famous medicine (see p. 42 - 45).

The premises of various old pharmacies have been "recycled". **All'Aquila**

Nigra, in San Zulian, was gutted to make way for the Cartier shop; **Alla Dogaressa**, in San Cassian, is a florist's; and the **Farmacia Italo-Inglese** in San Fantin was the official premises of the State Mint before becoming a shop. At Rialto, the site of the famous *spezieria* **Alla Testa d'Oro** (see p. 17) is now occupied by a shop of tourist knick-knacks. The wonderful pharmacy **Al Redentore** at St. Mark's (Calle Larga San Marco, 412-413) has also disappeared, even if the counter and some of the old decor have survived. The place now houses an art glass gallery.

THE MUSEUM OF THE PSYCHIATRIC HOSPITAL ❻

Island of San Servolo
• Fondazione San Servolo IRSESC (Istituto per le Ricerche e per gli Studi sull'Emarginazione Sociale e Culturale)
• Fax 041 2765460
• E-mail: servilio@provincia.venezia.ir
• www.fondazionesanservolo.it
• Guided tours by appointment at 041 5240119. Phone Sunday to Friday from 9:30am to 3:30pm • www.codesscultura.it
• Guided tours on specific themes relating to the psychiatric hospital (Monday and Wednesday) upon prior booking at 041 5264909 and 041 2765451. Phone Monday to Friday from 9:30am to 3pm

A museum of madness

Following the promulgation of what became known as the "Basaglia Law", after the name of the politician who introduced this bill to close all state-run mental asylums, the complex at San Servolo was redeveloped. It is now possible to visit the library, pharmacy (see p. 386) and the museum of the psychiatric hospital, where the archives have been carefully reassembled and catalogued. The collection contains registers, clinical dossiers and more than a hundred medical instruments used at the time within the asylum.

On the ground floor is a reconstruction of the original anatomy theatre, complete with 19th-century medical instruments and the stone slab used for autopsies. Note the extraordinary collection of skulls and encephala that have been *plastinated*, a special preservation technique that was developed at the University of Padua.

The therapy section traces the development in methods of treating mental patients. There are herbal medicines created in the island's famous *spezieria* (pharmacy), instruments for hydrotherapy and electric-shock treatment, and equipment inspired by an approach that was more concerned with patient "morale" (centred around the value of work and the beneficial effects of music).

Along with instruments used in scientific analysis and research, there is a section that illustrates the means used to restrain "difficult" patients: a grim-looking assortment of leather wrist straps and belts, protective gloves, handcuffs and strait-jackets.

Like most mental asylums of the day, San Servolo made ample use of segregation and isolation – auxiliary measures that were part of an oppressive, authoritarian regime that focused more on detention than treatment.

FROM AN ISLAND OF MADMEN TO A CULTURAL CENTRE

After the fall of the Venetian Republic in 1797, the island of San Servolo – previously a monastery and military hospital – became the home of "The Central Male and Female Lunatic Asylum for the Venetian Provinces", serving an area from Dalmatia to the Tyrol.

Known to the Venetians themselves simply as "The Island of Madmen", it had all the services it needed to function: a vegetable garden (kept by the patients), ironwork and woodwork shops, a printing shop, a shoemakers, a clothing factory, a mill and even a pasta factory.

After being a "European Centre for Architectural Restoration", the buildings on the island are now home to the Venice International University and host cultural events and international conferences.

THE DRIFTWOOD SCULPTURES OF MALAMOCCO

❼

The Murazzi seawalls

Sculptures thrown up by the sea

Not far from the village of Malamocco, going towards the Murazzi sea defences, can be found strange sculptures made from materials thrown up by the sea; the larger pieces were obviously left after storms. These works comprise not only branches and tree trunks, which have been curiously polished and fashioned by the action of the water, but also old clothes, torn fragments of fishing nets, floats, and other abandoned and forgotten objects. Created with a real artistic sense, the compositions are unfortunately ephemeral in nature, as they are often destroyed by the winter storms. However, at each new season, the materials that have once again been thrown up by the sea are used to produce entirely new creations.

Right at the end of Alberoni beach (after Malamocco) is a small kiosk near the mouth of the entrance to the lagoon. Here, too, the owner uses driftwood to create works during the course of the summer. There has even been an open-air exhibition of the pieces near the Rocchetta lighthouse.

SIGHTS NEARBY

PIECES OF ANCIENT CERAMICS FROM METAMAUCO

❽

Permanent Archaeological Exhibition
Palazzo del Podestà, Malamocco – Lido
• Visits by appointment: *Associazione Equipe Veneziana di Ricerca*
• Tel: 347 4144035

The exhibition in Palazzo del Podestà at Malamocco introduces you to the history of the ancient city of Metamauco. It was founded in 601 BC and was one of the first centres of power in the Venetian Lagoon. In AD 742, it even became the seat of a bishopric, which in 811 was transferred to Rivo Alto (Rialto), a site less vulnerable to invasion. It is said that Metamauco disappeared after exceptionally high seas in 1106, with a *Nova Metamauco* (the modern-day Malamocco) then being rebuilt not far from the site. The exhibition is dedicated primarily to ceramics, with a series of objects that date from a period running from the end of the 13th to the end of the 15th century. These ceramics were discovered during archaeological excavations in Piazza Maria Assunta in Malamocco. This permanent exhibition – the first part of a more extensive programme that will also include a library – bears witness to the historical importance of Metamauco, one of the oldest settlements within the lagoon.

AN UNDERWATER CRIB OFF THE VENICE LIDO

9

• Coordinated by WRMAC
Latitude: 45°21.936 N
Longitude: 12°26.608 E

> *The Holy Family on the seabed*

Venice never seems to do things the way other places do. For example, since 2005, it has been home to an amazing underwater Christmas crib.

On 23 December 2005, the divers of the *Club dei Moi* used steel cables to fix a small crib to the stern of a sunken ship. Measuring 50 cm by 50 cm, this depiction of the Holy Family is a copy of the crib that is displayed every year in the church of San Giobbe in Cannaregio. It was made by an artist who is a friend of the members of the club. Before being fixed to the wreck, the Holy Family was blessed in a short ceremony on shore that was held to commemorate a diver to whose memory it is dedicated.

The wreck itself is a Yugoslav merchant ship, the WRMAC (also referred to as the VRMAC or the WURMAK). Measuring some 80 metres in length, this vessel now lies roughly 17 metres deep about three miles offshore from the lighthouse at the San Nicoletto opening into the lagoon. The cargo ship was on its way from Croatia when it sank on 26 January 1961. Heavy seas raised by the violent north wind (the *Bora*) had shifted the massive load of over 1,300 tons of pyrites in the ship's hold. Of the 22-man crew, the helmsman and first mate were killed and two other men were declared lost at sea.

Given that it lay in shallow water close to the coast, the wreck soon became a sort of exercise facility for keen divers and an inevitable part in the training of any new enthusiast. Its ruined hull is now coated in seaweed and provides a home to a curious mix of marine fauna, from sea horses to scorpion fish, John Dory, sea bass and conger eels.

WHAT IS THE *CLUB DEI MOI* ?

The *Club dei Moi* is a group of Venetian diving enthusiasts who share a passion for underwater exploration. They make about one hundred dives a year on average. The club takes its name from *moi*, a small caplin fish that is frequently found living near wrecks. Served with polenta, these *moi* once formed the staple diet of local fishermen. They were not worth enough to take to market, so they ended up on the family table.
Polenta e moi is now recognised as a typical Venetian dish and is served in some restaurants that specialise in traditional local cuisine.

THEMATIC INDEX

ARCHITECTURE

CASINI

CURIOSITIES

HISTORY

THEMATIC INDEX

HOTELS / RESTAURANTS – SHOPPING

INSCRIPTIONS – GRAFFITI

LEGENDS

MUSEUMS

MUSIC

PAINTING

PHARMACIES – HEALTH

RELIGION

THEMATIC INDEX

SCIENCE – EDUCATION

SCUOLE (CONFRATERNITIES)

SECRET GARDENS

SYMBOLISM

TOPONYMY

TRACES OF OLD VENICE

TRADITIONS

Acknowledgements:
Thomas Jonglez: Thanks to Vitor Manuel Adrião, Giulio Alessandri, Bianca and Gilberto Arrivabene, Lucien d'Azay, Jacopo Barbarigo, Andrea Bastianello, Emmanuel Bérard, Toto Bergamo Rossi, Frank Billaud, Serena and Carlo Bombasei, Philippe Bonfils, don Natalino Bonazza, Isabelle and Louis-Marie Bourgeois, Giovanni and Letizia Bovio, Nani Bovolo, Umberto Branchini, Marie and Brandino Brandolini, Sabina Braxton, Séverine de Breteuil, Constance Breton, Catherine Buyse, Guillaume de Calan, Francesco Calzolaio, Barbara and Alberto Carrera, Danielle and Luc Carton, Karina and Pierre Casanova, Barbara Cavalieri, Elena Cimenti, Philippe Coffin, Angelo Comotto, Matteo Corvino, Frédéric Court, Marina Crivellari, Paolo and Aud Cuniberti, Frédéric Dib, Driss, cavalier Duilio, Gabrielle and Jean-Marie Degueldre, Anita Dolfus, Véronique Drucker, Enrichetta Emo, Franco Filippi, Antonio Foscari, Orsola Foscari, Massimo Foscato, Antonella Fumo, Alessandra and Filippo Gaggia, Irene Galifi, Gabrielle Gamberini, Jacques Garance, Paolo Gasparotto, Cristina Ghezzo, Benedetta and Giulio Gianelli, Gica, Giovanni and Servane Giol, Cintzia and Marco Giol, Donata Grimani, Romaine Guérin, Renzo Inio, Antoine Jonglez, Aurélie Jonglez, Guillaume and Stéphanie Jonglez, Timothée Jonglez, Isabelle Jordan, Frédéric Jousset, Koko and Samuel of Ca'Zenobio, Ziva Kraus, Giulio Lattuada, Hugues Le Gallais, Olivier Lexa, Sophie and Xavier Lièvre, Jean-Christophe Loizeau, Marco Loredan, Michelle Lovric, Marina Magrini, Marylène Malbert, Sylvie Mamy, Letizia Mangilli, Umberto Marcello, Veronica and Luca Marzotto, Monseigneur Meneguolo, Camille Merlin, Viretta and Massimo Micheluzzi, Marie-Louise Mills, Roger de Montebello, Sigried and Xavier de Montrond, Fabio Moretti, Jane and Francesco da Mosto, Élisabeth and Michel de la Mothe, Philippe Orain, Victoire and Olivier de Panafieu, Emanuela Pasti, Francesca Pasti, Tommaso Pezzato, David Philips, Dorit Raines, Giuseppe Rallo, Rav Elia E. Richetti, Niccolo and Paola Rinaldi, Béatrice and Pierre Rosenberg, Katarina Rothfjell, Giovanni Rubin, Justin Rubin, Elisa Rusconi, Pietro Rusconi, Guido Salsilli, Gérard-Julien Salvy, Valentina Sapienza, Luca Scappin, Daria Schiffini, Giorgio Scichellero, Marco Scurati, Jérome Siezeniss, Gleb Smirnoff, Claude Soret, Nori Starck, Antonis Stratoudakis, Alejandro Suarez, Aga Sudnikowicz, Bortolo and Daniela Suppiej, Angelo Tagliapetra, Sophia Taliani, Carla Toffolo, Delphine and Nicolas Valluet, Aude and Kees van Beek, Nicolas van Beek, Rita and Kees van den Meiracker, Franca Vanto, Natacha and Henri Villeroy, Hermann Walter, Margherita and Nicholas Ward-Jackson, Silvia Zabeo, Marcello Zannoni, Jérome Zieseniss, Alessandra and Alessandro Zoppi, Marino Zorzi as well as Alexandre, Inès and Louis.
Paola Zoffoli: Special thanks to Mariapia Brunori, Andrea Taddeo, Roberto Vianello, Sara Bardino, Stefano Corrà, Caterina Margherita, Luca, Tobia and Milo Bartolomei, Giulia and Matteo Cocon, Athos Zoffoli, Michele Bonaria. Also: Enrico and Maddalena Di Sopra, Rocco Fiano, Federico Andreolo, Pierandrea Malfi, Désirée Zellweger, Luigino Buratto, Paola Brasi, Alberto Benvenuti, Giovanni Burati, Enrico Venara, Renzo Venchierutti, M. Fiorangela Teruzzi, Stefano Regazzo, Giorgia Enzo, Maria Teresa Grison, Giuliana Grison, Franca Scarpa, M. Giacomina Andreolo, Mara Rosso, Claudia Cremonini, Cristiano Sant, Caterina Marcantoni, Cecilia La Monaca, Massimo Poggi, Vito Caputo, Elisabetta Rigon, Umberto Urbani, Elena Cerana, Guerrino Giano Lovato, Paola Pallieri, Olivia Cavallari, Robert Campello, Alessandra Althoff-Pugliese, Albarosa Ballarin, Annalisa Bacchin, Roberto Gianni, Mabel Sabadin, Michela Zalunardo, Antonella Busetto, Guido and Irene Fuga, Paola Bottalla, Cesare Peris, Ornella Zanella, Francesco and Sara Paolini, Mattia Baseggio, I Ciacoeoni, Rocco Ravagnin, Alessandro Claut, Roberto Vianello (Vecio Berto), Ettore Cavinato, Paolo Comin, Daniela Toso, Luigi Vicini, Augusto Gentili, Mario Infelise, Alessandra and Marisa Peri, Valentina Sapienza, Fabrizia Giongo, Ambrogio Barbieri, Laura Baldoni, Daniele Pighin, Giuliano Pavon, Sandro Bravin, Paolo Morsetto, Riccardo Vianello, Eugenio Simionato, Daniela Foà, Giulio Pozzana, Luigi Naccari, Marco and Alessandra Baseggio, P. Adriano Campesato, Carlo Semenzato, Gino Fontàna, Daniele Bonaldo, Marco Pagano, Liana Melchior, Giacomo Dorigo, Germano Da Preda, Marina Bassotto, Gigi Rannini, Luca De Stefano, Lorenzo Caner, Le Club dei Moi, Giampaolo Nadali, Stefania d'Este, Madeleine Chaize, Mariagrazia Dammicco, Antonietta and Cosimo Gorgoni, Gabriella Bondi, Isabella Campagnol, Gabriele Marchiori, Antonio Manno, Federica Zamboni, Silvia Freschin, Francesco Amendolagine, Valeria Caverzasi, Marco Centazzo, Marika di Mauro, Antonella Formentello, Alessandro Zago, Umberto Fortis, Gemma Silvestri, Marco Scurati, Jeanine Turpin, Christophe Pincemaille, Enrico Paganin, Alexandre Henriquez Delgado Salta, Dimitri Gris, Luca Lando, P. Manuel Paganuzzi, Grigore Arbore Popescu, Maddalena Jahoda, Mauro Bastianini, Piera Gustati, Michela Zanon, Patrizia Vachino, Elio Comarin, Lorenzo Sartini and the team from Mac Shop of Pesaro.

Photos: All photos by **Thomas Jonglez** except:
Pages 90, 92, 94, 96, 218, 233, 272 (Paola Zoffoli), page 232 (Rocco Ravagnin), page 240 (Casinò di Venezia SPA), page 248 (rabbi of the Venice Jewish community), page 389 (Désirée Zellweger), pages 118, 198 and 252 (Luca Bartolomei), pages 129, 211, 212, 214, 222, 223, 227, 306 (Andrea Taddeo), pages 204, 205, 217, 350, 351 (Luca Scappin), pages 164, 166, 167, 168, 170, 171 (Valentina Sapienza), page 367 (Claude Soret), pages 228, 264, 286 and 302 (Katarina Rothfjell), drawings of Corto Maltese, Ponte delle Tette and the inscription *Non Nobis* and photos pages 342 and 344 (Caterina Margherita), St. Mark's Basilica (Jacopo Barbarigo, with the kind authorisation of the Basilica of St. Mark of Venice), Lido underwater crèche (Stefano Corrà), Rubelli (copyright Rubelli SPA), projects never completed (Musée Correr).

Cartography: **Cyrille Suss** - Design: **Roland Deloi** - Layout: **Stéphanie Benoit**
English translation: **Jeremy Scott** - Proof-reading: **Caroline Lawrence**

In accordance with jurisprudence (Toulouse 14-01-1887), the publisher is not to be held responsible for any involuntary errors or omissions that may appear in the guide despite the care taken by the editorial staff.
Any reproduction of this book in any format is prohibited without the express agreement of the publisher.